£1,

5.

First published in Great Britain in 2012 by Unkant Publishing
First Floor Offices, Hoxton Point, 6 Rufus Street,
London N1 6PE

Designed by Keith Fisher
Cover illustration by Andy Wilson

British Library Cataloguing-in-Publication Data
A CIP catalogue record for this book is available from the
British Library
A Paperback Original

ISBN 978-0-9568176-7-9
1 3 5 7 9 10 8 6 4 2

Set in Unkant Jensen
www.unkant.com

1839
The Chartist Insurrection

David Black and Chris Ford

foreword
John McDonnell MP

Unkant Publishers

London, UK

David Black

David Black (born 1950) was brought up in
Newcastle-upon-Tyne. After leaving Middlesex
Polytechnic he worked for Roland and Claire
Muldoon's Cartoon Archetypical Slogan Theatre
(C.A.S.T.) and later for New Variety. In the 1980s
he got into freelance journalism. Since 1999 he
has been co-editor of *The Hobgoblin – a Journal of
Marxist-Humanism.*

His other books are *Acid: A New Secret History of
LSD, Helen Macfarlane: A Feminist, Revolutionary
Journalist and Philosopher in Mid-Nineteenth Century
England,* and *The Philosophical Roots of Anti-
Capitalism: Essays on History, Culture and Dialectical
Thought.*

Chris Ford

Chris Ford (born 1968) grew up in Hamilton, Scotland. A union activist since 1985 he works as a trade union education tutor for the Workers Education Association. For many years involved in solidarity work with the independent workers movement in Poland and Ukraine, he has written widely on aspects of critical theory, labour history and contemporary affairs. He is currently completing a study of the independent Social-Democrats and Communists in the Ukrainian revolution of 1917-1921. Works include: 'The Crossroads of the European Revolution: Ukrainian Social-Democrats and Communists (Nezalezhnyky), the Ukrainian Revolution and Soviet Hungary 1917-1920', *Critique*, 2010, 'Social Emancipation and National Liberation: The Dialectics of the Ukrainian Revolution', 'Introduction and Biography of Ivan Maistrenko', in *Borotbism: A Chapter in the History of the Ukrainian Revolution* by Ivan Maistrenko.

Contents

Dedication

To our friend and comrade Ian MacDonald
1957-2009

"After his life's fitted fever, he sleeps well"

Acknowledgements

The authors would like to thanks the following:

John Ford, Terry Liddle, Walter Kendal, Ray Challinor, Al Richardson, Allan Armstrong, Brian Higgins and Neil Cobbett.

Angela Ellis for great patience and support.

Val Pearman at the British Library and the staff of the British Library Newspapers, Colindale. The staff of the National Archives at Kew. Owen R. Ashton, professor of history and director of the Centre for the Study of Chartism at Staffordshire University for reading an earlier version of the manuscript and making a number of very helpful suggestions for improvement.

Andy Wilson, Ben Watson and Keith Fisher for editing, design, artwork and caring about the product.

Responsibility for the text is of course ours alone.

Chronology

1831   National Union of the Working Classes is formed to campaign for universal suffrage and trade union rights. Henry Hetherington founds the weekly *Poor Man's Guardian* and refuses to pay the newspaper stamp tax.

1832   Duke of Wellington's Tories fall from power. The Whig's Parliamentary Reform Act extends the electoral franchise to the middle-classes, but excludes the working class.

1833   The Whigs pass an Anti-Slavery Act for the colonies, and a Coercion Act for Ireland. Robert Owen's trade union forms co-operative workshops.

1834   The New Poor Law introduces the workhouse system. Trades unions are suppressed, the Tolpuddle Martyrs transported.

1835   The *Poor Man's Guardian* printing press is seized and destroyed by government officers. Printers and distributors of other radical papers are fined or imprisoned.

1836   Bronterre O'Brien translates *Buonarroti's History of Babeuf's Conspiracy for Equality*. William Lovett forms the London Working Men's Association to promote 'education'. John Frost is elected Mayor of Newport.

1837   The weekly *Northern Star* is founded in Leeds by Feargus O'Connor, the 'Lion of the North'. Lovett drafts the six-point People's Charter for Universal Male Suffrage. Onset of economic crisis.

1838   Mass meetings are held nationwide to elect delegates for a Chartist National Convention. Welsh miners elect John Frost and Henry Vincent. Chartist associations start springing up everywhere. Anti-workhouse campaigner Rev. J.R. Stephens is arrested and imprisoned for unlawful assembly. Home Secretary Lord Russell bans torchlit processions.

1839

Jan   The Chartist petitioning continues in earnest. In London Lovett launches a weekly newspaper, *The Charter*.

Feb   The National Convention opens in London, and goes into permanent session. Delegates debate what 'ulterior measures' they should call for in the event of Parliament rejecting the petition – as everyone knows it will. Pro-physical force supporters in London launch the *Chartist* newspaper as a rival to Lovett's *Charter*.

Mar   Convention delegates tour the provinces to build the campaign. Henry Vincent begins publishing the weekly *Western Vindicator* in Bristol. The Whigs' County Police Bill is seen by Convention delegates as a threat to Liberty. Radicals call for the arming of the masses. Several 'moderates' resign in protest against 'extremism'.

Apr   George Julian Harney launches the *London Democrat*. Lovett's 'moderates' complain about O'Connor's 'inflammatory' speeches and Harney's 'Jacobinism'. The Lord Mayor bans Chartist rallies at Smithfield. Intelligence reports indicate widespread arming and drilling by Chartists in the North. Home Secretary Russell appoints General Napier as Northern commander of the army. Napier complains he may not have enough troops to contain potential Chartist unrest.

May   Troops are sent to Llanidloes, mid-Wales, after Chartists seize the town and hold it for four days. A Royal Proclamation is issued against 'unlawfully assembly' and armed drilling. Henry Vincent is arrested in London and imprisoned at Monmouth, charged with making inflammatory speeches. Police raid the London Democrats headquarters. The National Convention moves to Birmingham. As Prime Minister Melbourne faces a vote-of-confidence crisis, hundreds of thousands turn out for peaceful Chartist demonstrations at Whitsuntide. The Chartist petition of 1.3 million signatures is submitted to Parliament.

Jun   Convention delegates tour the country to test opinion on ulterior measures, including a general strike.

Jul   The National Convention reassembles in Birmingham. Magistrates' attempt to enforce a ban on street meetings in Birmingham provokes massive riot. Lovett is arrested after issuing a proclamation defending the right to resist police violence. Parliament rejects the Chartist petition. The Convention moves back to London and votes for a general strike to begin 12 August, but disagreements persist about making it effective.

Aug   Operatives in Lancashire and miners in Northumberland and Durham come out on strike, but elsewhere support is weak. 'Physical-force' supporters blame lack of leadership from the Convention. A third of the Convention's 71 delegates are now either in prison or on bail.

Sep   The Convention, having lost its credibility, is divided on what to do next and votes to dissolve itself. Some delegates join a 'secret council' to plot insurrection. Frost returns to Wales and tries to reassert his leadership but the Chartist movement there is rapidly becoming a revolutionary army led by a shadowy 'Directorate'.

Oct   The Welsh Directorate makes plans for a Rising and organises procurement of pikes and muskets. The secret council in England, which is galvanising support for 'physical force', decides to follow the lead of the Welsh, whatever they choose to do. Dissident diplomat David Urquhart learns of the planned uprisings and holds secret talks with leading Chartists to try and stop them. He fails.

Nov   The Rising in south Wales begins with an attempt to seize Newport with thousands of men, mostly armed with pikes and muskets. When Chartists attack the Westgate Hotel, to free captured rebels, troops retaliate with deadly force. Frost is later captured. The Government sends troops to restore order in the Welsh valleys. Hundreds of Chartists are arrested or forced to flee into exile. Planned follow-up risings in Newcastle, Bradford and elsewhere are hastily called off.

Dec   As the treason trial of Frost and his Welsh co-leaders begins at Newport, O'Connor calls for a new Convention and a militant

'Save Frost' campaign. A new secretive leadership in England plans further risings. The Government employs spies and informers to try and stop them.

1840

Jan   Aborted risings in Newcastle, Sheffield, and Dewsbury end in more arrests of Chartists. In London *agent provocateurs* and informers try to stir up anti-Chartist hysteria and frame Chartist leaders. Frost and the other Newport defendants are condemned to death but the sentences are commuted to transportation for life. Despite the imprisonment of hundreds of Chartists, the movement begins to reorganise for future campaigns.

John Mcdonnell MP: Foreword

There is a school of Labour movement historiography that emulates the old Whig theory of British constitutional history. Just as the Whig theory of history views a succession of constitutional changes over centuries simply as a series of small steps in a linear progression to the perfection of the liberal democratic state (claimed by some as the 'end of history'), there have been fellow travellers in Labour History writing who have seen the individual struggles of groups of peasants and working people over recent centuries as merely the stepping stones on the path to the ultimate goal of the founding of the Labour Party, the TUC and the modern trade unions.

Those elements or key events in Labour movement history that have not conformed to the theory of the ineluctable evolution of the movement into a party committed to peaceful constitutional reform have been either written out of history altogether or relegated to mere historical footnotes. Often they are portrayed as deviations at best irrelevant to or, worse still, hindering the progress of effective working-class political representation.

Those historical actors or movements that in Britain explored or attempted other routes to political change are generally considered condescendingly as primitives or patronisingly as naïve as soon as they ventured down the path of physical force or large scale resistance associated with Revolution rather than Reform.

Consequently, in most histories of the British Labour movement the story of the Chartists has focused on the large-scale mobilisations of petitioners, the development of mass-circulation radical newspapers for working people and the promulgation of the tactic of the general strike, the 'sacred month' or 'big holiday'. The Newport Uprising and other attempts to use physical, as opposed to moral force have been, if not hidden from history, then at least pretty heavily disguised.

With its meticulous attention to detailed sources, its comprehensive scope and its exacting research, this book doesn't just address the neglect of this important and interesting episode in Labour movement history, but more importantly it also challenges us to think again about the revolutionary potential of the British Labour movement.

Black and Ford evidence in a way others have failed to do the scale of the threat to the British establishment in 1839. Less than two centuries after an unlikely coalition of small landholders, Puritans, Ranters and Diggers had severed the head of an English king, this equally broad new alliance of Free Traders, Republicans, early Trade Unionists, proto-socialists and working people oppressed by poverty and the Poor Law raised again the standard of rebellion.

Just as in 1648 the intransigence of Charles I forced his opponents to explore other means to bring about change, as the events of the year 1839 unfold the failure of the nineteenth-century state to budge on any of the basic demands of the Chartists produces a mounting frustration that inevitably leads to the exploration of other means of forcing change. The seemingly endless and at times frustratingly meandering debates of the Chartist Convention on the options for action reflect the class forces, differing life experiences and different ideological stances represented within the early Chartist coalition. This work depicts so well the debates and debaters, warts and all.

Of course, as this book demonstrates, contingency always plays a part in any historical sequence of events. We witness the political manoeuvrings of the different factions within the Convention, the role of its leaders, with their strengths and weaknesses; the determination of some and the loss of nerve and lack of judgement of others.

However, the discussions on strategy prefigure many of the future debates and controversies in the Labour movement both here and across Europe. The use of the general strike in the form of the 'sacred month' foreshadows the advocacy by Rosa Luxembourg of the general strike weapon and her emphasis on the spontaneity of mass action, which has an echo of the swift mobilisations of mass protests by the Chartists. The divisions in the Convention between those adhering to moral force and those advocating physical force, if only in extremis, are repeated time and again in many major class struggles over the following century from Czarist Russia to Paris 1968.

In most accounts of the course of the Chartists' campaigns it seems preposterous to compare the uprisings of 1839 with the revolutions that were to follow in many European states, and in Russia and China, over the next century. Thanks in part to the spin within the contemporary media and the received wisdom replicated in subsequent historical accounts, the Chartist revolutionaries are looked upon largely as incompetent blunderers or fantasists.

Certainly, it is evident that many of the Convention leaders, such as John Frost of Newport, were out of their depth when it came to organising a revolution, and many were orators rather than street fighters. However, this book makes clear that all the evidence points to an extremely fragile British state that was unprepared for a rebellion on any serious scale, and indeed was stretched to its near limits in containing protest—let alone armed insurrection.

At the same time, despite the exaggerated claims of some of the Chartist leaders and Convention representatives of the level of support for armed revolt in their areas, it is obvious from this research that there was sufficient combustible material amongst the working class in 1839, particularly in the industrial areas of Wales and the North, to catch the fire of revolt.

Black and Ford describe how this spark failed to light the fire of revolution, but also show how close an alternative revolutionary route nearly opened up for the forward march of Labour in Britain. Decade after decade of Labour movement historiography has overlaid the Chartist story with the concept of an overwhelmingly conservative British working class and a solely reformist British Labour movement. The message has been consistently drilled into us that revolution was and is futile.

This book offers another perspective. Revolution in Britain in 1839 was closer than we have been previously taught. There is nothing inherently conservative in the British working class, as generation after generation have mobilised to prove. What may be missing, however, is the learning of the lessons of each revolt and each mobilisation for change. By challenging the prevailing hegemony relating to the events and significance of 1839, this book assists us greatly in understanding the potential for future challenges to the system.

John McDonnell MP

1839
The Chartist Insurrection

The New Radicals

Yes, vain all arts will tyrants find
To cramp or bind the human mind,
For onward with resistless force,
The stream of mind will hold her course
Robert Peddie, 'Dungeon Harp'

O n Christmas Eve 1838 Major-General Sir Henry Bunbury, Whig Member of Parliament and former Under-Secretary of State for War, wrote a letter to Home Secretary Lord John Russell. It began: *"Dear Lord John, I am not in general an alarmist; but I must confess that the present state of the kingdom gives me much uneasiness".*[1]

Lord Russell had been nicknamed 'Finality Jack' for his statement that since the Reform Act of 1832 the electoral system was as perfect as it ever could be, with 700,000 voters in a country of 25 million. But millions of the disenfranchised were now demanding universal male suffrage, and many of them were–literally–up in arms about it. Sir Henry said that since he had left office he no longer had the means to assess the balance of forces between the government and the 'disaffected', but he was now able to view the prospects at his leisure, *"undisturbed by the hopes or fears or bias of party politicks"*. In his estimation *"a wide-spreading insurrection of the working people"* was *"far from improbable"*, and might result in *"so much destruction of property, and such a shock to trade and credit and confidence as would be ruinous to this Commonwealth"*.[2]

---

1. 'Dungeon Harp' is quoted in Timothy Randall, 'Chartist Poetry and Song', *The Chartist Legacy*, ed. Ashton, Fyson and Roberts.
2. *Chartism and Society: An Anthology of Documents*, ed. F.G. Mather (London, 1980), pp. 147-50

Sir Henry conceded that the Whigs' Reform Act of 1832 had united the propertied classes against the advocates of 'democratical government'. By giving the vote to the middle classes, the Whigs had made the propertied classes a *"vast power"*, which was *"widely diffused and intermingled throughout the country"* and unparalleled anywhere else in the world. But unfortunately, he pointed out, the manufacturing areas were infected with the *"spreading notion"* that *"everything is being produced for the rich by the labour of the poor"*. This *"notion"* wasn't just about the exploitation of workers by employers. As Sir Henry would have known, half of all tax revenue ended up in the coffers of rich 'fundholders' as interest payments on the national debt accumulated during the Napoleonic Wars. The Poor Law Amendment Act of 1834 had abolished the old obligation of parishes to look after the unemployed and had established the hated workhouse system. In the North and Midlands there had been fierce resistance to the new law: workhouses had been attacked and burned; and the Poor Law commissioners sent to implement the Act subjected to hostile demonstrations and intimidations.

The dangers were not confined to the manufacturing areas, for in general, Sir Henry pronounced, the 'mass' was 'rotten'. In rural areas in the South there had been serious disturbances. Sir Henry would have known of the Battle of Bossenden Wood in Kent on 31 May 1838, in which troops fought a mob of half-starved agricultural labourers, led by 'Sir William Courtenay', a self-styled Christian messiah and gentleman-revolutionary, whose real name was John Tom. A Cornish confidence trickster, John Tom had been a disciple of the ultra-radical Thomas Spence in his youth, but more recently, in 1832, had stood as a Tory parliamentary candidate; he had also spent some time in a lunatic asylum. Tom told the Kent labourers that he would end oppression by the wealthy and would cancel all debts. He administered a sacrament and anointment to his followers which would, he assured them, make them immune in fighting. When the police tried to arrest him for stirring up a rebellion, Tom shot a constable dead and carved up his body with a sword. The authorities, in response, called in a 150-strong company of the 45th Infantry to confront Tom and forty of his followers, who were armed with clubs. When Lieutenant Henry Bennett demanded they surrender, Tom shot him dead as well, at which point the troops opened fire. Tom was killed along with nine of his followers.[3]

The 'disaffected' were, however, not led by sabre-wielding lunatics for the most part. In Sir Henry Bunbury's own constituency of Suffolk, the new Ipswich Working Men's Association launched the Chartist petition for universal male suffrage in the summer of 1838, and extended its influence to the agricultural labourers of the county. According to the *Ipswich Journal*, at one large meeting the speakers felt free to *"blurt out their venom at those who have amassed property and call them knaves and plunderers of the working classes"*. The newspaper alleged that the Chartists had as a *"covert object"* a *"general confiscation of property, to be effected under the pretext of securing equal political rights, or in other words: to bring all men to the same level"*.[4]

In Sir Henry's own estimation, farmers in disturbed areas were too *"selfish and timid"* to unite and stand up to their labourers; and the gentry were *"helpless"* and inclined *"to flock with an esprit moutonnier behind the hurdles which they expect the State to interpose between them and the wolf"*. He had seen how Justices of the Peace allowed *"two or three hundred men, women and boys to bully half a county"* and waited on the orders of an absentee Lord Lieutenant to call in the troops. It was essential, he argued, that regular soldiers should be used only *"for the purpose of holding central points in districts"* and not be *"frittered away in garrisoning every rich man's well-furnished mansion"*. Sir Henry also feared that troops billeted in the distressed manufacturing districts might be vulnerable to the arguments of the radicals. Therefore the government needed to establish local armed militias which, he stressed, should consist not of *"hot-headed Tories"* who might endanger the peace but of enlightened men of the gentry and middle classes, even *"radicals"*.

---

3. P.G. Rogers, *Battle in Bossenden Wood: The Strange Story of William Courtenay* (London, 1962). Barry Reay, *The Last Rising of the Agricultural Labourers: Rural Life and Protest in Nineteenth-century England* (London, 1990)
4. Hugh Fearn, 'Chartism in Suffolk', *Chartist Studies*, ed. Asa Briggs (London, 1962), p. 159. *Ipswich Journal*, 18 Aug 1838.

Many of these latter, he was certain, *"would be found amongst the most forward to maintain the cause of law and good order"*.

A t the very time Sir Henry was writing to the Home Secretary, one of the leaders of the 'disaffected', a twenty-one-year-old Jacobin-socialist named George Julian Harney, was on a 300 mile stagecoach journey from London to Newcastle-upon-Tyne. In the coming year Harney would play a leading role in building a new type of political movement, organised throughout the kingdom, the aim of which was to establish democracy—if possible through 'moral force' and peaceful persuasion or, if this not possible, through what Sir Henry Bunbury feared the most: a *"wide-spreading insurrection of the working people"*. A brief summary of Harney's political development up to this point in his young life provides a useful survey of the events, ideas and personalities that shaped him, and which led to the great confrontations of 1839.

Harney was born to working-class parents in Deptford in 1817. At the age of nine he was taken by his father to see a parade for the Reform candidate in the Southwark parliamentary election, General Robert Wilson. The general had been a champion of the ill-fated Queen Caroline, whose 'cause' most working-class Londoners had fervently supported. A banner carried in the procession by anti-slavery campaigners showed the figure of a black man in chains with his hands clasped, and bore the inscription 'Am I not a Man, and a Brother?' Harney later recalled, *"there needed not the speeches of a Wilberforce or Clarkson, or the writings of Granville Sharp, to make me an Abolitionist forthwith"*. Harney's parents had a great love for books, which they passed on to young George Julian: *The Pilgrim's Progress, Robinson Crusoe, The Castle of Otranto* and *The Sorrows of Young Werther* stimulated his dreams and whetted his thirst for knowledge. As his father had served as a Royal Navy rigger in the Napoleonic Wars, George Julian was able to enter the Greenwich School for training with the merchant navy. In 1831 he was taken on as a cabin boy, but he had been just six months at sea when his ship, en route from Lisbon to London, was hailed by an outward-bound vessel and told that the House of Lords had thrown out the parliamentary Reform Bill. On arriving home, Harney found the country plunged into political turmoil that he found more interesting than life at sea. He abandoned his naval career and threw himself into political struggle.

Harney joined the National Union of the Working Classes, which had been born out of the struggle for Reform; but as soon the Whigs took power in 1832 they reneged on the promises they had made concerning working-class rights and representation. In the words of Harney's biographer, A.R. Schoyen, *"The political union*

George Julian Harney, leader of the London Democrats

of the middle and working classes which had achieved the Reform Bill was destroyed so thoroughly that it was not to be constructed for three decades". In May 1833 a large meeting to plan a national convention for universal suffrage was attacked by the Metropolitan Police. This finished off the National Union of the Working Classes, and as a result working-class interest shifted from political agitation to organising trade unions and cooperatives.[5]

Since the 1820s working-class radicals had upheld the 'rights of labour' against the claims of the 'profit-mongers'. London had a host of small-scale manufacturing industries, employing skilled

5. A.R. Schoyen, *The Chartist Challenge* (London, 1958), pp. 1-8.
Newcastle Weekly Chronicle, 15 Nov 1890, 25 June 1896.

workers such as shoe-makers, tailors and furniture-makers. But the old artisan proletariat of the 'honourable' trades, which supplied the luxury goods market, was no longer protected by regulation and apprenticeships. By the 1830s increased demand for their products was being met not by mechanisation but by sweated 'slop' production in the 'dishonourable' sector of non-apprenticed workers and by foreign imports that were flooding into the London docks.[6]

In September 1833 the 'utopian socialist' Robert Owen, addressing the Operative Builders Union, proposed that workers organise in favour of co-operative production. This led to the formation of the Grand National Consolidated Trade Union, which campaigned for a ten hour day and aimed to create co-operative enterprises through 'labour exchanges', thus cutting out the capitalist 'middleman'. The Owenites also sought to challenge the power of Parliament in Westminster with a 'House' of the Trades. The Owenite paper *The Crisis* claimed in 1834: "*There are two Parliaments in London and we have no hesitation in saying that the Trades Parliament is by far the most important, and will in the course of a year or two be the more influential*".[87] But in 1834 London building workers and tailors were defeated in industrial actions, and the Dorchester labourers known as the Tolpuddle Martyrs were transported to Van Diemen's Land for swearing loyalty to the union. An enormous demonstration was held at London's Copenhagen Fields to support the Tolpuddle men, but the Grand National Union was unable to withstand the defeats and collapsed in 1835.[8]

After the demise of the Grand National Union, many of Owen's followers decided that there could be no practical solutions to the problems of industry unless the working class gained the necessary political power to oversee them. Bronterre O'Brien, an Irish lawyer who edited *The Poor Man's Guardian*, praised Owenite so-

---

6. David Goodway, *London Chartism 1838-48* (London, 1982), pp. 8-9.
7. Quoted in Asa Briggs 'The Local Background to Chartism', *Chartist Studies*, ed. Asa Briggs, p. 13.
8. Goodway, op. cit., p. 10. Goodway points out that although it is commonly believed that the Grand National had half a million members (the Fabian historians Sidney and Beatrice Webb originated this myth), its real dues-paying membership was just 18,000.

THE PIONEER;

OR, GRAND NATIONAL CONSOLIDATED

TRADES' UNION MAGAZINE.

"THE DAY OF OUR REDEMPTION DRAWETH NIGH."

No. 34.	SATURDAY, APRIL 26, 1834.	[PRICE 2d.
	Printed by B. D. Cousins, 18, Duke Street, Lincoln's Inn Fields, London.	

GREAT PUBLIC MEETING OF THE LONDON MEMBERS OF THE GRAND NATIONAL
TRADES' UNION, ON MONDAY, APRIL 21, 1834.

*The above View was taken by a Member of the Miscellaneous Lodge, from the upper part of Copenhagen-fields.
The Procession consisted of from forty to fifty thousand Unionists, was between six and seven miles in length; and it is estimated
that no less than four hundred thousand persons were assembled on the occasion.*

Last Monday was a day in Britain's history which long will be remembered; for labour put its hat upon its head and walked towards the throne. Labour has been a thing of late which politicians thought possessed no soul; a thing of nerves and muscle without morality, and void of intellect. But wherefore did its footsteps shake the judgment-seat? and why did warriors put their bucklers on awaiting its approach? Its heavy tread made statesmen tremble, and as it shook its locks, ferocious scribes grew tremulous. Law held its jaws aghast and showed its teeth, but offered not to bite. Doubt, wonder, and suspense made many hearts uneasy, and far and near an anxious people awaited the result. The sun cast down its eyelids for an hour while labour gathered up its strength, then looked upon its majesty in full magnificence.

Ah, who can tell the mixed emotions which nerved each artizan that lovely morning! The crimson badge

Owenite Trade Union rally, London Copenhagen Fields April 26 1834

cialism as a new idea for *"a complete subversion of the existing world"* in which *"the working classes aspire to be at the top instead of at the bottom of society—or, rather that there should be no bottom at all".*[9] But O'Brien, who was also a Francophile admirer of Robespierre and Babeuf, thought that Owen lacked a historical understanding of the question of political power. O'Brien saw the conduct of the

9. *Poor Man's Guardian,* 19 Oct 1833.

Whigs in the Reform Crisis of 1832 as akin to the manoeuvres of the Girondists in the French Revolution: both had given political power to the *"small middlemen... in order to more effectively keep down the working classes"*.[10]

In 1836 O'Brien translated Philippe Buonarroti's *Gracchus Babeuf et la Conspiration pour l'égalité dite de Babeuf*. Publisher Henry Hetherington put it out under the title *Buonarroti's History of Babeuf's Conspiracy for Equality* and sold it in twenty parts at 2d a copy. In 1796 Babeuf and Buonarroti were members of the Society of the Pantheon, which met in the crypt of the Paris Convent of Saint Géneviève. They both served on a Comité Insurrecteur within the Society which attempted to organise a coup d'etat against the Directory in order to have the Constitution of 1793 implemented, and fulfil what they saw as the logic of the revolutionary class struggle: economic equality and common ownership of property. Babeuf's plot was betrayed and he was executed, but Buonarroti survived to tell the tale.[11] In O'Brien's 'Babouvist' view, the problem with both the American and French Revolutions was that they left the *"institutions of property"* intact as *"germs of social evil to ripen in the womb of time"*; the great democratic gains were subverted by counter-revolution from *"within and without"*. Therefore the next revolution had to be social as well as political: *"from the laws of the few have the existing inequalities sprung; by the laws of the many they shall be destroyed"*.[12]

Owenism and French Babouvism were not the only socialistic doctrines to influence young radicals. Harney was introduced by Allen Davenport, a poet and journalist, to the ideas of the late Thomas Spence. Spence had proposed a radical reform of agriculture, which would turn the land into the 'People's Farm'. But he was convinced that all attempts at land reform would fail without democracy; and by the same token real democracy would be impossible unless the power of the landowners was broken. He

10. Quoted in E.P. Thompson, *The Making of the English Working Class* (London, 1963), p. 903.

11. Alfred Plummer, *Bronterre: A Political Biography of Bronterre O'Brien* (London, 1971), pp. 59-72.

12. Ed. Max Morris, *From Cobbett to the Chartists* (London, 1947), p. 160.

envisaged a 'New Republic' overseen by an elected Convention, in which local authorities would rent land to co-operative enterprises. After Spence died in 1814 his followers organised the Society of Spencean Philanthropists to promote his ideas. Several Spenceans were tried and acquitted for high treason after a riot at Spa Fields, London, in 1817. More seriously, some were involved in the 1821 Cato Street Conspiracy. The conspirators, in reaction

Stamp-tax officers breaking radical printing presses

to the Peterloo Massacre of 1819, planned to start a revolution by assassinating the Cabinet at a banquet, then seizing the armouries and firing ships on the Thames. But from the outset the plot was penetrated and 'ripened' by government *provocateurs*, and it ended in a violent showdown in Cato Street. Five of the conspirators were executed and another five were transported. Despite this disaster for Spenceanism, Spence's social theories retained their influence. In the 1830s his disciple and biographer, Allen Davenport, took on board Robert Owen's schemes for co-operative workshops, and extended Spence's programme for land nationalisation to industry as a whole–arguing that it could be just as fruitfully applied to manufacturing.[13]

Harney entered the world of radicalism when he became a 'runner' for Bronterre O'Brien on the *Poor Man's Guardian*. This paper, owned by Henry Hetherington, was published from 1833 to 1835, with a weekly circulation that reached a peak of 22,000. It was one of hundreds of illegal publications that came and went between 1830 and 1836–illegal because they refused to pay the 3d Stamp Tax that was levied on periodicals carrying news reports. Brought in by a previous Tory administration, this was in effect a tax on knowledge, which made news too expensive for working people. Radical publishers employed an army of sellers and distributors who used every ruse available to evade the watchful stamp officers: papers might be carried over rooftops, or carted through the streets in a funeral hearse, then handed to customers in a shop through a hole in the wall by an invisible vendor. Anyone caught selling a newspaper without the red government stamp could be arrested and fined, or imprisoned for up to six months; Hetherington, who also published the popular *Twopenny Despatch*, himself served two terms. In 1830-36 probably a thousand publishers, printers, distributors and sellers were imprisoned throughout the country in what became known as the War of the Unstamped.[14] In 1834 sixteen-year-old Harney was arrested by stamp officers, and served his first London prison term at Coldbath Fields. A second term followed at Borough Compter Prison within less than a year. By 1836 the War of the Unstamped in London was getting too hot for Harney, so he moved to Derby and joined a distribution network of the *Political Register* (not connected with the journal of the same name founded by the late William Cobbett). Harney was working under a false name, but a stamp officer from London recognised him. Raided in the middle of the night, he was hauled before the Derby magistrates, to whom he declared:

---

13. Schoyen, op. cit., p. 12. E.P. Thompson, *The Making of the English Working Class* (London, 1963), pp. 672-74.
14. Stanley Harrison, *Poor Men's Guardians* (London, 1974), pp. 75-103.

*These laws were not made by me or my ancestors, and therefore
I am not bound to obey them… knowledge should be untaxed.
I have already been imprisoned for selling these papers, and am
ready to go to prison again, and my place will be supplied by
another person devoted to the cause. I defy the government to put
down the unstamped… I have no goods to be destrained upon
and if I had, neither his majesty, or any of his minions should
have them.*

Harney's gall got him a stiff six-month sentence, and when he
was released from Derby Gaol in August 1836 he fainted from
starvation on the highway to London. He resolved, *"If I ever for-
gave the scoundrel who caused this misery then might I never be forgiven
myself"*.[15]

  By this time the Whig government, having failed to stem the tide
of the Unstamped, had decided to reduce the newspaper stamp to
1d. This was excellent news for the large circulation daily newspapers. *The Times* and the *Morning Chronicle*, having had to sell at
6d or 7d a copy to cover the 3d stamp, could now almost halve
their prices and capture a good part of the unstamped press's
readership. Those unstamped penny papers that simply provided harmless entertainment and useful knowledge also welcomed
the reform: having been left alone by the government because of
their political inoffensiveness, they were prepared to pay the tax
and clean up the competition. Another aspect of the new legislation was that it gave greater powers to the stamp officers and
increased the penalties for illicit printing, distribution and hawk-
ing. This left the radical unstamped press facing virtual annihila-
tion by competition and repression. O'Brien, in Hetherington's
Twopenny Dispatch, denounced the reform as *"a declaration of war
against the working classes"*. John Cleave, in his *Weekly Police Gazette*,
wrote that *"you the toilworn, the trampelled, the unrepresented, will
have no legal newspaper under the new system, any more than you had
under the old one"*.[16]

---

15. Schoyen, op. cit., pp. 9-10. *Derby Mercury*, 24 Feb 1836. *Northern
Star*, 29 Dec 1839.
16. Joel H. Wiener, *The War of the Unstamped: The Movement to Repeal
the British Newspaper Tax 1830-36* (London, 1969), pp. 260-77.

Henry Hetherington, radical publisher

The Whig parliamentary reformers, having reneged on giving the working classes any say in elections, had now reneged on giving them a free press. Working-class radicals increasingly saw the 're-formers' as incapable of reforming anything, and turned to independent working-class organizations as the way forward. In April 1836 the Association of Working Men to Produce a Cheap and

Honest Press reconstituted itself as the London Working Men's Association (LWMA) under the leadership of William Lovett, supported by the radical publishers John Cleave, James Watson and Henry Hetherington. The LWMA planned to build *"a political school of self instruction… to examine great social and political principles"*, and membership was restricted to *"honest, sober, moral and thinking"* working men–although middle-class sympathisers were admitted as non-voting honorary members. The aim of the organisation was to *"seek by every legal means to place all classes of society in possession of their equal political and social rights"*. Lovett, as secretary, organised enquiries into conditions of work in the trades and arranged deputations to Parliament to acquaint sympathetic MPs with working-class grievances.[17] An important ally was Francis Place, who acted as a parliamentary lobbyist for trade unions. Place, having made the transition from Jacobinism in the 1790s to moderate radicalism in the 1820s, was of a generation of artisans who were self-educated in the political economy of Adam Smith and David Ricardo. But by the 1830s, under the influence of Thomas Malthus, the leading exponents of political economy had become what Marx later called the *"ideological prize-fighters"* of the cotton magnates. In 1835 the political economist Andrew Ure declared war on the skilled worker in his notorious *Philosophy of Manufacturing*. He conceptualised the ideal factory as *"a vast automaton, composed of various mechanical and intellectual organs, acting in uninterrupted concert for the production of a common object, all of them being subordinated to a self-regulated moving force"*. Because of the unwillingness of the 'traditional' artisans to work in such environments, *"the constant aim and tendency of every improvement in machinery [is] to supersede human labour altogether, or to diminish its cost, by substituting the industry of women and children for that of men; or that of ordinary labourers, for trained artisans"*.[18]

By the mid-'30s the cheapened workforce in cotton manufacturing was turning out more products than the owners could sell.

17. 'Address and Objects of the London Working Men's Association, June 1836', reprinted in David Jones, *Chartism and the Chartists* (London, 1975), pp. 191-96.
18. E.P. Thompson, op. cit., pp. 395-96. Andrew Ure, *Philosophy of Manufacture* (London, 1835), pp. 13-23.

When prices collapsed the ensuing downturn depressed the engineering industry that supplied the mills, and in turn hit metal trades, coalmining, shipbuilding and railway construction.[19] For huge numbers of the newly unemployed, the workhouse beckoned. Some of the radical liberals in the parliamentary Whig Party had supported, or accepted, the New Poor Law, because in principle they adhered to the argument of the Rev. Thomas Malthus, that 'pauperism' was simply a product of population growth. This view was shared by some working-class radicals such as Place, who only differed with Malthus on the remedy; whereas Malthus advocated sexual abstinence, Place advocated sex education and contraception. William Lovett of the LWMA had less faith than Place in the laws of the market according to Malthus, and believed that *"surplus labour is at the mercy of surplus wealth"*. But many radicals, such as Harney, were suspicious of Lovett's associations with Place and his friends in Parliament, whom they despised as 'Whig-Malthusians'.[20]

In those areas in the North where the New Poor Law was being implemented, Malthus was universally hated by working-class radicals. In 1838 the mysterious writer 'Marcus' published a mischievous Swiftian pamphlet entitled *On the Possibilities of Limiting Populousness*, which drove the arguments of Malthus to what he saw as their logical conclusion: a 'rational' argument for mass extermination. Not until the appearance of Marcus's next pamphlet, the *Book of Murder*, published in 1839, did it become obvious to most that his writings were satirical. Nonetheless, the *Book of Murder* stoked the suspicions of many people that the Malthusian agenda was indeed murderous; and what began as a satirical idea spread as a rumour. In 1839 the Ashton Female Chartist Association called on countrywomen *"to do all that in you lies, to prevent the wholesale murder of your new born babies, by the Malthusian method of painless extinction"*.[21] When Seymour Tremenheere, a government agent, was sent to South Wales in 1840 to investigate the

19. S.G. Checkland, *The Rise of the Industrial Society in England 1815-1885* London, 1964, pp. 17-21.

20. Joel Wiener, *William Lovett* (London, 1989), pp. 40-47.

21. Jutta Schwarzkopf, *Women in the Chartist Movement* (London, 1991), p. 93. *Northern Star*, 2 Feb 1839.

causes of the Rising of November 1839, he was beset by a rumour that he had been sent to *"take account of the number of children, and that the government intended to have one in ten put out the way"* and that he was *"to be shot, or treated as they proposed to treat the Lord Lieutenant"*.[22]

Despite misgivings about Lovett's moderation, most London radicals joined the LWMA as the only game in town. Nevertheless, some of the radicals decided that the democratic cause in London also needed a 'Jacobin Club'. On Tom Paine's birthday, 29 January 1837, an organisation called the East London Democratic Association was founded, with headquarters at the back of an umbrella shop in the Minories in Swan Lane. Many of the founding members were veteran disciples of Thomas Spence, such as Allen Davenport, Charles and Elizabeth Neesom, and the suspected Cato Street plotter Thomas Preston. Samuel Waddington, a veteran of the London Corresponding Society of the 1790s, also joined, as did younger activists like Harney and James Cane Coombe. Whereas Lovett's LWMA had a membership fee of 1s a month, the East London Democratic Association had a fee of just 4d a month. And whereas the LWMA restricted recruitment to *"the intelligent and useful portion of the working classes"*, i.e., the better-off artisans, the East London Democratic Association recruited amongst the shoe-makers and the Spitalfield weavers, many of whom lived on a weekly wage of just a few shillings.[23] Lovett's LWMA also found some rivalry in the west of the metropolis from the Marylebone Radical Association, founded in 1837 and led by the firebrand former Member of Parliament Feargus O'Connor.[24]

Feargus O'Connor was born in 1796 into a moderately well-off family of Irish Protestant landowners in Cork who claimed descent from Roderick O'Connor, King of Ireland in the eleventh century. O'Connor's father, Roger, and his uncle, Arthur, had been Jacobin sympathisers and leaders of the United Irishmen in the 1790s. O'Connor studied law and was admitted to the Irish bar, but soon turned his efforts to politics. In 1822 he published a

22. John Humphries, *The Man From the Alamo* (St Athan 2004), p. 36. Kenrick papers loc. cit., p. 90, Tremenheere, 'I Was There', p. 37.
23. Schoyen, op. cit., pp. 14-17.
24. James Epstein, *The Lion of Freedom* (London, 1982), pp. 24-25.

pamphlet entitled *The State of Ireland*, which denounced landlordism, church tithes and corruption in the courts. In 1832 he stood for Parliament in Cork on a program of universal suffrage and repealing of the Act of Union. In his campaign O'Connor showed great talent as an orator and got excellent press coverage by bribing reporters. Elected, he took his seat at Westminster as a member of Daniel O'Connell's Home Rule Party. But in 1835 O'Connor was disqualified when it was found that the annual income from his property fell below the £600 necessary for any member to sit in the House.[25] O'Connell was less than sorry about O'Connor's disqualification, as it had already become clear that the Irish Party was not big enough for both of them.

Feargus O'Connor, 'The Lion of Freedom'

Much to O'Connor's distaste, O'Connell had formed a parliamentary pact with the ruling Whigs, promising not to push for repeal of the Act of Union in the current Parliament in return for a promise of limited reforms. The gap between them widened with O'Connell's statement, intended for the ears of the Whigs, that *"Ireland is so discontented... that it is impossible to keep the people quiet. They would agitate with the radicals of England if I did not throw their exertions into another and better channel"*.[26] For O'Connor, in contrast, to *"agitate with the radicals of England"* was precisely what the Irish Repealers needed to do—for the benefit of both. After losing his Irish seat, he attempted to fill the parliamentary shoes of the recently deceased William

25. Donald Read and Eric Glasgow, *Feargus O'Connor: Irishman and Chartist* (London, 1961), pp. 2-22.
26. Quoted in Goodway, op. cit., p. 62.

Cobbett, celebrated radical journalist and member for Oldham, Lancashire. Cobbett's son, John Morgan Cobbett, was poised to 'inherit' the seat, but some of the religious dissenters in his party, who wanted the separation of Church and State, thought him a bit soft on this question. O'Connor allied himself with the dissenters and stood against Cobbett Junior, but this split the radical vote and allowed the Tory candidate to take the seat. O'Connor was unfazed, however, having seen a glimpse of his future as a leader of the northern industrial workers.[27] He recalled: *"I saw England for the first time with the naked eye... the pallied face, the emaciated frame, and the twisted limbs, wending their way to the earthly hell"*.[28]

O'Connor continued to agitate throughout the North of England, in alliance with Anti-Poor Law campaigners. George Weerth, a German poet and communist who later lived in England, wrote of O'Connor's *"powerful and metallic"* voice and the *"lively and meaningful"* physical motions he performed during his speeches:

> One can see at once that he does not belong to the ranks of the ordinary, one can divine that there is something wild and ungovernable about the man, one is convinced that one is going to listen to an extraordinary speech when one sees him mount the rostrum with joy shining in his eyes. There is his proper place![29]

Having learned his trade holding crowds of Irish peasants in windswept fields and bare-knuckling his entrance into hostile hustings, O'Connor seemed to English workers the type of leader they had been waiting for since the recent demise of the famous radical orator Henry Hunt. O'Connor also sought to emulate the success of William Cobbett's popular journalism by launching in 1837 the weekly *Northern Star* newspaper, published in Leeds. Despite paying the Stamp Tax and having to sell for a hefty 4½d, the paper was a huge success. By January 1838 the circulation was heading for 20,000 and in 1839 it would average 36,000, with peaks of 50,000. The actual readership was much more, because it became the custom for subscribers to pass the paper around their neigh-

---

27. J. Epstein, op. cit., pp. 22-23.
28. *Northern Star*, 16 Jan 1841.
29. Epstein, *Bulletin of the Society for the Study of Labour History*, no. 24 (1972), p. 112.

bourhoods, where it could be read aloud in taverns and meeting halls for the enlightenment of the illiterate.[30]

In 1837 Lovett's LWMA sent missionaries to the provinces to encourage workers to found their own associations on similar principles. This mission was successful, and Working Men's Associations sprouted up in various parts of the country.[31] But in Yorkshire O'Connor had a strong power base in the militant Radical Associations, and drew the Working Men's Associations into the Great Northern Political Union—which he founded for the purpose of *"uniting together, upon the general principle of justice all those who, though loving peace, are resolved to risk their lives in the attainment of their rights".*[32]

Bradford became one of the most militant strongholds of the Great Northern Union. At the turn of the century Bradford had been a small town surrounded by green fields and country lanes; by the late 1830s it had become one of the dirtiest, ugliest and worst administered towns in the country. In the first two decades of the nineteenth century hand-spinning had been ousted by machinery, and by the end of the 1830s Bradford had sixty-seven steam-powered worsted mills employing over 10,000 hands. By this time mechanisation had begun to eliminate hand-loom weaving as well, with wages for weaving declining by a third between 1831 and 1838.[33] Wool-combers, the last of the outworkers (wool-combing machinery had not yet been invented) became enthusiastic Chartist supporters. According the memoirs of W. Cudworth:

> the wool combers… received O'Connor's gospel with enthusiasm. Unlike the more taciturn hand-loom weavers they worked in batches, and the discussion of the affairs of the nation, so far from hindering their work, deprived it of its monotony… the combing shops rang with wild denunciations of wrongdoers, or of fervid admiration of the champion of democracy. In the depression

30. Epstein, *The Lion of Freedom*, pp. 68-69.

31. Weiner, op. cit., p. 43.

32. Quoted in Max Beer, *History of British Socialism, vol. III* (London, 1953), p. 13.

33. A.J. Peacock, 'Bradford Chartism 1838-1840, *Borthwick Papers no. 36* (York, 1969) pp. 1-3.

years of 1837-40, the wool-combers could earn no more than six
to eight shillings a week.[34]

In 1837, just as the depression hit, the government sent Poor
Law commissioners to Bradford to implement the new legislation
and acquaint the unemployed with the workhouses. They were
immediately attacked by a mob, and troops had to be called in
to protect them. Soon thousands of workers joined the Bradford

Opening of the Chartist National Convention in London, February 1839

Radical Association, a branch of O'Connor's Great Northern Union set up by a former wool-comber, Peter Bussey, now owner of
a beerhouse. Bussey's beerhouse became a kind of popular theatre of radical propaganda, with the landlord often reading aloud
press reports of his own speeches amid cheers and laughter.[35]

In early 1838 hostilities erupted between William Lovett and
Feargus O'Connor over events in Scotland. The Glasgow spinners
had struck in the summer of 1837 against a 50 per cent wage cut,
and fought a violent struggle with the authorities and employers–
during which a strike breaker had been shot dead by an unknown
gunman. After the strike, the elected members of the strike com-

34. W. Cudworth, 'Rambles Around Horton', quoted in Peacock, ibid.
35. Peacock, op. cit., pp. 5-12.

mittee were prosecuted for conspiracy and complicity in murder. Five of them were sentenced to seven years' transportation on 11 January 1838. Trade unionists throughout the kingdom saw this as a rerun of the show trial of the Tolpuddle Martyrs; but in a debate on the sentences in the House of Commons, Daniel O'Connell, an honorary member of the LWMA, condemned the strikers and moved successfully for a select committee to investigate trade unions. In March 1838, at the behest of Francis Place, Lovett was appointed as paid secretary to a London Trades Committee, set up to put the case of the trade unions to the select committee.[36] However, when Lovett said that in his view some of the Scottish trade unionists had been guilty of violence and deserved punishment, O'Connor alleged that he and his fellow leaders of the LWMA were helping Francis Place and O'Connell push an anti-union agenda.[37] Harney, siding with O'Connor, wrote O'Connell an open letter, which was published in *The Times*, demanding that he either *"substantiate or repudiate"* his attacks on the trade unions. Harney wrote, *"I am one determined to stand by my order, and to denounce… any apostatising miscreant, who vauntingly proclaims himself the champion of liberty, while he thwarts her potency and prevents the developments of her energies"*. O'Connell responded by saying he had sent a letter explaining his views to the LWMA, with permission to publish it as they saw fit. When the LWMA refused to publish, Harney said that *"the real motive… is that they wish to shield O'Connell from the just indignation of the people"*. He demanded that the organisation expel O'Connell from its ranks as a *"vile slanderer of the working classes"*, and added provocatively, *"If I have acted unbecoming a member of that body [the LWMA], why does not the Association censure, or expel me from their ranks? This they have not done…"* When, on 6 March 1838, the LWMA did pass a motion of censure against Harney, his response was to resign from the organisation along with Charles Neesom and Thomas Ireland. They immediately published an 'Address to the Working Millions', in which they accused the LWMA of collaborating with *"sham patriots"* like Daniel O'Connell; of seeing education as a panacea for all the ills of society, whilst ignoring the lack of political rights;

36. Ibid., p. 54.
37. *Northern Star*, 24 March 1838.

and of failing to recognise that the interests of the middle class and working class were in direct opposition to each other. Lovett, who responded to O'Connor's taunts by referring to him as *"the great I AM of politics"*, appeared unruffled; and with good reason, for it was he and not O'Connor who had just drafted the historic petition for the six-point People's Charter, which called for universal male suffrage, equalisation of constituencies according to population, abolition of property qualifications for MPs, payment of MPs, annual parliaments and the secret ballot.[38]

The LWMA published *The People's Charter* on 8 May 1838. Crucially Lovett's Association soon found common cause with the Birmingham Political Union (BPU), which had united the city's operatives and masters in the Reform Bill agitation of 1830-32. Led by Thomas Attwood MP, the BPU was revived when the depression hit Birmingham in 1837, and grew to 5,000 members. Those militant operatives who embraced the Charter campaign were impatient for action, including a 'National Holiday', or 'Sacred Month', in other words a general strike. Surprisingly, Attwood accepted strike action in principle as a means to put pressure on Parliament–if all else failed. The campaign for the Charter took off nationally and spread very rapidly. On 21 May 1838 an estimated 200,000 marched in support of it to Glasgow Green, behind the actual banner that had been carried by the revolutionary Covenanters at the Battle of Drumclog in 1679. At this meeting Thomas Murphy of the LWMA and Attwood of the BPU proposed that a National Convention should be elected at mass meetings throughout the land to press the case of the Charter, centralise the campaign and present the petition to Parliament.[39]

On 27 June 60,000 gathered in Newcastle. As the procession through the town passed the *Northern Liberator* offices on The Side, political editor Thomas Ainge Devyr stuck a musket out of an upstairs window and let off a fiery salute skywards–horrifying his colleagues, who wisely dragged him away from the window. At the big meeting on the Town Moor a company of dragoons from the nearby barracks came too close for comfort and the crowd became agitated, shouting *"Off! Off!"* One man pushed away an

---

38. *The Times*, 13 Feb 1838.
39. Epstein, op. cit., pp. 103-10.

officer's horse and shouted, "*Get along you scoundrel, is it not enough for us to support you, but must we also be insulted and trampled upon?*"

William Lovett, leader of the London Working Mens Association

O'Connor, who was making a speech, played the crowd. Simultaneously keeping order and provoking authority, he declared of this "*contemptible display*" of military force that "*I only regret that the men around me are not in condition to respond to it in the only language it deserves and to repel force by force... let the brats of the aristocracy take care lest they dare the people to assemble, and bring their arms too...*"[40]

In July 1838 Attwood's BPU and Lovett's LWMA issued a joint call for the National Convention of elected delegates to meet in early 1839. However, as the very name National Convention conjured up the spectre of the French Revolution, a more congenial one was chosen to allay the fears of potential middle-class allies: the General Convention of Industrious Classes. As it turned out, this made no difference, because the body became popularly known, by friend and foe alike, as the National Convention. The organisers of the Convention had to avoid giving the Convention any status as a political society with branches, which would put it in breach of the Corresponding Acts of 1798 and 1819, so it was decided that the delegates would be elected at large public meetings, not at meetings of an association.

40. Thomas Devyr, *The Odd Book of the Nineteenth Century* (New York, 1882), p. 162.

It was also decided that the Convention required a nationwide collection of money for a National Rent, to fund its proceedings and lecture tours by political missionaries. A further series of mobilisations took place to build up the Convention: reportedly 200,000 at Holloway Head, Birmingham, on 6 August; 300,000 at Manchester's Kersal Moor on 24 September; and 250,000 at Peeps Green, West Riding, on 5 October.[41]

In our own time the art of addressing a crowd of upwards of 10,000 without a microphone has long been lost, and it may be wondered how the Chartist orators could do it. Robert Lowery recalled his first attempt, at an open-air meeting of over 10,000 in North Shields:

> *in my excitement I made no calculation of the volume of voice requisite to extend over such a crowd, and had no knowledge then of the pitch of voice from which its rising or falling may be regulated, but I began at the highest pitch and soon was obliged to stop from exhaustion and take a mouthful of water. This enabled me to get into lower key, but still too high; my voice became hoarse, still I gradually acquired confidence as I observed the effects of my remarks, which were very well received. I managed to continue to speak for upwards of twenty minutes… I became a marvel of admiration among the working classes, who always feel proud of the speaking talent of their own order.[42]*

In the much larger mass meetings of the period, attended by hundreds of thousands, there were several speakers, mounted on carts, addressing sections of the crowd simultaneously.

By the end of 1838 there were 608 organisations—Working Men's Associations, Female Political Unions, Radical Clubs, Political Unions and Democratic Associations et al.—collecting signatures for the Petition and money for the National Rent. Whatever 'alternative' visions there were to the existing order (and there were many) all the adherents to Chartism accepted that the future society could only come through democracy; and democracy had

---

41. Peacock, op. cit., p. 18.
42. 'Robert Lowery: Radical and Chartist', serialised in the *Weekly Record of the Temperance Movement in 1856*. Republished, eds. Brian Harrison and Patricia Hollis (London, 1979), pp. 79-80.

to be embodied in a central institution. The National Convention thus appealed to many people as a legitimate alternative to an un-representative Parliament, as well as the means to win *The People's Charter*: 'Peaceably if we can, Forcibly if we must'. But this slogan was ambiguous–seemingly reasonable, but potentially explosive. 'Peaceable' means might include withdrawal of labour, but effective strike action might involve disabling the boilers in mills, turning off furnaces in foundries, and intimidating 'blacklegs'. Force might include arming for self-defence, as the God-given right of every peace-loving citizen; but self-defence might include insurrection, should the government turn its armed force against the people. This ambivalence was embodied in Feargus O'Connor, the 'Lion of Freedom', who told prospective members of his Great Northern Union that they:

> should distinctly understand that in the event of moral force failing to procure those privileges which the Constitution guarantees... and should the Constitution be invaded, it is resolved that physical force shall be resorted to, if necessary, in order to secure the equality of the law and the blessings of those institutions, which are the birthright of free men.[43]

Less ambivalent was the stance of George Julian Harney. On 10 August 1838, the anniversary of the overthrow of the French monarchy, his East London Democratic Association transformed itself into the London Democratic Association (LDA) at the Green Dragon tavern in Fore Street. The LDA membership card bore an inscription from Buonarotti: *"Let each of us depend only on institutions and laws, and let no human being hold another in subjection"*. The Democrats addressed each other, in true Jacobin style, by the term 'citizen' and at meetings decorated themselves with French revolutionary emblems and dress, much to the annoyance of the moderates in the LWMA. In their constitution they quoted *"the incorruptible Robespierre's"* call for a society:

> in which each individual shall enjoy with pride the prosperity and glory of his country; in which each soul shall be elevated by the continual intercommunication for democratical sentiment, and

43. Epstein, op. cit., p. 104. *Northern Star*, 5 May 1838.

by the wish to merit the esteem of a great people; in which the arts shall flourish as the decorations of the liberty that enabled them and in which commerce will be a source of public riches, and not of the monstrous opulence of a class only.

The LDA stood for *"social, Political and Universal Equality"*, unity of *"all classes into one bond of fraternity, for the attainment of Universal Suffrage"* through equal electoral districts, annual elections and payment of representatives. Other objects of the As-

Reverend Joseph Rayner Stephens, anti-Poor Law campaigner

sociation were removal of tax on newspapers; repeal of the New Poor Law; abridgement of the hours of labour in factories and workshops to eight hours and the total abolition of infant labour; support for *"every rational opposition made by working men against the combination and tyranny of capitalists"*; and promotion of *"public instruction and the diffusion of sound political knowledge"*. Ultimately, the Association declared, *"the great object, end, and, aim, of this association is the destruction of inequality and the establishment of general happiness"*.[44]

Harney differentiated his socialism, or 'social equality' as Babeuf called it, from Robert Owen's rather abstract visions, which seemed to suggest that in the new society everything would be rationalised and uniformity would be the order of the day. Harney said in one of his speeches:

44. 'The Constitution Comprising the Address, Objects and Rules of the London Democratic Association' (London, 1838), HO 44/52.

> Do I mean that we should have their food dressed alike, our hous-
> es built in parallelograms, our coats having one uniform cut?...
> God bless you no such thing. I only mean that all men should
> have what they earn and that the man who "does not work,
> neither should he eat".[45]

Organisationally, the LDA adopted the methods of the 1790s
London Corresponding Society and the later Spencean Philanthropists. Its central council was based at rented premises in Ship
Yard, Temple Bar, and consisted of 'tribunes' elected from seven
London divisions, with each division to be subdivided into sections of twenty-five members led by organising secretaries. Any
member could vote and attend the central council as an observer.
With no fixed membership subscription, money collected would
be divided equally into local expenses, association expenses and
members' welfare. The LDA constitution sought to put into practice "the beautiful theories of Babeuf, Buonarotti, Bronterre, &c, by making the Tribunes, the deliberators and perfectors only of the will of the
people, whilst in the people themselves is the ultimate decision, by retain-
ing in their own hands the ultimate sovereignty". Within months the
organisation would claim an estimated 3,000 members: some 20
per cent were shoemakers and 12½ per cent silk-weavers, with
tailors, furniture-makers, printers, building workers and brass-
founders making up the rest.[46]

  Legally, the LDA was on dangerous ground in trying to build an
all-London political organisation. The Corresponding Act stipu-
lated that any club or society composed of different branches
which communicated to each other through their officers "shall be
deemed and taken to be unlawful Combinations and Confederacies". The
Act also forbade correspondence between societies, and between
societies and individuals. In short, this meant that the political
party in its modern form was outlawed. Excepted from these laws
were freemasonry, charities and religious organisations, so some
radical groups circumvented the law by registering as 'Rational
Religionists' or charities to protect their funds; another means

45. *Northern Star*, 13 June 1839.
46. Jennifer Bennett, 'The Democratic Association 1837-1841: A
Study in London Radicalism', *Chartist Studies*, ed. Edward Epstein
(London, 1982), pp. 91, 107.

of circumvention was organising through 'correspondence' in a newspaper. Feargus O'Connor's paper, the *Northern Star*, had such an 'organisational' aspect; and Harney had plans to launch a paper to build the LDA.[47]

The LDA, as good Jacobins, naturally supported the plan for a National Convention and wanted to be part of it. On 17 September 1838 a meeting of 15,000 was organised by William Lovett at Palace Yard, Westminster, to elect delegates for London. LDA supporters were excluded, because the event was stage-managed by Lovett's Association, which had a monopoly on ticket sales: Lovett's liberal allies from Parliament were thus allowed to participate in the deliberations while the Democrats were kept out of them. But Lovett also excluded from the platform Feargus O'Connor and Robert Lowery, who had both been elected as delegates for important districts in the North. O'Connor spoke *"from the crowd"* and rather spoiled the aura of moderation with *"extremist"* speechifying—as did Lowery.[48] As O'Connor, now even more distrustful of Lovett, had decided that more radical voices from London were needed in the Convention, he decided to promote Harney and the Democrats in the *Northern Star*, praising the LDA as *"extensive and organised beyond our expectations. We never saw a finer set of men, nor yet determined to be free"*.[49]

Harney's reputation in the provinces did not depend solely on O'Connor's support. Outside London there were other Democrat associations (in contact with the LDA), formed in Norwich, Leeds, Nottingham and parts of Scotland.[50] With the support of the weavers and mechanics in Norwich, Harney was invited to stand for election in November as their Convention delegate. William Lovett tried to block this by sending John Cleave, the celebrated radical publisher, to run against Harney, in front of a crowd of 10,000. But also standing was the Rev. J.R. Stephens, from Ashton-under-Lyme, a popular leader of the campaign in Lancashire against the New Poor Law—a campaign much closer to

47. Eileen Yeo, 'Christianity in Chartist Struggle 1838-42', in *The People's Charter*, ed. Stephen Roberts (London, 2003), pp. 361-62.
48. Schoyen, op. cit., pp. 36-37.
49. *Northern Star*, 27 Oct 1838.
50. Bennett, op. cit., p. 111.

Harney's heart than Cleave's or Lovett's. Stephens, who had led a radical split from the Methodist church in south Lancashire, was both a Tory and a revolutionary: Tory in the sense that he wanted to go back to the paternalist and Christian values of old rural England, and revolutionary because he was convinced that the factory system–run by men he regarded as blasphemous murderers and swindlers–would have to be uprooted as thoroughly as Sodom and Gomorrah. Lowery recalled Stephens telling a large audience: *"I am no Chartist, that for your five points"* (snapping his fingers) *"I am no O'Connor's man, but while I live and where I live there shall be the law of God and righteousness"*. Stephens agreed with the former Lord Chancellor Lord Eldon's opinion that the New Poor Law was unconstitutional and had been enacted illegally, except that Stephens drew the implications:

> *England stands on a mine–a volcano is beneath her… If the New Poor Law comes your way then, Men of Norwich, fight with your swords, fight with pistols and daggers. Women fight with your nails and your teeth, if nothing else will do and wives and brothers and sisters will war to the knife. So help me God.*[51]

Harney's speech did not match the messianic power of the preacher's but he put across his arguments well, stressing that *"We have petitioned too long… Will we have the Charter or die in the attempt to obtain it?"* Standing with a red cap on his head and tricolour ribbon round his neck, he reminded his listeners that in June 1792, 30,000 Frenchmen had petitioned, armed with pikes and muskets, and had inaugurated a rising of the masses two months later. The scenario he had in mind was clear and simple: demand democracy, arm and prepare to seize power when the demands were rejected. Harney and Stephens were elected to represent Norwich, as was Bronterre O'Brien who didn't attend. Cleave, who was all but ignored, was not elected.

On hearing of the outcome at Norwich, Attwood's BPU condemned the speeches of both Harney and Stephens as dangerously irresponsible and attacked similar statements by Feargus O'Connor.[52] These protestations were echoed at a mass meeting

51. Yeo, op. cit., Lowery, op. cit., p. 111-12.
52. *Northern Star*, 10 Nov 1838.

THE
NEW POOR LAW BILL
IN FORCE.

why did not you die too, you good-for-nothing old son of a rascal !-- because nobody would not kill me Mr. Blubberhead.yes Sir, get a barrow and tie this old man to the legs of it, and tell Tom Sweatwell, to drive him to the New Workhouse, sixteen miles off, and tell him when he comes back he shall have a basin of water Gruel for his trouble.

Now (if a man has got a Wife, &c.

Now Mr. Blubberhead, is there any likelihood of a rest outside ? why Sir, there is old Bellyskin a bones, and old Peter Broken Back grumbling. Put them in the Stocks side by side till to-morrow, at Eleven o'Clock, and they shall have three months each at the Treadmill. Let in another. Who are you ma'am ? why Sir, my name is Jenny Frolicksome, and you appear in a Frolicksome way ? yes Sir I am very queer. so it seems, who is the Father of it ? Blubberhead the Beadle, Sir, the deuce he is, is that true Blubberhead ? perhaps so Sir, then kick her out. and how much is your pay One Pound per week. well for the future it shall be Thirty Shillings, thank he Sir, Let in another, who are you ma'am ? Why Sir, my name is Betsy Begenough, so it seems, have you the dropsy, why, why, why, why the devil don't you speak up, Sir, I am, I am, I am, What are you ? I am in the family way, Sir, the devil you are. Are you not ashamed of yourself ? No Sir, the devil you are not. Who is the Father of it ? slabberhead, the beadle Sir, Where did he get it ? Behind the tombstone in the church-yard, Sir. Kick her out Blubberhead, and for the future your salary shall be two guineas per week. Thankee, Sir.

Now (if a man has got a Wife &c.

All round the country there is a pretty piece of work All round the country against poor people's will, Feeble, and borne down with grief, They ask the Parish for relief, (Law Bill. They tell you to go home and try to learn the Poor

CHORUS.

Now, if a man has got a Wife and some Children Starving, Distress should only seize him, he his got no work to do, and if to the Overseers go, Ground down with Sorrow, Grief, and Woe, they will tell you to go home and try to learn the Poor Law Bill.

SPOKEN.--Now, Mr. Blubberhead the Beadle, fetch in the Overseers' and Churchwardens 12 bottles of the best Port Wine, yes Sir, and Blubberhead, is there any Vagrants outsi'e wants examining? why, Sir, there is a wonderful lot of people outside, and I think they are all Bones, for there is very little flesh upon them.---Now, Mr. Blubberhead, the Beadle, let in one of those Rascals--Who are you pray, Why Sir, my name is John Pineway, who is been ill Seventeen long months, I have a Wife Confined, and eight Children Starving.--Well, what odds is that to me ? Go home and sell your bed I have no bed ; I sleep upon straw. Well, poor man, I pity you.-- When had you any food ? Last Saturday, Sir, Mr. Blubberhead. Yes, Sir, Get a truck and put this old man and his family into it, and have them removed to the New Workhouse. Put the man in 114 cell, and the woman in 395 ward ; and take the children six miles from thence, and tell them not to let them see each other for once in six months.

Now (if a man has got a Wife, &c.

SPOKEN.--Now, Mr. Blubberhead, let in another. Who are you, pray ? Why. Sir, my name is Bill Fastamonth. Aye, and I expect you will have to fast three months. How old are you ? 122 next Friday week. Where is your wife ? She is dead, Sir And

SPOKEN.--Now Mr. Blubberhead, let in another. Who are you Ma'am ? Why sir, my name is Mary Neversweat. What the devil do you want ? Why sir, my husband is very ill, and I have nine children starving. Who sent you here ? The magistrate. Mr. slabberhead, send all the paupers and vagrants home to their homes; and them that has got no homes must go to Farmer muffnose's cart-house to sleep ; and take this old man and his wife in our dung cart to the New Workhouse. Put the man in 115 cell, and the woman in 394 ward, and take the children to the barn twelve miles from there, and tell them not to let them see each other for once in two years, for we must enforce the rule of the New Poor Law Bill.

Sharp, Printer, 30, Kent Street, Borough.

Anti-Poor Law handbill

called by the Scottish Radical Associations on Edinburgh's Calton Hill. The Scottish moderates proposed that tactics involving physical force be ruled out, and won the vote despite spirited opposition from the 'Jacobins'. This effectively split Chartism in Scotland, and was a serious blow to the unity of Chartism in Britain as a whole—from which, as Harney recalled years later, it never really recovered.[53]

Following the election to the Convention by the Marylebone Radical Association of Harney's friend William Cardo, the war of words between Lovett and O'Connor intensified. At a debate on 20 December at the Hall of Science on Commercial Road, Lovett, outraged by the use of *"violent language"*, threatened to leave and split the movement. But he did not do so because, given the current strength of the 'Jacobins' and 'O'Connorites', a split would have left the 'moderates' outside the mass movement, and less able to influence the course of the events that were now unfolding.

Since the winter nights had set in, the Chartists—as they were now called—had been holding night rallies all over the country, marching silently by torchlight to their meeting places. Often they carried pikes, and fired off the occasional musket salute. O'Connor told a meeting in Rochdale that *"One of those torches is worth a thousand speeches. It speaks a language so intelligible that no one could misunderstand"*.[54] In response to middle-class alarm, Prime Minister Lord Melbourne banned torch-lit processions.[55]

On 23 December 1838 Harney, having been invited to stand for election to represent Newcastle-upon-Tyne at the Convention, boarded the stagecoach.

---

53. G.J. Harney, *Northern Star*, 2 March 1850.
54. Donald Read, 'Chartism in Manchester', *Chartist Studies*, ed. Mather, p. 45.
55. Ibid., p. 377.

The Northern Liberators

Words are things and a small drop of ink
Falling like dew upon a thought produces
That which makes thousands, perhaps millions think.
Byron, 'Don Juan'–the *Northern Liberator* masthead

T he coach left London at eight o'clock on the evening of
23 December 1838. George Julian Harney recalled, fifty
years later, that he travelled on the top deck with no protection from the elements, save the overcoat he was wearing and
the leather apron attached to the seat which was buckled across
his knees. There were twelve hours of darkness ahead before the
first stop, and soon Harney began to feel as if his legs were *"encased in ice"*. After stopping at Grantham for breakfast the coach,
lashed with rain and snow, passed through Doncaster and Selby,
then stopped at York, where a late dinner was provided for those
who could afford it, which Harney could not. By the time the
coach reached Durham, with its cathedral shrouded in darkness,
the cold Harney felt in his feet gave him *"a deadly-lively appreciation, though not much comfort, from the philosophy of Locke on the Understanding"*. At about one o'clock on the morning of Christmas
Day, and some thirty hours after leaving London, the driver gave
the horses an extra whip-up, *"the traveller incurring no small risk,
overpowered by somnolency and benumbed into the helplessness of pitching headlong from his seat and breaking his neck"*. Finally the coach
was *"driven at a rattling pace"* down from Gateshead, then over the
stone bridge which spanned the River Tyne and up the steep hill
from The Side to Collingwood Street, where it disembarked at the
Turf Hotel. After checking in, Harney was given a candlestick,
"something hot" and a bed. On Christmas morning his breakfast

was interrupted by a welcoming committee from the Northern Political Union (NPU), who took him down to the office of the *Northern Liberator* on The Side. There he made his first personal acquaintance with the Northern leaders.[1]

The *Northern Liberator*, a stamped weekly newspaper, had been founded in 1837 by the Anglo-American publisher Augustus Beaumont. Until 1836 Beaumont had lived in Jamaica, where he campaigned for independence, fought anti-Jewish discrimination and was accused of inciting a slave rebellion. At a Newcastle meeting held in November 1837 for the defence of the Glasgow spinners, he declared, "*We abhor Civil War, but if we cannot obtain freedom without it, then welcome the barricades*". In 1838 Beaumont planned to raise an armed force of 500 to fight for the rebel democrats in Canada, but died of typhoid during a fundraising tour that year, and the campaign came to naught. To fund this campaign Beaumont had sold the paper to Robert Blakey, Mayor of Morpeth, philosopher and political disciple of the late William Cobbett.[2] Blakey, as new owner of the *Northern Liberator*, employed the poet and novelist Thomas Doubleday as editor and Thomas Ainge Devyr, an Irish Land Reform activist and son of a Donegal United Irishman, as local political editor. The readership base of the *Liberator* was the NPU, which had 7,000 members. With a circulation of 4,000, it outsold the other five papers in Newcastle.[3]

The NPU of Newcastle organised throughout Northumberland and in some of the Durham villages just south of the River Tyne; whilst the Durham County Chartist Association, based in Sunderland, organised in the rest of Durham and as far south as Stockton and Middlesbrough. The NPU had first been founded during the Reform Bill Campaign of 1830-32, but in its revived form it was shunned by its former middle-class radical leaders, who had

---

1. The account of Harney's trip to Newcastle is taken from the *Newcastle Weekly Chronicle*, 5 Jan to 30 Jan 1889, except where otherwise referenced.
2. Lowery, op. cit., p. 123.
3. Joan Hugman, 'A Small Drop of Ink: Tyneside Chartism and the Northern Liberator', in *The Chartist Legacy*, eds Ashton, Fyson and Roberts (London, 1999), pp. 24-47.

now become civic dignitaries in the local Whig administration.[4] In Newcastle at the end of 1838, recalled Thomas Devyr, "*We were now fairly in a storm of agitation. Almost the entire working element was on our side, and almost the entire middle class (we called them 'profitmongering' class) was against us*".[5]

Harney made arrangements for the 'big meeting' later in the day and took a stroll around the town. He recalled: "*The morning of Christmas Day 1838, broke fresh and fair. It was cold, but crisp cold, such as sets the blood dancing in the veins*". Immediately attracted by Grey's Monument, he admired the town's new neo-Classical buildings, designed by John Dobson for the property developer, Richard Grainger:

> *setting aside the best of London… Bath, Cheltenham, Leamington, and other show places; also places of antiquarian interest, like York, Canterbury and other Cathedral cities, I know not so pleasant a place as Newcastle. As an industrial and commercial centre, it, to my mind, is far handsomer and cheerier than larger manufacturing towns and cities it would be invidious to name. Frankly, I don't like large towns; but all large towns in England I have any knowledge of, commend me to canny Newcastle.*

The Town Moor was too bleak and windswept for a meeting that day. The chosen venue was The Forth, a tree-lined space overlooking the steep river bank and bordered on the north by Westgate Road (Newcastle Central railway station was built on the site a few years later). The procession of friendly societies, political and trades organisations took off through the main streets of the town, with bands playing and colours flying. There were the stone masons of the Grainger renaissance, the miners, metal-workers and a host of other trades, along with their wives and families; and delegations from as far as Hexham and Carlisle in the west. Most of the workers in the Carlisle district were handloom weavers, many of whom earned as little as 5 or 6s per week. Robert Lowery, who knew that area well as a Chartist lecturer, found

---

4. William Henry Maehl, Chartism in the North East', *International Review of Social History*, vol. VIII, part 33 (Amsterdam, 1963), pp. 390-414.
5. Devyr, op. cit.

it *"peculiarly painful to observe so many of the females who, for want of a sufficiency of blood-forming food, had sunken cheeks and dim eyes, instead of the beaming brightness and ruddy glow which belonged to their ancestors"*. But despite this poverty, he observed, the weavers were often intelligent, well read, and well acquainted with the political issues of the day: *"This arises from the facilities which their employment gives them for conversation"*.[6] In this respect the Carlisle weavers were like the equally beleaguered wool-combers of Bradford, inclined towards militant physical-force politics.

On the banners, Harney recalled:

> *figurative adornments and mottoes showed the still surviving influence of the great French Revolution: 'Liberty, Equality, and Fraternity', 'The Rights of Man' etc; whilst the old Cromwellian spirit found utterances in Biblical denunciations of the Oppressors of the Poor, such appeals as "He that hath no sword, let him sell his garment and buy one!"*

At the Forth, Thomas Doubleday chaired the great meeting of an estimated 60,000. Young-middle-aged, slightly dandyish and mellow voiced, Doubleday knew his listeners would not want long speeches as they stood in the cold, so his opening speech came straight to the point. The movement had advanced, and the inauguration of the National Convention was near. Their business that day was simply to elect the delegates: there was no need to debate the petition, since *The People's Charter* had already been generally adopted at previous meetings without any question as to its principles or details. But first there was a vote of thanks for Feargus O'Connor and the Rev. J.R. Stephens (in their absence) proposed by Mr Hanson, a weaver from Carlisle. Hanson, with the half-starved gaunt and pale look that was all too typical of his trade, spoke in condemnation of the Birmingham and Edinburgh moral-force leaders who had denounced O'Connor and Stephens for violent language. This vote of thanks was carried unanimously. Then James Ayr, a short, middle-aged stone mason, moved the resolution to appoint delegates to the National Convention. This was seconded by another mason, Edward Charlton, who behind the scenes was engaged in procurement of muskets. He observed

---

6. Lowery, op. cit., pp. 113-15.

that *"if the Convention were attacked, the cry should be 'To your Tents! O Israel!'"*[7]

Harney was nominated along with Dr John Taylor and Robert Lowery as one of the delegates to the General Convention, and then they addressed the meeting. Lowery, who walked with a permanent limp after an injury he had sustained working on a merchant ship, had also worked as a tailor, and now, aged thirty, worked for the *Northern Liberator* as agent and publicist. He told the crowd:

> *We are to have no sham work; we are to tell the Government and Parliament that if we have no part in making the laws, we will not obey the laws (Cheers)… if after all legal means have been tried and after all our arguments have been used, if we can not get our rights, then we might use our arms.*

Lowery's memoirs describe Harney as *"a fluent speaker"*, who had *"evidently read with avidity the history of the French Revolution, and was smitten with admiration for the social theories and sentiments of Robespierre and St Just…"*[8] Lowery also knew that Harney was closely associated with Feargus O'Connor and that Augustus Beaumont had warned him, *"O'Connor is not to be trusted. He's a coward and if we should have to fight he is not to be depended on".*[9] But there was no tension between Lowery and Harney that day. In appearance Harney was a blue-eyed London youth, with brown hair hanging down to his shoulders, of slim medium height, slightly stooped owing to childhood illness. According to R.G. Gammage, who was no great admirer,

> *his dark piercing eyes were shaded by a rather moody brow, and were never at rest, but constantly changing from one object to another, as though he distrusted all around him. About his lips there was an appearance of strong vindictiveness, which pointed*

---

7. Terry McKinney, *Bedlington Iron and Engine Works 1736-1867*: *www.pitwork.net/terrymcbedl.htm*

8. Lowery, op. cit., p. 119.

9. Ibid., p. 123.

> him out as a dangerous enemy, and experience only served to
> prove the correctness of that impression.[10]

Harney recalled of himself that he was *"Of a fiery temperament,
not much possessing, as possessed by an enthusiasm in more need of
experience, discipline and regulation. Not generally a good speaker…
But capable at times of making effective speeches"*. Confiding with his
friend Friedrich Engels, a few years later, he compared himself
with O'Connor: *"A popular chief should be possessed of a magnificent
bodily appearance, an iron frame, eloquence, or at least a ready fluency
of tongue. I have none of these. O'C[onnor]—at least in degree has them
all"*.[11]

Harney told the assembly on the Forth that the Charter would
be theirs within a year, but only through the action of the men
of the North. In a guarded forewarning of things to come, and
drawing allusions to the Girondin-Jacobin conflict in the French
National Convention of 1793, he suggested that the Convention
in itself might not achieve the goal, since in it there would be two
parties: *"one party to do for the people, one party to do for themselves"*.
He also issued a challenge to his audience: *"you are met with your
feet on God's own earth, with God's own sky for their canopy… will you
take the oath to live free or die?"*[12]

Dr Taylor, the third delegate, was a surgeon who had completed
his medical training in Paris. A resident of Ayr, he had also been
nominated to represent Renfrewshire at the Convention, much to
the alarm of the Scottish moral force advocates—who regarded him
as an extremist and a bit too fond of the drink. Aged thirty-four,
he was a tall man with a dark complexion, the grandson of a Scottish general who had married an Indian woman. With his shock
of long curly hair parted in the middle, Taylor was dressed in a
green hunting coat, white breeches, top boots, a broad-brimmed
hat and an open-neck red shirt. He seemed to Harney the kind of
man Byron *"would have deemed an admirable presentment of Corsaire,
or Lara—ready to take to the field against any odds"*. Taylor told the

10. Robert Gammage, *History of the Chartist Movement* (London, 1894),
p. 29.
11. Harney to Engels 30 March 1846, published in ed. F.G. Black and
R.M. Metevier, *The Harney Papers*, (Amsterdam, 1969), pp. 239-42.
12. *Northern Liberator*, 29 Dec 1838.

crowd that he had fought with the pen and at the hustings, but, he added, "*I would part with the sabre only with my life, and when all else have forgotten me my own hand will write my epitaph upon a tyrant's brow, in characters of blood with a pen of steel*".[13]

All three–Harney, Lowery and Taylor–were elected by a show of hands. Finally, Chairman Doubleday underlined the physical-force message, saying that the people had a legal and constitutional to possess arms and to use them in self-defence. The bands played as the people dispersed.

Two days later Stephens was arrested in Lancashire for making seditious speeches. Harney and O'Connor had been warning for some time that the verbal assaults by moderates on campaigners like Stephens would make government repression more likely. The Manchester courthouse at which Stephens was committed for trial was besieged by his supporters, and the news soon reached the North East, where there was great indignation, and the *Northern Liberator* replaced the lines from Byron on its masthead with a quote from Blackstone's Commentaries on the Law of England, confirming "*the right to bear arms for self-preservation and defence*". The paper also gave advice on making ball and buckshot and stated that "*moveable barricades are recommended for street fighting… hand grenades can be cast by any workman of the thousands of the NPU employed in the iron foundries*".[14]

The extreme militancy of the North East in this period seems to belie the received wisdom that revolutionary sentiment tends to rise and fall in parallel to levels of economic deprivation. The depression that began in 1837 had a severe impact on the textile trades of Lancashire and the West Riding, as well as the workshops of Birmingham which supplied them with machinery. But the North East was not so badly hit. New mining technology had broken through the deep layers of magnesium limestone above the seams of the Durham coalfield, and there were now dozens of new collieries, costing up to £100,000, which had access to newly constructed harbours along a network of railways. Even in the

---

13. Lowery, op. cit., p. 118. W. Hamish Fraser, 'Dr John Taylor, Chartist, Ayrshire Revolutionary', *Ayrshire Monographs #33* (Ayr, 2006), p. 49.
14. *Northern Liberator*, 12 Jan 1839.

depression, sales of coal continued to rise and the North East's railways continued to expand, despite a spate of company failures which wiped out many first-wave investors. In nearby Sunderland shipbuilding continued to grow, with sixty-five shipyards by 1839.[15]

As the New Year began Harney did a speaking tour of the outlying villages of Newcastle. The foundrymen at the iron works of Winlaton and Swalwell, just across the river in Durham county, were in Harney's opinion 'exceptional'. The ironworkers comprised a sizeable establishment of small craftsmen, founded as far back as 1690 by Ambrose Crowley, but the industry was now facing decline because of competition from more modern works in other areas of the country. Winlaton was a hotbed of insurrectionary plotting and secret manufacture of weapons such as pikes, knives, caltrops (spikey metal contraptions for disabling horses' hooves), and even cannon and grenades. Winlaton also had a lively Female Chartists branch. These women invited Harney to rest in their parlours and partake of their spice cakes cooked on the stove, known as 'singing binnies', and held dances in his honour. His party trick was to take a local girl on his arm, place his Jacobin red cap on her head, then dance with her and sing 'When this Old Cap Was New', a popular song written by Thomas Doubleday. Harney's audiences in the North generally seemed to contain as many women as men, and he would tell them that he thought women were superior. In return the Northern women frequently presented him with an embroidered silk scarf.[16]

Historian Edward Royle suggests that despite the armed militancy of the Winlatonians, the "*potential danger*" was minimised by the buoyancy of the North East's economy and other forces, which had "*institutionalised*" the revolt of the trade unions in the collieries.[17] It is also true, however, that the miners, precisely because they were comparatively well paid, were able to direct their minds towards ideas and political solutions that would improve their lot further. Two major strikes at the time of the Reform Bill, in 1831 and 1832, had drawn the miners into the Reform

15. Checkland, op. cit., pp. 157-69.
16. Schoyen, op. cit., p. 72.
17. Edward Royle, *Revolutionary Britannia* (London, 2000), pp. 94-95.

campaign, and thus encouraged them to act in the political field as well as the economic. Their organisational practices were influenced by the local Primitive Methodist tradition, from which they borrowed the model of organising into classes of ten as well as the holy *"enthusiasm"* of the outdoor meeting.[18] Lowery thought the colliers of Northumberland and Durham to be intellectually a *"century in advance of their class in any other mining district"*. This, he explained, was because enterprises were bigger and more lucrative than elsewhere: in the large pits there were no intermediate contractors to complicate relations between proprietors and men; and there was no 'truck' system of company shops and beerhouses to re-appropriate the wages of the workers. Because the colliers' work-day was no more than eight hours, they had time for leisure, especially horticulture and reading. Lowery said of one such man: *"... as he walked along his flowerbeds he would sound their scientific names in his provincial tones, intermingling his conversation with remarks on the philosophy of Locke, or quoting passages from Milton, Byron, Shelley or Burns"*. Others, he recalled, had a passion for mathematics:

> *While there was much occasional intemperance and ignorance amongst them, yet there was a large number of reading, thinking, and ingenious men; you would often meet with a good library in their cottages. There were superior mathematicians, and the booksellers were known to sell, chiefly among the workmen of the North, a larger number of works on that science than were sold in any other district of the country.*

The physical-force tendency in the North East had not been invented by the Chartists, but by the local Whigs during the Reform Bill agitation in 1831-32:

> *No part of the country exceeded in fervour the district around Newcastle-upon-Tyne for the Reform Bill [1832]. Nor did any association surpass that of the Northern Political Union in talent and influence. Its principal leaders combined astuteness, literary ability, oratorical powers, and social standing rarely equalled... It is well known that the language was often violent, and the opposition threatened with physical resistance if they should proceed*

18. Maehl, op. cit..

to enforce any laws to stop the unions in agitating for their demands... At that time the masses of Newcastle presented a state
of mind peculiar to themselves... Thus, while the intelligence of
the people was strong and they had their literary and philosophical institutions and a number of public libraries, and every week
public lectures on various subjects, the old tavern system still pre-
vailed. All classes met there to compare notes and to hear individual remarks and criticisms on what occupied public attention,
and there was in consequence much intemperance. Every branch
of knowledge had its public house where its disciples met. Each
party in politics had their house—there was a house where the
singers and musicians met—a house where the speculative and
freethinking met—a house where the literate met—a house where
the artists and painters met—also one where those who were men
of science met.[19]

After some weeks in the North East, Harney moved on to
Lancashire and Yorkshire and then to Derby on 21 January
1839—his first visit to the town since coming out of its prison.
Local press reports put the attendance for the Derby gathering at
5,000, whilst the Chartist press claimed several times that number. Mounting the platform to loud cheers from familiar faces,
Harney spoke with passion and relish:

Three years ago on a winter's evening, I was dragged from my
home without the least notice and consigned to a dungeon by the
magistrates of Derby, because I had committed the heinous of-
fence of selling an unstamped newspaper, because I had strove to
set the press of England free. Yes my friends, I was for six months
confined in a Bastille because I dared, in defiance of wicked and
infamous laws, to give the working classes that untaxed knowledge which they have the right to enjoy. The Tyrants bound me,
but could not subdue me... but I return to Derby not as I departed. I come back to look tyrants in the teeth, in the proud
character of a leader of the people—as one of the chosen chieftains
of the brave men of the North. What is it that we want? Not to
destroy property and take life, but to protect our own lives and
to protect our own property—viz, our labour... I say, we are for

19. Lowery, op. cit., p. 82.

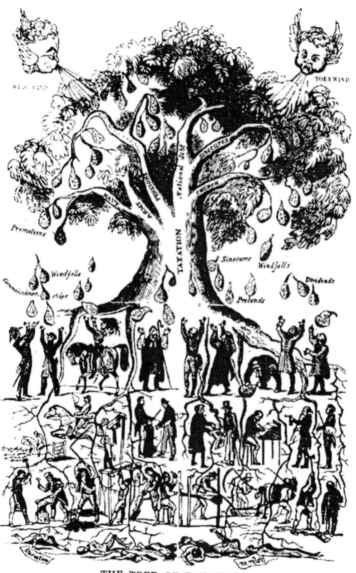

THE TREE OF TAXATION.

Cartoon from the Northern Liberator *13 Oct 1838*

peace, but we must have justice—we must have our rights speedily, peaceably if we can, forcibly if we must.

Turning to the Malthusian theories, Harney continued:

They say we are too many—that population increases faster than the means of subsistence, if so, let those leave the land who do not love labour—let those who work not leave the country, and when the Aristocracy betake themselves to Van Dieman's Land, and the money mongers to the devil, take my word for it, there will be enough left for you and me. But we will not leave the land of our sires—we will not quit the soil that gave us birth.

With the inauguration of the Convention fast approaching, Harney echoed the insurrectionary talk that had cost Stephens his freedom a month earlier: *"You will get nothing from your tyrants but what you can take. I say 'Arm for peace, Arm for liberty, Arm for justice… and the tyrants will no longer laugh at your petitions'".*[20]

Harney was again elected as a delegate to the Convention, which was scheduled to begin on 4 February 1839. He was now a delegate for three of the most important districts of England: Northumberland, the city of Norwich and the borough of Derby. He had wanted, in the first place, to be a delegate for London but, as we have seen, he had been blocked by the manoeuvres of Lovett and the LWMA. One of those 'approved' by the LWMA for London was Henry Vincent, a twenty-five-year-old printer, also elected for Hull and the West Country. Vincent was, however, his own man, or rather a man of the people he came to represent. As in the West Riding of Yorkshire, the woollen industry of the West Country was in decline and wool-workers' wages were being cut; and towns like Trowbridge, Devizes and Bath were becoming as radicalised as Bradford and Dewsbury in the West Riding of Yorkshire. At a meeting in Bath organised by the local Working Men's Association Vincent spoke on a platform with the Association's patron, Sir William Napier (brother of General Charles Napier, who we shall meet later). Vincent, referring to the fact that the people were kept down by knaves, proceeded to name them: *"Lord John Russell is a knave, Harry Brougham is a knave, the*

20. Lowery ibid., pp. 48-49, *Derby and Chesterfield Reporter*, 23 Jan 1839.

BLACK SLAVES VERSUS WHITE SLAVES.

Caricature from the Penny Satirist *10 Feb 1838 of Whig reformer and anti-Chartist Lord Brougham in a special constable's uniform*

Duke of Wellington is a knave". This was too much for Sir William, who protested that such language injured the cause: "*I deny that. The Duke of Wellington is no knave; he fought for his country nobly, bravely, honourably, and he is no knave*". Vincent replied: "*I say that any man, be he a Russell, a Wellington, or a Napier, who denies me the right to vote, is a knave*".

Vincent's writings lacked the intellectual spark of Harney, but with his fine passionate speaking voice and handsome looks, he exceeded Harney in the number of silk scarves he collected from the Female Chartist Associations–at one 4,000-strong women-only meeting in Bath he was even given a fine gold watch. Having made such a big impression in the West Country, Vincent extended his influence further to the west when he was also appointed by the National Convention as touring missionary lecturer for South Wales. His involvement in the heady affairs of the South Wales coalfield was to have dramatic consequences for him and for the whole movement.[21]

21. Gammage, op. cit., pp. 77-79.

The South Wales Cauldron

A more lawless set of men than the colliers do not exist… It requires some courage to live amongst such a set of savages.
Reginald Blewitt, Whig MP for Monmouth boroughs, 1839

Т he last medieval-style castle round-towers to be built in Britain were completed in 1822, near Brynmawr, Monmouthshire.[1] The builders were the brothers Crawshay and Joseph Bailey, who along with a small number of other families owned most of the mines and iron-works in South Wales. Today one the towers is half-demolished, but the other is still standing and has been restored. Along with the remaining ruins of the foundries, the towers are monuments to the class war of the South Wales coalfield in the first half of the nineteenth century. Completion in 1822 was timely, because that year Joseph Bailey started what was nearly a civil war when he cut the wages of his colliers from 2s 4d to 1s 3d per ton. Only with the help of the army and yeomanry could he force the colliers back to work.

Between the censuses of 1801 and 1831 the populations of Monmouthshire and Glamorgan doubled, mainly through migration from neighbouring counties and from Ireland. During the course of the 1830s iron production in the furnaces of South Wales doubled to almost half a million tons per year, and coal mining expanded to meet the demands of the industry. By 1839

---

1. **Reginald Blewitt,** quoted in Ivor Wilks, *South Wales and the Rising of 1839* (London, 1984), pp. 38-39, 155

a quarter of a million people in the valleys of South Wales were dependent on these two industries.[2]

The first generation of coal and iron magnates in the Principality had no sense of civic paternalism. Their new company towns were simply rows of shacks and cottages adjoining the mines and works, devoid of adequate drainage and sanitation, education for children or medical services. For the inhabitants life was hard, dangerous and short: there were regular outbreaks of typhus, scarlet fever and cholera; the infant mortality rate was a disgrace to any civilisation; and the mines claimed a hundred lives a month in accidents. Women were employed in the iron-works and mines, as were children as young as six, who were carried to work on their fathers' backs. But the masters, as good Benthamites, saw no responsibility to their employees beyond paying them wages. As Englishmen (which most of them were), they saw no point in providing schools for people who spoke an archaic Celtic language; as Anglicans they did not want to encourage dissenting chapels in the community; and as monopolistic capitalists they did not want street markets or shops which might take business from their company stores. In these company stores the employers operated an extortionate 'truck' system, which re-appropriated workers' wages by charging 30 per cent (or more) above the market prices for goods and paying workers in company-store vouchers. Independent traders were kept out: whilst the capitalists had canals and tram-roads, there were not enough roads in the valleys to service free trade in consumer goods. The English iron-masters, who also owned the largest mines, lived away from their workers in their fortified mansions. Beneath the owners in the hierarchy were their agents, managers and contractors, who were also mainly English-speaking and Anglican.[3]

As industrialisation in South Wales took off in the first decades of the century, workers' self-organisation took the form of friendly societies, which also acted as union clubs. In 1831 serious rioting broke out in Merthyr Tydfil over a reduction of wages at

2. David Williams, *John Frost: A Study in Chartism* (Cardiff, 1939), p. 111.
3. David J.V. Jones, *The Last Rising: The Newport Insurrection of 1839* (Oxford, 1985), pp. 10-12.

Cyfarthfa ironworks. Twenty-one people were killed in the town when Scottish troops opened fire on a large crowd. The union was effectively crushed after a two month lock-out, and one of the leaders, Dic Penderyn, executed for his part in the rioting. The workers, in response to this repression, organised secretly as the 'Scotch Cattle'. The word 'Scotch' referred not to the nation but the verb, which means to thwart or to stop. The Scotch Cattle made and enforced a number of rules in the coal and iron industries, such as trade secrecy, solidarity with sacked workers and refusal to work with non-members. To frighten transgressors the 'herd' went about at night in disguise, sometimes in women's clothes or wearing horns, and making cattle noises. Usually such theatrics and anonymous threatening letters were sufficient to intimidate strike-breakers and other enemies of the Cattle; if not, terroristic methods were sometimes employed, such as house-burning or 'accidents' at work.[4]

By the late 1830s a tiny proportion of the middle-class and better-off workers in the larger towns, such as Newport, were organised into radical reform groups. These radicals saw the old 'Norman' oligarchy which still effectively ran Wales as the class enemy holding up reform. Many of them found it hard to accept the hostility of the middle 'industrious' classes, but the fact was that the iron and coal masters, since they had received the vote in 1832, had become more hostile to reform than the old feudal grandees. Wales, whose gentry had been in decline for hundreds of years, still did not have a 'national' bourgeoisie, with aspirations for political hegemony. Although there were a number of Welsh coal-owners in the Principality and a sizeable 'shopocracy' in places like Cardiff, Swansea and Newport, these native entrepreneurs lacked the capital accumulated by the old aristocrats and new English capitalists, who owed much of their fortunes to the slave trade as well as the new industries.[5] Parliamentary elections in Monmouthshire were still dominated by the clans of the old feudal order–the Morgans, Somersets and Salisburys–who were more concerned with inter-family rivalries than with public policy.

---

4. Williams, op. cit. 112-18.
5. Wilks, op. cit., p. 47.

In parliamentary elections their candidates spent fortunes bribing the voters with feasts and free beer.[6]

Some radicals of the middle class served on Newport town council. In 1836 John Frost, a prosperous middle-class draper, was appointed to the magistrates' bench. In this role he did his utmost to obstruct the implementation of the New Poor Law. That same year he was elected Mayor of Newport, and made a name for himself as the scourge of the old regime of Thomas Protheroe (the chief agent for the Tredegar estates of the Morgan family) and his business partner Thomas Phillips. In 1838 Frost failed to get re-elected as mayor and was replaced by Phillips. This struggle between Frost and Phillips before long became a matter of life and death for them.[7] In the meantime Frost assumed leadership of the new Working Men's Association in Monmouthshire, and was elected as delegate to the Chartist National Convention in late 1838 along with two other WMA leaders: solicitor Hugh Williams (Carmarthen and Merthyr) and former cleric Charles Jones (Montgomeryshire).

At first the Working Men's Associations avoided the coalfield and recruited the artisans, tradesmen, schoolmasters and dissenting ministers of the larger towns. But with the onset of *The People's Charter* campaign in autumn 1838, signatures for the petition were needed and the lecturers of the WMA were sent into the valleys, where they preached the democratic ideas of Thomas Paine and set up radical associations. On New Year's Day 1839 Henry Vincent, Convention delegate for the West Country, addressed 7,000 near Pontypool, then went on to Bristol, where he announced to the WMA his intention to publish a paper in the city. As a former printer he knew how to do it, and as a friend of Hetherington and Cleave, the leading radical London publishers, he had access to their contacts in the printing and news-vending trades. In order to avoid the status of a newspaper, which would incur the stamp-tax, Vincent gave it the title *The Western Vindicator; or, Memoirs and Correspondence of an Editor*. With its feature entitled 'The Life and Rambles of Henry Vincent', beginning on 9 March, Vincent was able to effectively report on his activities

6. Williams, op. cit., pp. 6-7.
7. Ibid., pp. 86-94.

and speeches on his missionary tours in the West Country and South Wales, which he undertook with William Burns of Dundee. Through his tours he was able to recruit a number of WMA supporters as leader writers and correspondents, who contributed similar 'Life and Rambles' features. One 'Hibernicus' addressed Irish readers; 'Junius' championed the iron and coal workers against the masters and coal agents and their aristocratic allies; 'A Young Republican' advocated use of arms in self-defence; and John Frost contributed a weekly letter in which he consistently called for an alliance of artisans, tradesmen and farmers to take on the corrupt industrialists and landed families. The political writings of Cobbett, Paine and Volney were extracted for the paper, and literary contributions included short stories, songs and poems. Local industrialists, aristocrats and clergy who expressed views hostile to Chartism were denounced and insulted. In one of the few cartoons to be printed in the *Vindicator*, Newport Mayor Thomas Phillips appeared on the front page as a chimpanzee in a gentleman's suit. By August 1839 the paper had sales of 3,400 at 2d a copy, more than enough to break even.[8]

 Henry Vincent had witnessed a frantic level of agitation on the part of the Welsh and West Country Working Men's Associations by the time the Convention delegates gathered in his native London in February 1839. To Lovett and the 'moderates' of the LWMA, the 'extreme' agitation in the North and West was a symptom of the disease, not the cure, and endangered efforts to find common cause with the 'enlightened' elements of the middle class. Even in South Wales there were some in the WMA who agreed with Lovett's moderate position, but they were losing ground to the physical-force advocates. According to an anonymous correspondent in *The Welshman*, the WMA in South Wales had originally consisted of:

> really intelligent men, overlookers and operatives in the Iron and Coal Works, etc, who thoroughly acquaint themselves with the principles of political economy, are well versed in the history of their country, including its government… they seek a change…

8. Owen R. Ashton, 'The Western Vindicator and Early Chartism', *Papers for the People—A Study of the Chartist Press* (London, 2005), pp. 54-81.

but they seek it only by employing the moral powers of evidence, argument, union and perseverance... These we may venture to denominate the original and legitimate Chartists.

But by 1839, he continued, these moderates had been usurped by a new breed of Welsh physical-force supporters. He was astonished—and appalled—by their new-found political consciousness:

It is astonishing to what extent men, who do not understand a word of English, are informed, and accurately too, of practices in church and state... They know all about the Civil List, and the spiritual rent-roll—they can give undeniable detail of sinecures, pensions, jobs, and official salaries of fat Bishoprics and lean Curacies—they compute the amount of national taxation, and by a practical arithmetic of their own, divide its charge among the community, giving themselves, at least, their full quota—and then seeing that they are not all consulted in laying on the burden, they are seized with strong desire to fling it off... These are the physical force, or spurious Chartists; who think a Revolution would be a good thing, because it would get rid of all the aforesaid grievances, by a grand explosion...[9]

By March, the *Western Vindicator* could claim, "there is now more political feeling in this country than ever existed, perhaps, in any nation in the world. It would seem that every man has become a politician".[10] As in the North East, there was no simple correlation between political consciousness and wage levels. In South Wales miners earned about 24s a week and ironworkers often earned twice that amount. Even labourers' wages, at 12s to 14s, were twice that of textile workers in some areas of northern England.[11] The *Western Vindicator* observed:

there is something more in hand with the people at the present time than a mere question of a rise or fall in wages. They feel the degradation of being bound by laws, oppressive and tyrannical in their nature made by persons who know nothing of their condi-

9. Quoted in Wilks, op. cit., pp. 99-100. *Shrewsbury News*, 21 December 1839.

10. *Western Vindicator*, 3 March 1839.

11. Williams, op. cit., p. 118.

tion and their wants. They have felt there is no security for their rights–no respect for their feelings–no hope of any amelioration from a Parliament elected by you–the middle classes. They have been robbed of the fruits of their labour, and their poverty and misery laughed at by worthless and wicked men. They have been slaves, and from all appearances they are determined to be so not much longer.[12]

There was also a growing understanding of the conflict between labour and capital. The Swansea Working Men's Association declared:

the wealth procured is made the slave to the possessors of the wealth that he laboured to create; power is transferred from labour to capital, and the producer sinks into a mere instrument to be used as needed, and thrown aside as soon as a more efficient one is presented.[13]

By February 1839 there were over twenty Chartist associations in Monmouthshire alone, claiming a total of 15,000 signed-up supporters.[14] By the summer, membership was estimated to be around 25,000 in Monmouthshire and Glamorgan. Unlike the London Chartists, those in South Wales had no problem finding meeting places; the beerhouses were beyond the control of any licensing authorities. Women's associations, as elsewhere, were active, but in South Wales the level of radicalisation was greater. Mary Ferriday, one the widows of the Rising later that year, said, "*I used to quarrel on Mondays with my husband about his going to the Chartist club… The women used to mob me because I would not join them and called me a Tory and abused me whenever I met them*".[15] This reign of democratic 'terror' affected relationships at work: managers and clerks who signed up for their employers as special constables were intimidated, as were shopkeepers who refused to support the Charter. In many parts of the valleys anyone who didn't sign the petition was subjected to as much contempt as a strike-break-

12. *Western Vindicator*, 24 Aug 1839.
13. Jones, op. cit., p. 56.
14. Jones, ibid., pp. 61-65. *Western Vindicator*, 3 March 1839.
15. Jones, ibid., p. 68, Newport Public Library, *Chartist Trials* 9, M. Ferriday.

Henry Vincent, editor of the Western Vindicator

er. In March 1839 Newport magistrate and mayor, Thomas Phillips, wrote to the Home Secretary about Chartist agitators, who were telling audiences in the valleys that *"if their demands are not conceded they will be justified in resorting to force and that they need not fear bloodshed because the soldiers will not act"*. He added:

> *I cannot say to what extent these appeals may influence the conduct of the working classes in this neighbourhood—I am loath to believe that they will be hurried into actual insurrection but it is certain that sullen discontent marks their appearance that they look with aversion and dislike at their employers and that the moral influence which ought to belong to the government and without which the government itself cannot exist is altogether at an end amongst a very numerous class of the community.*[16]

Crawshay Bailey was alarmed to overhear talk by his employees that they wanted a stake in the company, and to make him and his friends dig the coal themselves.[17] Not surprisingly, Bailey saw Chartism as behind such talk, and when Henry Vincent came to agitate the iron workers at Nantyglo, Bailey confronted him. All the land and industry in the area and everyone on it belonged to him and his family, he boasted, and he intended to keep it that way. *"I would risk my life rather than lose my property"*, he declared at an anti-Chartist meeting.[18]

But even coal-owners could be radicalised. In 1838 Zephaniah Williams, a former coal-owner and minerals agent, discovered that a colliery at Cwrt-y-Bella owned by Phillips and Prothero was mining coal from under the land of his in-laws. When Phillips and Prothero refused to pay royalties Williams sank a shaft on his in-laws' land and brought down the roof of the tunnel in the mine. Williams only escaped prosecution because he was charged under the wrong statute. Having made himself *persona non grata* with the leading iron and coal magnates, he changed profession by renting a beerhouse, the Royal Oak, in Blaenau. The first record

16. Dorothy Thompson, *Early Chartism* (London, 1971), pp. 226-27. 'Letter to the Home Secretary from a Newport Magistrate', HO 40/45.
17. Jones, op. cit., p. 81.
18. Ibid., p. 16.

of any political involvement by him dates from 31 March 1839, when he addressed a Chartist meeting of 1,000 on the land attached to his beerhouse. Vincent, who met Williams at the end of April, described him as *"one of the most intelligent men it has ever been my fortune to meet with"*,[19] and Williams had a similarly high opinion of Vincent. They were both to pay a high price for their common cause.

---

19. John Humphries, *The Man From the Alamo: Why the Welsh Chartist Uprising of 1839 Ended in a Massacre* (St Athan, 2004), pp. 68-75.

The Convention

A political party only truly exists when it is divided against itself.
G.W.F. Hegel

he drawing by an unknown artist of the opening of the National Convention at the British Coffee House, Cockspur Street, shows a large room with paintings, fine drapery and chandeliers. The delegates are smartly dressed and looking statesmanlike and solemn, as if they were preparing to determine the fate of the nation. The Convention began its proceedings at 10 a.m. on 4 February, the day of the Queen's opening of Parliament. Robert Lowery, delegate from the North East, recalled:

> *The British Coffee House being close by, those of us who had never seen her Majesty made a general rush to see her and her procession. Some of the gentlemen in waiting would have been astounded at the free criticisms and remarks made upon the beef-eaters and paraphernalia of the procession.[1]*

So far over a half a million signatures had been collected for the petition and almost £1,000 had been raised for the National Rent, to finance the work of the Convention. The Convention met with fifty-three delegates in attendance, all of them men. Out of a total of seventy-one who attended during the Convention's seven-month existence, forty were working men, fifteen were newspaper editors or publishers, and the rest were small businessmen or professionals in law, church or medicine. There was, however, usually a disproportionate middle-class presence at any given

---

1. Lowery, op. cit., p. 119.

time, because the working men often had ties to home and work which were difficult to break.[2] For example, Dorchester delegate George Loveless, the Tolpuddle Martyr now back from Van Dieman's Land, had to return home after attending for four days. He explained in a letter: *"I find it utterly impossible under present circumstances to leave home. If I did I must hire a man to supply my place which at present I cannot afford to do"*.[3]

On 6 February the Convention moved to a cheaper venue at Dr Johnson's Tavern, Bolt Court, Fleet Street. John Frost was elected as chairman, a move which led to the Home Office terminating his position as a magistrate weeks later. The atmosphere of the early Convention is captured in the memoirs of the French feminist Flora Tristan, who gained admittance to its proceedings accompanied by a female friend close to the Chartist leadership. The two women turned off Fleet Street into a narrow passage leading to a beer house, where they were challenged for the password by a pot-boy sentry. On providing it, they were led through a back parlour into a small courtyard, and along a corridor to the door of the meeting-room. Tristan wrote:

> *nobody was admitted except after being vouched for by two known members. These wise precautions prevented spies from slipping inside. The first thing that impressed me was the expression on the faces of the delegates… each head had a striking individuality of its own. There were about thirty or forty members of the National Convention present and about the same number of young working-class sympathisers. I was pleased to find five French working men and two women of the same class among them. Every one present followed the discussion with alert attention.*[4]

On 11 February the Ayrshire tailor Hugh Craig proposed that the Convention urgently needed to make a clear pronouncement on what ulterior means they should recommend to the people, should

---

2. Thomas M. Kemnitz, 'The Chartist Convention of 1839', *Albion*, vol. 10, no. 2 (summer 1978), pp. 161-64.

3. Dorothy Thompson, *The Chartists* (London, 1984), p. 65.

4. Quoted in Alfred Plummer, *Bronterre—A Political Biography of Bronterre O'Brien 1804-1864* (London, 1971), pp. 106-7.

"it unfortunately happen that the delegates fail to convince the members of the House of Commons of the justice of the principles of The People's Charter".[5]

Feargus O'Connor supported Craig's motion, but others did not. Rochdale delegate James Taylor, a Unitarian minister, said that it would be wrong to assume that Parliament would ignore the wishes of the people. If the Convention ruled out a positive result in Parliament from the start, then how would the Convention maintain an amicable working relationship with the two dozen or so MPs who were needed to present and propose the petition to the House of Commons? Bronterre O'Brien agreed, arguing: *"At present the Convention stands as mediator between the suffering people and the House of Commons... and it would be absurd to talk of ulterior measures unless they had two or three millions of signatures".* He also believed that the people would only support ulterior measures if and when Parliament rejected the petition. At this point Henry Vincent put forward a compromise: to appoint a committee to consider what measures to undertake in the event of the failure of the petition. But even this was too much for some of the moderates. James Paul Cobbett, a solicitor from the West Riding (and son of William Cobbett), demanded that the Convention restrict itself to presentation of the petition. He got little support for this, because delegates knew that such a restriction would curtail their political discussions and would mean, in effect, that once Parliament rejected the petition the Convention would have to dissolve.

O'Connor dismissed the idea that discussion of ulterior measures would lessen parliamentary support for the petition. He was convinced that popular support for the Convention depended on

5. We have referenced the proceedings of the Convention only by date, and in the text. There are numerous sources for the proceedings of the Convention. Kemnitz cites the *Champion*, the *Charter*, the *Chartist*, the *Northern Star*, the *Operative*, the *Sun*, and police reports filed in HO 40/44. As well as these we have used reports in the *Morning Chronicle* and the account of the proceedings in Robert Gammage, *History of the Chartist Movement*. In the publications of the time the spoken words of the delegates were reported as indirect discourse. For readability we have taken the liberty of rendering them as direct discourse.

making it clear that the petition would be their *"last notice to the House of Capitalists"*. If Parliament rejected it, he promised, *"the Convention would do something, within the law, which would afford a demonstration of the people's strength and determination"*. Dr Matthew Fletcher argued that petitioning was simply a legal cloak for such a demonstration: *"the men of the North hold their meetings under this cloak, because the right of petitioning is almost the only constitutional right they have left"*. O'Brien concurred, likening the petition to a *"notice to quit"*; failure to obey the notice would bring about the ejection of the capitalists from the House.

One delegate who had no doubt that ulterior measures would have to used rather than just talked about was Dr Peter McDouall. A surgeon in Ashton-under-Lyme, Lancashire, McDouall had presented a paper to the British Association describing the conditions of Ramsbottom and nearby towns: a very low rate of literacy; high infant mortality (in some areas 50 per cent of children never reached the age of five); millworkers' wages as low as 4s a week; and families of seven or more living in single rooms—*"rags, starvation and death were the fate of these unfortunate people"*. McDouall had been elected to the Convention because he had been proposed by the Rev. J.R. Stephens, who had stood down following his arrest in December for an inflammatory speech. In answer to the delegates who wanted to restrict the Convention to petitioning and moral force, McDouall insisted that the people had a right to bear arms and withdraw their labour in a general strike. *"I did not come to the Convention merely to present a petition,"* he said. *"If you are not prepared to recommend ulterior measures I had better go home"*. When the vote was taken, Henry Vincent's amendment to establish a committee on ulterior measures was passed. Cobbett resigned from the Convention on 14 February, as did the middle-class Bolton delegate Joseph Wood.[6]

These first defections would not be the last. But for the majority who remained there was agreement on the need to get more signatures for the petition. The Convention assigned some of its members to travel as missionaries to parts of the kingdom where it had not yet been circulated. For example, in March Rob-

6. Kemnitz, op. cit., pp. 161-64.

ert Lowery and Dumfries delegate Abram Duncan were sent as missionaries to Cornwall, a region thoroughly cut off from radical thought by the combined forces of impassable roads from England, class domination and Methodism. In Truro no landlord dared give Lowery and Duncan a meeting room, so they decided on an open-air meeting and got the Truro town crier to go around and announce it.[7] The two Chartists were given a fair hearing by those who hesitantly approached their soapbox. Lowery's first impression was that the Cornish were *"a simple primitive people, with strong religious feelings"*, and he thought that *"The Methodist style of preaching, however good to work on their feelings, wanted some Presbyterian reasoning to cultivate their understanding"*. In his speeches he *"generally took some acknowledged principle in religion or morals, and endeavoured to show that the evils we complained of, and sought to remove, were opposed to it, and that resistance to such wrongs was obedience to God"*.

Duncan sent a report on Cornwall to the radical *True Scotsman*, telling his cultured Scottish readers:

> you can have no conception of the ignorance of the people upon general politics… they might just as well have sent missionaries to the South Sea islands, to instruct the natives there in the principles of a free government, as to Cornwall… The people have no dreams of the past—no historical epochs to fall back upon, calculated to light the torch and inflame the soul anew for the battle of liberty. They never fought, bled, or died for liberty. They have never been taught to know that knowledge will improve their social and political condition.[8]

Throughout their tour of Cornwall the two missionaries refused all donations of money offered by their audiences and made no collections, which gave some of the Cornish the impression that they were *"noblemen in disguise"*. Some refused to believe that they were working-men even when assured that this was the case. In St Ives Lowery asked another town crier if they had any radicals in the town:

---

7. Lowery, op. cit., pp. 128-32.
8. *True Scotsman*, 30 March 1839. Lowery ibid.

"A what, Master?" *said he with a vacant stare.* "Any Radicals or Chartists?" *said I. I shall never forget the vacuity and bewilderment of his countenance.* "No", *answered he, with a grave shake of the head,* "they catch no fish here but pilchards and mackerel". *I burst into a convulsion of laughter...*

In the event there was a large and enthusiastic meeting in St Ives and also at Penzance. When they arranged a meeting at a village near Falmouth, the town crier informed them that the clergyman

THE RURAL POLICE;
'OR, THE LAND OF LIBERTY IN THE 19th CENTURY!

Cartoon Penny Satirist *22 Aug 1840 on government plan to establish county police forces. Shows police raiding a pub, stealing chickens and pigs, and demanding to see a man's passport.*

had told him he was not to cry it, but he was willing to go round the houses and tell people that this was the case! This made the townsfolk more eager to come.

The tour culminated at Gwenapp Pit, where Wesley had once been stoned for preaching. Despite a downpour 14,000 attended. The *Falmouth Express* referred to Lowery and Duncan as *"these poisonous and prowling animals"*, and a magistrate sent a report to the Home Office on 16 March about *"certain miscreants calling themselves deputies from the National Convention"*, who were attempting to inculcate *"treasonable"* principles *"destructive of life and property"*. Most alarmingly, these delegates *"on the one hand... recommend the deluded people to buy a musket, telling them how well it looks on the chimney piece if kept clean and ready to use—and on the other hand urging them to resist the Poor Law—knowing the feeling against that law, I fear more from that doctrine than any other"*. Duncan's dour assessment of the Cornwall mission notwithstanding, it seems to have caused great alarm amongst the Cornish establishment, who felt that the *"deluded"* and *"backward"* population of Cornwall were, as elsewhere, ripe for the Chartists' radical and dangerous ideas.[9] Lowery wrote to the Convention on 26 March that *"the little Kings are all in an uproar here, we have invaded and overturned their dominion"*.[10]

As well as the extension of the Chartist campaign into new areas of the country, there was an intensification of efforts within the movement's existing strongholds which drew in a huge wave of female support. If the huge estimates for attendance at mass meetings in 1838–39 were remotely accurate, then there must have been a great number of women present. Women had already made their presence felt in mobilisations against the New Poor Law as they felt threatened by the state's new power to destroy families, by separating wives and children from husbands in the new workhouses—which became known as 'Whig Bastilles'. Although *The People's Charter* only called for male universal suffrage, Chartism gave women a number of roles, such as collecting signatures for the petition and money for the families of political prisoners, adorning the banners with striking images and slogans, enforcing exclusive dealing with pro-Charter shopkeepers, organising Chartist tea parties, teaching at Chartist Sunday schools and organising public meetings of the new Female Chartist Societies.[11]

There were more than a few male Chartist leaders who praised women's capacity to absorb ideas as superior to men's. Robert

9. National Archives HO 40/41.
10. British Library, Add. MSS. 34,245A. ff. 169-70.
11. Eileen Yeo, 'Practices and Problems of Chartist Democracy', *The Chartist Experience, Studies in Working-Class Radicalism and Culture, 1830-1860*, eds James Epstein and Dorothy Thompson (London, 1982), p. 348.

Lowery, for example, describing his audiences in 1839, *"found the average mind and manners of the women much superior to the men among the poor. Their powers of thinking and observing had evidently been more exercised".*[12] He found that male attitudes to the need for exclusive dealing were often deficient when compared with their female counterparts: *"the man that will not go to the length of the street to spend his money in the shop of a friend or a store the profits of which he may be sure, will never walk ten miles with the musket on his shoulder to fight for freedom".*[13]

Feminist historian Jutta Schwarzkopf argues that despite the important mass activity of women which marked the beginning of Chartism, and the praise of some of the male leaders, the failure to fight for female suffrage and the circumscribing of women's ambitions to being 'good homemakers', had the effect of holding back the radicalising process for the long term. Certainly the articles and addresses published by Female Chartist Associations during this period show that the writers had, as Schwarzkopf puts it, *"absorbed the movement's political creed"* that the workers were the real producers of wealth, that the *"class legislation"* of *"aristocratic misrule"* should be replaced by democracy.[14] Schwarzkopf says: *"In the context of general working-class insubordination, Chartist women's refusal to let themselves be excluded from the public sphere heightened the threatening aspect of Chartism to the ruling classes".* As the Newcastle Female Chartists declared,

> We have been told that the province of woman is her home and that the field of politics is to be left to men; this we deny; the nature of things renders it impossible and the conduct of those who give the advice is at variance with the principles they assert.[15]

Schwarzkopf points out that, although the rebellion of women against their 'mission' to stay in the home was welcomed by Chartist men in the organisational sense, they expected women to accept their mission in the ideological sense, though *"infused with a sense of class consciousness"*. The December 1838 address by the

---

12. Lowery, op. cit., p. 132.

13. *Northern Star*, 14 Sept 1839.

14. Schwarzkopf, op. cit., p. 96. *Northern Star*, 8 Dec 1838.

15. Schwarzkopf ibid., p. 97. *Northern Star*, 9 Feb 1839.

Nottingham Female Political Union said: *"At a time like the present, our energies are required in aid of those measures in which our husbands, fathers, brothers and children are so actively and zealously engaged"*. Schwarzkopf comments: *"This pose severely hampered women's political self-expression. It effectively prevented them from establishing themselves as political agents in their own right with needs and aspirations specific to them as women"*. Furthermore:

> *this pose implied that the women were happy to support a struggle, the primary object of which—universal male suffrage—ostensibly did not affect themselves… Common social origin, regardless of gender, was to ensure that working-class women's grievances would be considered sympathetically. Far from addressing any forms of sexual antagonism, such gender-blind political representation helped remove them from the agenda of class politics.*[16]

Although Chartist 'ideology' never recognised women's role as *"political agents in their own right"* with specific needs and aspirations, Schwarzkopf points out that not all women in this early period towed the line. The Female Chartist Association of Ashton, for example, fully expected female suffrage to follow automatically from the enactment of the Charter.[17] Certainly some Chartist men 'privately' agreed with this view. William Lovett later claimed that when he drafted *The People's Charter* in 1838 he had included a clause for the extension of the franchise to women, but this was removed in the face of arguments that it would hold up the enfranchisement of men. But as historian Dorothy Thompson has shown, it was after the draft of the Charter was circulated nationally to associations that the proposal to include women's suffrage was put forward, presumably by groups from the provinces. Lovett, in a second printing of *The People's Charter* that same year, took note of the suggestion as a *"reasonable proposition"* but expressed *"fears of entertaining it, lest the false estimate man entertains for this half of the human family may cause his ignorance and prejudice to be enlisted to retard the progress of his own freedom"*. Since, as Thompson points out, the LWMA did not admit women as members, the *"fears"* were not surprising. Thompson also points out that whilst

---

16. Schwarzkopf ibid., pp. 89-90.
17. Schwarzkopf ibid. *Northern Star*, 5 Feb 1839.

the LWMA did not admit women members, the 'Jacobin' LDA did and established 'autonomous' female organisations.[18] In May 1839 Elizabeth Neesom, of the London Female Democratic Association, said—in a clear 'feminist' tone:

> [we] consider it our duty to co-operate with our patriotic sisters in the country to obtain the Universal Suffrage in the shortest possible time [and] to annihilate the cruel, unjust and atrocious New Poor Law (miscalled!) Amendment Bill, to support with any means in our power any patriot engaged in the great struggle for freedom who may need our assistance and to destroy for ever this cruel murdering system of transporting our children to the burning sands of Africa or immuring them in the horrid cotton hells and treating them worse, for no other crime than that of being poor. Sisters and friends, we entreat you to shake off that apathy and timidity which too generally prevails among our sex (arising from the prejudices of a false education)... To those who may be, or appear to be, surprised that females should be daring enough to interfere with politics, to them we simply say that, as it is a female who assumes to rule this nation in defiance of the universal rights of man and woman, we assert in accordance with the rights of all, and acknowledging the sovereignty of the people our right, as free women (or women determined to be free) to rule ourselves.[19]

The East London Female Patriotic Association (also backed by the Democratic Association) called for a campaign of *"exclusive dealing"* with *"friendly"* (i.e. pro-Chartist) shops and businesses, and made it clear that the Association was self-determined as regards which men should be allowed to address it. The Association would consist of *"females only"* and would let *"no gentleman be admitted without the invitation of a majority of the members present"*.[20]

The Chartists' failure to support women's suffrage in 1838 left a legacy that lasted throughout the century. The level and militancy of women's involvement during the period we are concerned with was not sustained in the movement's later years. In Schwar-

---

18. Dorothy Thompson, *The Chartists* (London, 1984), p. 124.
19. *Northern Star*, 11 May 1839.
20. *Operative*, 14 April 1839.

zkopf's view, "*It could be argued that, after the demise of Chartism [in the 1850s], women dropped out of working-class politics not least because of the movement's obvious failure—given its inability to arrest the pace of industrialisation—to reinstate them into what was commonly agreed to be their proper position of wives and mothers*".[21]

---

21. Schwarzkopf, op. cit., p. 287.

The London Montagne

When delegates arrived from the provinces to attend the National Convention in mid-February many were dismayed at how apathetic the capital seemed to be in comparison with other parts of the country. True, 8,000 Londoners did attend a welcome meeting for Convention members on Clerkenwell Green; and when Feargus O'Connor asked another meeting that month outside White Conduit House in Pentonville what they would do if the government arrested the Convention members, they heartily shouted *"We'd rise–we'd rise and we'd fight"*. But such voices represented only a minority opinion of the London working classes. Some delegates complained that the Convention was spending a lot more money on propaganda and organisation in London than elsewhere; and yet the fractious London Chartists had collected less National Rent money and signatures for the petition than had some small northern towns. O'Connor, on the other hand, saw London Chartism as so important that it warranted all the support the Convention could muster.[1]

One of the problems facing Chartism in the capital was the social geography of the city itself. The population, of perhaps two million, was still crammed into a metropolis that only extended as far as Paddington and Kensington in the west; Camden and Islington in the north; Hackney Marshes and India Docks in the east; and Lambeth and Southwark south of the river. There had

1. Goodway, op. cit., p. 28.

been considerable movement of the well off from the centre to the west, leaving behind their dirt-poor neighbours in the rookeries of Seven Dials and Moorfields. There had also been migration by better-off artisans from the even worse areas of the East End to the north and west, because anyone who could afford to get out of the East End did so as soon as possible. The railways were only just beginning to have an impact on the lives of Londoners. North of the river the new Euston Arch greeted passengers on the new London and Birmingham Railway, and from Paddington the Great Western ran as far as Maidenhead. On the south bank the London and South Western ran from Nine Elms to Woking, and the London and Greenwich now extended to Croydon. But the big railway termini and the extension of the commuter networks were still to come and outlying villages, such as Tottenham, Highgate, Putney and Wandsworth, were still untouched by urban sprawl. As late as 1840 Francis Place could still claim:

> London differs very widely from Manchester and, indeed, from every other place on the face of the earth. It has no local or particular interest as a town, not even as to its politics. Its several boroughs in this respect are like so many very populous places at a distance from one another, and the inhabitants of any of them know nothing, or next to nothing, of the proceedings in an other, and not much indeed of those of their own.[2]

The LDA, led by Harney's 'Jacobins', tried to overcome this parochialism. By the time the Convention began, the LDA had broken out of its strongholds in the East End and set up new sections in Shoreditch, Deptford, Lambeth, Bermondsey, Old Kent Road, St Pancras, Islington, Westminster, Hammersmith, Chiswick and Kensington. Another breakthrough was the decision of Marylebone Radical Association to expand itself as the West London Democratic Association and affiliate to the LDA in April.[3] The

2. Francis Place to Richard Cobden, 4 March 1840 'Papers: 1839-40', London Radicalism 1830-1843: 'A Selection of the Papers of Francis Place', pp. 203-18 (London, 1970) [www.british-history.ac.uk].

3. Jennifer Bennett, 'A Study in London Radicalism: The Democratic Association 1837-1841', *Chartist Studies*, ed. Epstein (London, 1982), pp. 92, 104.

LDA was organising fairly large meetings to argue for ulterior measures. In February a meeting on Stepney Green saw 10,000 in attendance, and another, at the George public house on Commercial Road, sponsored by the Tower Hamlets Rent Committee, drew 7,000.

In the Convention, LDA leader Harney sat with a group who loosely constituted themselves as the Jacobin 'Montagne' of the Convention: Dr John Taylor from Ayr; William Burns, Dundee shoemaker; William Cardo, London trade unionist; William Rider, Leeds weaver; Peter Bussey, Bradford publican; Richard Marsden, Preston weaver; Robert Lowery, former seaman from Newcastle; and Charles Neesom, the LDA intellectual who represented Bristol.

On 28 February Harney and Neesom got resolutions passed at a public meeting of the LDA at the Mechanics Hall in Marylebone, calling for the Convention to organise resistance to all acts of government repression. William Rider and Richard Marsden proposed to the meeting that *"we hold it to be the duty of the Convention to impress upon the people the necessity of an immediate preparation for ulterior measures"*. Other members of the Convention, not all of them 'moderates', regarded this as unacceptable pressure by the Democratic Association. Dr Matthew Fletcher alleged that *"self-styled Jacobin Clubs"* with *"purely foreign"* politics were conspiring to dominate the Convention, and John Cleave similarly denounced the LDA as *"Marats"*; while J.R. Richardson of Manchester accused Harney and his allies of constituting a *"junta"* which was pushing for *"ulterior measures independent of the Convention as their principal objects"*; and even the 'extremists', Dr Taylor and Dr McDouall, called the LDA's actions an affront to the authority of the Convention and injurious in the fight for public opinion.[4]

In the middle of this fracas, Feargus O'Connor, who by this time clearly saw himself as the leader of the movement, assumed the role of mediator and unifier. Harney, Neesom, Ryder and Marsden, he insisted, were *"as good men as we have"*; and he added that *"if Jacobin Clubs, or the Democratic Association, can infuse fresh zeal into the Convention, so much the better"*. O'Connor proposed that discussion of ulterior measures should take place at simultaneous

---

4. *Operative*, 10 March 1839.

mass meetings to be called a week before the presentation of the petition to Parliament. For present purposes, he proposed—much to Harney's approval—that a meeting should be held at the Crown and Anchor on the Strand on 16 March, to explain the Convention's thinking on this issue. At this very well-attended event, chaired by John Frost, the speakers—Vincent, Harney, O'Connor, O'Brien, Dr Taylor and George Rogers—all argued that the Convention should encourage preparations to use force.

A police spy in the LDA reported that an anonymous pike seller met Harney, Coombe, Ireland and Beniowski at the Hole-in-the Wall public house in Fleet Street on 20 April, offering pikes at 4s each (very expensive, at twice the going rate). The spy claimed that he overheard Harney say to the man on the stair that *"he must have them ready by next Thursday [25 April]"*. But it seems that the LDA was not in any position financially to buy pikes from suspicious hawkers. Another spy, who attended a council meeting of the LDA in April, reported that treasurer Thomas Ireland had received less than 11s in subscriptions, out of which 7s had to go on rent—leaving not even enough to pay the cost of printing the membership cards.[5]

The LDA managed to get James Cane Coombe to finance the launch, on 13 April, of the *London Democrat*. In the first issue of the paper Harney announced that he would be writing on the lessons of the French Revolution of 1789 under the name 'Friend of the People'—the same title assumed by his hero of the French Revolution, Jean-Paul Marat. In the next issue (20 April) he said that *"in the Democratic Association, the Jacobin Club again lives and flourishes"* and urged his readers, *"Your country, your posterity, your God demands of you to ARM! ARM! ARM!"* Coombe argued for a march on the Metropolis from Birmingham, Manchester, Liverpool and the surrounding districts.

Chartist activists and trade unionists in the outlying villages of London had local concerns and voted for delegates they knew best. But the LDA was more concerned with getting those delegates elected who would fight all the way for the Charter. Because of some clumsy attempts by the LDA to get its members elected by stacking meetings, Harney and Neesom were accused

by the *Charter* newspaper of attempting to take wholesale control
of Chartism in London. On 22 April, at a meeting on Kennington
Common to elect a delegate for East Surrey and Lambeth, the
moderate Charles Westerton lost the vote to Joseph Williams of
the LDA. The vote was disputed and the Convention upheld the
challenge, refusing to allow Williams to take his seat. Similarly,
after a 1 May meeting on Stepney Green to elect a Convention
member for Tower Hamlets, the vote for LDA supporter William
Drake was overturned by the Convention.[6]

London delegates Hartwell and Vincent identified with what
might be called a 'centrist' current in the metropolis, represented
by the *Chartist* newspaper. Launched on 2 February 1839, in rivalry to the weekly *Charter*, the mouthpiece of the LWMA, the
Chartist was prepared to support physical force if all else failed,
but also argued for an alliance with the middle-class against the
"*vermin-breeding squires*".[7] After the departure of the Birmingham
moderate faction in April, the O'Connorite majority and the
Chartist newspaper got the Convention to back a new Metropolitan Charter Association to pull London Chartism together, with
Hartwell as its secretary.[8]

Assemblies in Smithfield on 22 and 29 April frightened the Lord
Mayor of London into issuing a proclamation banning a planned
outdoor meeting on 6 May at Smithfield. The LDA defied the
ban and met at Smithfield, but when the police were sighted they
marched off, 5,000-strong, and gathered on Islington Green.
Harney urged them to arm, but when he unwisely asked those
who had armed to show their hands he got a very poor response,
and shouts of "*Oh! Oh! That's going too far!*" Harney's stance should
not, however, be seen merely as an example of his alleged infantile
Jacobinism; he was simply trying to express the majority position
of the Convention, which was getting a very different response
elsewhere in the country.[9]

_____

6. Bennett ibid., p. 98.
7. *The Chartist*, 23 February 1839, reproduced in *Chartism and Society*,
pp. 194-95.
8. Bennett, op. cit., pp. 102-3. Schoyen, op. cit., p. 65.
9. *Operative*, 13 May 1839.

The Prayer
and the Blunderbuss

*I would remind you [of] the story of Gil Blas—where a famous
beggar who levied his blackmail under the name of charity used
to present his petition with one hand whilst the finger of the other
was applied to the blunderbuss to assist the prayer of the petition.
That was a style of petition that never failed.*
Bronterre O'Brien, 1837

Feargus O'Connor argued that whatever form the coming
clash would take, the Convention would have to *"bring itself
morally into collision with the other authorities"*. He thought that
simultaneous mass meetings would stretch the capacities of the
army and police to contain them and strike fear into the government. He even implicitly went so far as to justify incendiarism as
a form of self-defence, citing the torchlight processions of the
last winter as an effective test of the legal right of assembly, and
said he was not *"going to counsel the people with pikes and pistols without barrels, and guns without locks to unfold their breasts to armed soldiery… No, when the people make their attacks it will be upon property"*.
O'Connor warned that *"the wadding of the first cannon which might
be fired on the people will ignite all the property in the country"*, and
added: *"let them fire one shot upon the people, and I would not give them
two-pence for all the property within two miles march"*. But although he
showed himself as quite prepared to use the veiled threat of violence, he consistently stopped short of actually calling for armed
revolution.[1]

However serious the threat, the government had by this time
decided to beef up the forces of law and order in the provinces.
Although London had a large police force of 3,000, the provincial
towns and cities had nothing like such a strong police presence.
In March the Whigs proposed a centralised plan for policing the

---

1. *Northern Star*, 6 April 1839.

country in the County Police Bill, sometimes called the Rural Police Bill.[2] William Villiers Sankey, Anglo-Irish aristocrat, author
and Convention delegate for Edinburgh, said of the Police Bill:

> *this system was first tried in Ireland... Ireland has been for a long*
> *period the nursery in which the future legislators of England are*
> *sent unfledged to develop the powers of mischief... and now the*
> *Lord Lieutenant of Ireland is in fact the independent general of*
> *an army appointed by himself, commanded by officers chosen by*
> *himself...*

Dr Taylor declared:

> *You may submit to it in the South of England—the men of the*
> *North, I tell you will not... before such a system can be put in*
> *force there, you will hear of many a bloody struggle, and when all*
> *else has failed and England is subdued, every valley in Scotland*
> *will be a battlefield...*

For a minority of delegates such talk made it impossible for them
to remain in the Convention. The BPU, having failed to divert
Chartist energies into a campaign against the Corn Law, sub-
sequently failed to defeat the physical-force arguments in the
National Convention.[3] At the end of March the middle-class
Birmingham delegates, Hadley, Pierce and Salt, resigned, as did
Patrick Mathew, a landowner from Perthshire and Fife, and the
Rev. Arthur Wade, Nottingham delegate, Church of England vicar

---

2. *Chartism and Society: An Anthology of Documents* (London, 1980),
ed. F.C. Mather, p. 57. Malcolm I. Thomis and Peter Holt, *Threats of
Revolution in Britain 1789-1848* (London, 1977), p. 98
3. *Derby and Chesterfield Reporter*, 30 Jan 1839. The Corn Law forbade
imports of corn unless the home price exceeded 80s a quarter, and
thus kept food prices high in comparison with manufactured goods.
Chartists argued that the Corn Law repealers only wanted to make
bread cheaper so they could lower wages. At an anti-Corn Law
meeting at Birmingham Town Hall in January, a thousand businessmen
and merchants had found themselves joined by a larger number of
Chartists, who voted to 'amend' the repeal motion into one that stated
reforms of trade were impossible until *The People's Charter* had been
realised.

and sometime Home Office informer.[4] The seats of the defecting Birmingham delegates were filled weeks later with the election of pro-physical force men: Edward Brown, John Powell and Henry Donaldson.[5]

On 9 April the Convention debated the people's right to arm. R.J. Richardson, citing a whole list of learned sources from Aristotle and Cicero to Dr Johnson and William Cobbett, argued:

> *The laws are complicated in themselves and hard to be understood… Yet not one of those laws denies the constitutional right of Englishmen to be armed… I am not in favour of secret arming, neither, on the other hand, am I in favour of a display of arms at public meetings, yet I wish it to be known to the Government that we are armed, and I would even say I have no objection to a registration act, provided it is founded upon the principle of the 33rd of Henry VIII, which allowed the undoubted right of men to be armed.*

Alexander Halley, of Dunfermline, one of the remaining moderates, argued that *"speaking of arming has done havoc in the North"*; *"I suppose we will next have a commissariat department and drill sergeants. Very few of the country have yet joined us. Very few have signed the petition. I will have nothing to do with anything but moral means. I do not consider the entertainment of this question one of them"*. William Cardo disagreed. He said, *"I have been through a great part of the North lately, and can assure the Convention that it is quite the reverse"*. Richard Marsden from Preston agreed with Cardo, saying *"I know of one street alone where twenty muskets have been procured"*. The Convention then voted that it was *"fully convinced that all constitutional authorities agree on the undoubted right of the people to bear arms"*.

The Liberal Government took note of these proceedings, considered the reports from the provinces of growing disturbances, and began to react, carefully but in earnest. General Charles Napier was appointed commander of the army in the North, arriving at Nottingham Castle to take up the post at the beginning of April 1839. This was quite a shrewd move on the

---

4. Schoyen, op. cit., p. 89.
5. Kenmitz, op. cit.

part of the Government; for politically, General Napier was a reforming radical. Napier wrote of his assignment:

> conscience should not wear a red coat. When I undertook the command of the Northern District under Lord John Russell, I put all my Radical opinions in my blue-coat pocket, and locked the coat in a portmanteau which I left behind me. I told Lord John this when I went to see him on taking the command.[6]

The standing army at this time consisted of only 11,000 troops for the whole country, 6,000 of whom were under Napier's Northern Command at Nottingham. Napier soon found himself inundated with requests from the terrified magistrates of the 'disturbed areas' to send troops. He regarded many of these magistrates as cowardly and incompetent, and usually responded by telling them that their requests would only be considered if they were prepared to provide barrack accommodation, which he saw as essential to protect his troops from attacks and corruption by radicals.[7]

Napier was receiving intelligence from the Home Office on the doings and plans of the Chartists. In the West Riding of Yorkshire, Bradford magistrates reported that armed groups were being led by old soldiers, but charges could not be brought because no one could be found *"to prove them on oath"*. Guns were selling at between 12s and 35s a piece and locally made hand grenades for a trifling 1s a piece.[8] One James Partington of West Houghton, Yorkshire, wrote to the Home Office on 3 April:

> Honoured Sir,
>
> I consider it a duty incumbent upon me to inform you of the Chartist proceedings on Monday last. About four o'clock p.m. five very splendid flags, Caps of Liberty, Death with Cross Bones, mounted upon poles, a band of music, accompanied with a great number of men, women, boys and girls armed with pikes, some with swords, pistols, firelocks with fixed bayonets arrived and halted opposite the Chapel from Hindley and Wigan road, which

---

6. ed. Dorothy Thompson, *Early Chartism*, p. 24. Lord Broughton, *Recollections of a Long Life*, 1909.

7. Thomis and Holt, op. cit., pp. 112-13.

8. Peacock, op. cit., pp. 28-29.

Motley Group was joined by a number of the 'West Houghton Fleet'. After brandishing swords, and discharging fire-arms several times in front of the Red Lion Inn, they returned by the same road...[9]

On 20 April a Home Office report sent to General Napier described Dr Peter McDouall of Ashton, Lancashire, as *"one of the most violent of Chartists"*. On 22 April, in Hyde, near Manchester, McDouall spoke to 3,000 people, many from the Female Radical Association. According to the prosecutors at his trial three months later, he told the crowd that fifty determined men could overthrow the government by seizing the armoury at the Tower of London and handing out arms to the masses. It was also alleged that, along with several accomplices, he had purchased muskets and bayonets from a Birmingham gunsmith.[10] In Newcastle an arms dealer, having procured fifty muskets from a Birmingham gunmaker, placed a darkly humorous advertisement in the *Northern Liberator*:

> *Important Notice.—Whereas a large fleet of war ships is now concentrating on the Southern coast of Russia, within three days' sail of Newcastle or Hull... and might take it into his head any day to try and reach India by a march through England to the utter subversion of the liberties we have not, and the paternal government that does not exist among us. Therefore, and for those reasons, it becomes the duty of every patriotic Englishman to provide himself with the requisite arms, and to be ready at a moment's warning to vindicate his liberties and the independence of his country. In view of this imminent danger, a consignment of muskets and bayonets has arrived in Newcastle and is now on sale at No.—The Side. Price for the individual outfit one pound sterling.*[11]

---

9. David Jones, *Chartism and the Chartists* (London, 1975), p. 156. HO 40/37.
10. Owen Ashton and Paul Pickering, 'The People's Advocate: Peter Murray McDouall (1814-1854)', *Friends of the People: Uneasy Radicals in the Age of the Chartists* (London, 2002), pp. 9-12.
11. Devyr, op. cit., p.171.

On 23 April Napier wrote in his diary: *"These poor devils are in-clined to rise, and if they do what horrid bloodshed! This is dreadful work, would be to God I had gone to Australia"*.[12]

Further south, outside Napier's area of command, there was a serious disturbance in mid-Wales. Working Men's Associations had been founded in the flannel-manufacturing towns of Llanid-loes, Welshpool and Newtown in 1837 after a visit to the area by Henry Hetherington, acting as a missionary from the LWMA. In April 1839 Hetherington returned to the district as a missionary of the National Convention, and when he got back to London he reported to the Convention that these towns had 600 armed men drilling regularly. His report, when published, scared the Mont-gomery magistrates into asking the Home Office for troops. Lord Russell instead sent officers of the London Metropolitan Police to support the special constables at Llanidloes. When, on 30 April, the police arrested three Llanidloes Chartists, a mass meeting was hastily assembled at the call of a bugle, and weavers marched on the magistrates' headquarters at the Trewythen Arms to free the prisoners who had been lodged there. On seeing a considerable force of police and specials forming up in front of the hotel they withdrew, but only to gather weapons for a return visit. A wit-ness, Edward Hamer, recalled:

> some of the women who had joined the crowd kept instigating the men to attack the hotel—one old virago vowing that she would fight till she was knee-deep in blood, sooner than the Cockneys should take their prisoners out of the town. She, along with others of her sex, gathered large heaps of stones, which they subsequently used in defacing and injuring the building which contained the prisoners. When the mob had thus armed themselves, the word 'Forward!' was given, and as soon as they were within hearing of the police, they imperatively demanded the release of their friends, which demand was of course refused.[13]

---

12. eds R. Brown and C. Daniels, *Chartist Documents and Debates* (London, 1984). William Napier, *Life and Opinions of General Sir Charles Napier* (1857).
13. Wilks, op. cit., pp. 93-94, 127.

The weavers then stormed the building. Many of the specials fled the scene and those who remained, along with the London police, were overpowered. The prisoners were set free. Bottles and

Bronterre O'Brien, founder of the Poor Man's Guardian

barrels of beverages from the hotel were taken out and either drunk or spilled into the gutter. As Hamer put it, *"Destruction alone seemed to relieve the intense feeling of hatred which they experienced against the police and the house which sheltered them"*. The Mayor was dragged from his hiding place under a hotel bed and brought out to face the crowd in the street. A surgeon by trade, he acquitted himself by telling them that, considering he had brought many of them into the world, it would be unfortunate if they were to send him out of it. Touching their better nature, he was allowed to go home.

The Times headline declared, 'Chartist Outrage–The Town of Llanidloes in the Possession of Revolutionists,' and on 3 May a Royal Proclamation was issued against those in the country who *"unlawfully assembled together for the purpose of practising military exercise, movements, and evolutions"*. On Saturday 4 May, after the Chartists had held Llanidloes for four days, a force of troops, yeomanry and special constables entered the town in force. The Chartists, warned of their approach, had fled. The Convention delegate for Birmingham, John Powell, shoved a policeman off the chaise he was escaping on, but was arrested in nearby Welshpool and charged with seditious speaking. A dozen others were arrested when, as the Times reported, the troops went out into the countryside to *"beat the bushes for Chartists"*. Few arms were found, as they had probably been buried.[14]

On 7 May Home Secretary Lord John Russell wrote to the Lord Lieutenants of the English counties, encouraging them to organise the middle classes into armed associations at the government's expense. But the argument that every free-born Englishmen had the right and duty to bear arms whenever 'liberty' was endangered was also taken up by the Chartist physical-forcers, who argued that the working-class democrats, not the squires and shopocrats, represented freedom and patriotism. They asked: if the people were forbidden from organising for their own self-defence against the New Poor Law and the proposed County Police, why not prosecute the middle classes for attempting to form militias? When, in May, O'Connor and James Cobbett brought a prosecution against some *"'Respectable' Peace Preservation Physical Force Men"* in Barnsley who tried to form a militia, the quarter sessions found in O'Connor's favour–but the verdict was overturned two months later in Rotherham.[15]

Thomas Phillips, the Mayor of Newport, Monmouthshire, reported in mid-March to the Home Office that gun-purchasing clubs were being set up by South Wales Working Men's Associations, and that consignments of muskets made in Birmingham

---

14. *Early Chartism*, pp. 222-25. Edward Hamer, *The Chartist Outbreak in Llanidloes* (1867).

15. *Chartism and Society*, pp. 152-54. *Sheffield and Rotherham Independent*, 13 July 1839: *Sheffield Iris*, 9 and 16 July 1839.

were being delivered to Chartist hot-beds such as Pontypool and Tredegar.[16] When the Lord Lieutenant of Monmouthshire, Capel Hanbury Leigh, was given Home Office approval and funding for 'Associations for Protection of Life and Property', the *Western Vindicator* carried an open letter to Lord John Russell, the main point of which was to give an estimate of armed Chartist strength in the South Wales coalfield:

> *I do not know exactly the number you want… but I would suggest the following as a commencement:*
>
> | | |
> |---|---|
> | *Newport; arms, etc. for* | *… 5,000 able-bodied men* |
> | *Pontypool and vicinity, arms for* | *… 8,000 ditto* |
> | *Carleon and vicinity, arms for* | *… 500 ditto* |
> | *Blackwood, Tredegar, etc. arms for* | *… 10,000 ditto* |
> | *Nantyglo and its vicinity, arms for* | *… 10,000 ditto* |
> | *Merthyr Tidvil and neighbourhood, arms for* | *… 20,000 ditto.* |
>
> *And so on. These will form a small company of fifty-four thousand, five hundred men, ready to turn out in a moment's notice to defend 'life, labour and property'.*[17]

For the first four months of 1839 Home Secretary Russell had left the Chartist leadership unmolested, whilst collecting reports from magistrates on their speeches for possible use in prosecutions for libel and sedition. One difficulty here was that most Chartist leaders spoke in such a way as to avoid laying themselves open to prosecution. One stratagem speakers used was to quote the seditious words of other speakers (naturally not named), whom they said they had heard speaking in other districts.[18] A shift in the government's softly-softly approach was signalled when Lord Russell, acting on a request from Monmouth, agreed to the arrest of Henry Vincent for holding a meeting that had been banned by Welsh magistrates. While he was on Convention business in London on 9 May, Vincent was hurriedly seized by the Metropolitan Police and taken to Newport, along with the South Wales Chartist leader William Edwards, who was known for the

16. Wilks, op. cit., pp. 123-24. HO 40/45.
17. *Western Vindicator*, 8 June 1839.
18. Royle, op. cit., p. 99.

violence of his speeches against the workhouses and the Poor Law Guardians. The Convention immediately instructed John Frost to go back to Monmouthshire and make sure the local leaders didn't do anything rash. But when the two prisoners were delivered to the Newport magistrates, a pitched battle broke out between 300 special constables and a large crowd. Several were arrested after stones were thrown, and a woman led a charge against the specials guarding the court. Frost, who was present, played the role of pacifier and successfully urged demonstrators to go home.[19] In his report to the Convention, he condemned the provocative actions of the authorities and said, *"I have had the greatest difficulty in keeping the people within bounds, and I am convinced that nothing but my presence could have restrained them"*.

The Metropolitan police, having delivered Londoner Henry Vincent into the hands of his enemies in South Wales, next turned their attentions to the LDA. On Friday 10 May plain-clothes officers observed a meeting organised by the Association on Clerkenwell Green. James Cane Coombe was speaking and according to the police there were just few hundred in attendance, although press reports suggest that there were actually a few thousand. After the meeting ended, Superintendent Massey, who claimed to have *"received information"*, went to The Crown pub on the Green and asked the landlord if anyone had left a bag. Someone had, and the bag was found to contain five pikes. The landlord gave a description of the man who left them and the superintendent went off with his plain clothes squad to find him. The first place they looked was the LDA headquarters in Ship Yard, Temple Bar where, upstairs, in a room capable of holding 300 people, the police found thirteen men standing by the fire, including Thomas Ireland and Samuel Waddington, a seventy-year-old who had been associated with Thistlewood's Cato Street Conspiracy in 1821. According to police, one of the men, Richard Cornish, tried to stab an inspector with a pike head. Having secured the prisoners with chains, the police seized documents, a tricolour flag and banners bearing such slogans as 'Free We Live and Free We Die' and 'For Children and Wife We War to the Knife'. The next day defendants told the examining magistrate that the pike head had

19. Jones, op. cit., p. 83.

been planted and that there had been no attempted stabbing. They also claimed that a police superintendent had pointed a gun at Waddington's head and shouted, *"You old rogue. I'll blow the brains out of the first that stirs"*.[20]

After five days in gaol the thirteen prisoners faced the magistrate again, this time with lawyers who included Richard Cobbett. When Cobbett said that Thomas Ireland had an *"irreproachable character"*, Superintendent Massey produced an anonymous letter written about the prisoner, but Magistrate Roe stopped him from reading it, saying that he *"never attended to anonymous letters"*. As there was insufficient evidence that the pikes were intended for illegal purposes, the magistrate restricted his deliberations to 'advice'. He told the prisoners that he was certain that ten of them were members of the LDA, and though they may have been induced to believe that it was a legal organisation it *"touched so closely on illegality… that all those who belonged to it were placed in considerable peril"*. He advised them *"for the future, to have nothing to do with such a society as might lead them into seditious and treasonable practice"*. They were bound over for good behaviour on 30s each in bail bonds. Waddington protested that he was too poor to pay, but Roe commented: *"from what I know of his past history, I believe him to be a very vain and foolish old man… utterly incapable of producing mischief, and I shall therefore, discharge him without bail"*.[21]

Harney, speaking at a meeting in Birmingham three days later, denounced the Metropolitan Police: *"If the government began a reign of terror, the people would end it… It might be that the people would end it with the musket and the pike"*.[22] These words did not endear Harney to those in the movement who saw him as dangerous. Some of his enemies in the radical press insinuated that he might be spy or agent provocateur when they reported the Ship Yard raid. The *Chartist* newspaper, blaming the incident on the *"stupid and dangerous proceedings"* of Harney and Coombe, noted that when the arrests had been made they had *"managed to be out of the way"*.[23]

20. *Morning Herald*, 13 May 1839.
21. *Morning Chronicle*, 16 May 1839.
22. *Northern Star*, 18 May 1839.
23. Schoyen, op. cit., pp. 68-69.

HE LONDON DISPATCH;

AND

People's Political and Social Reformer.

WITH WHICH IS INCORPORATED,

CLEAVE'S POLICE GAZETTE.

SUNDAY, FEBRUARY 26, 1837.

[PRICE THREEPENCE HALFPENNY.

OF GHENT.—LETTER TO THE | MANIFESTO OF THE POLES. | liberty combined will overthrow the old world of privilege and | WORKING MEN IN THE POLITICAL ARENA.
NG MEN OF LONDON. | The Polish Committee at London have published a de... | erect a new world of equality.

THE PLANET.

No. 80.   SUNDAY, JULY 21, 1839.   PRICE 4½d.

THE FIRST EDITION OF "THE PLANET" is published in time for transmission to all parts of the Country by the Post and Mails on Friday night—that it may arrive in any town or village on the Saturday morning.—The SECOND EDITION is published on Saturday Morning with the Gazette of Friday night, and delivered by the News-venders in the Metropolis; and by the General Post on the Sunday Morning.—And, THE THIRD and LATEST EDITION, for circulation in the Metropolis and its Environs, is published every Saturday night at Twelve o'Clock on the Saturday night.—Applications for "THE PLANET"—specifying which of the THREE EDITIONS is required—may be made to all Newsmen and Booksellers, in Town and Country; or to the Office of the Paper,—addressed to the Printer and Publisher—No. 30, Holywell Street, Strand, London.

SCENES IN THE SESSION. | tinguary, for the purpose of grumbling on it a Bill. | THE SYSTEM or COLONIZATION
THE PENNY POSTAGE, A BOON TO | thorpes, the Peels, and the Wetenaults, in either | The South Australian system is founded on this
THE POOR. | house, the opportunity of interposing all imaginable | main principal—that the public land of a colony
We believe that there is no one great public | obstacles, in addition to every species of practicable | should be disposed of, not by grant or gift,

---

THE OPERATIVE.

(*Established by the Working Classes for the Protection of the Rights of Labour.*)

SUNDAY JULY 14, 1839.

PRICE 4d.

ATROCIOUS OF
OF THE RUSSELL POL
BIRMINGHA

Mr. Earing—It is needed
tion to read your
provoked outrage committed
police-army upon the working
tion, and I would avail m
fearless of class, which is th
organ of neighbouring observ
offering some further obser
important subject. The
can never be popular, be
ciple upon which it is est
couple of individuals, insta
the rate, in legitimate direction
police plan is an improved
system of constables and
decoy, but each will never la
public knowle...

Above and opposite: Chartist Weeklies

In Birmingham, every day in April had seen meetings in the Bull Ring (a triangular commercial area of the town centre) in which speeches were made and stories from newspapers were read out to large crowds. The Birmingham magistrates, many of whom were members of the BPU, were at first reluctant to suppress the mass meetings, but were forced to issue a ban on 8 May under pressure from the local military commander. Short of police and troops, the Birmingham authorities got London to send a detachment of sixty Metropolitan Police officers to help control the town's 200,000 inhabitants. By this time moderates of the BPU had largely lost control of Birmingham Chartism, and had been replaced by the new Convention delegate Edward Brown and local workers' leaders such as J.A. Fussell. In Manchester on 9 May several thousand met at Stephenson Square to elect stonemason Christopher Dean to the Convention, as replacement for James Wroe, a moderate middle-class journalist/bookseller who had resigned.[24]

Two days after the Royal Proclamation forbidding military exercises, four men were arrested in McDouall's constituency, Ashton, for drilling, and Chartist leaders in the West Country were arrested at Westbury. In Trowbridge there were serious riots, with many injured and a policeman wounded with an air-rifle. Trowbridge leader William Potts, a chemist, was arrested for arms possession.[25]

At the Convention in London delegates were hoping that the Melbourne government, which had a shaky majority and was under fire for its suppression of the rebellions in Canada and Jamaica, might fall. A general election, it was hoped, would channel discontent into what the delegates regarded as lawful political struggle on a truly massive scale. One plan to which the delegates gave serious thought was mobilising their supporters to attend election hustings en masse, to demand of all parliamentary candidates that they pledge themselves to support the Charter. If no standing candidate agreed to do so, the Chartists would 'elect' their own candidate on a show of hands. The 'elections' would be

24. Owen Ashton and Paul Pickering, op. cit., pp. 9-12.
25. Ibid. *The Times*, 6 May 1839.

followed by a million-strong march on London. Harney, writing in the *London Democrat*, set out the scenario:

> *When parliamentary elections take place let all the unrepresented elect Chartists. There is no doubt that nine-tenths of the elected will be Universal Suffrage men. To elect representatives without enabling them to take their seats in the legislature would be the veriest farce imaginable. To complete the good work it will be necessary that each representative should be furnished with a bodyguard of sturdy sans-culottes, some thousands strong. By the time the whole of the representatives arrives in the environs of the metropolis they will have with them not less than a million men. This will settle the matter. They will encamp for one night on Hampstead Heath and then march to Parliament Street. Should the plutocratic-elected scoundrels be fool enough to have taken their places in the tax trap, the voice of the people, crying 'Make place for better men!' will scatter them like chaff before the wind, or should they hesitate to fly the job will soon be settled by their being tied neck and heels and flung into the Thames!*[26]

Davenport considered the implications of a general election, if at the hustings any candidate should fail to support *The People's Charter*:

> *Would it not be tantamount to saying that four-fifths of the adult population of this country are either idiots, lunatics, or criminals in the eye of the law? Who will deny that it would?… Shall we tamely lick the foot upraised to trample on our rights, shake our chains, and find melody in their horrid clank? Or shall we meet the enemy of our rights in a trial of strength, and prefer being buried in one common grave beneath the ruins of our country, if they will have it so?*[27]

On Tuesday 7 May Prime Minister Melbourne's alliance with Robert Peel's Conservatives collapsed, leading to a government defeat in the House of Commons. Melbourne offered his resignation. But, as it turned out, the Peelites were highly exercised by the number of Victoria's bedchamber staff who were Whigs and

26. *London Democrat*, 27 April 1839.
27. *London Democrat*, 8 June 1839.

suspected of exercising an undue influence on the young impressionable sovereign. Melbourne agreed to ask Queen Victoria to replace some of them with Tories and Peelites. In the event Victoria refused to make any changes to her staff, but Melbourne's deal with the Peelites held. The survival of the Whig government meant that the Chartists could not carry out their plan to intervene at election hustings. Other courses of action would now have to be considered.

On 12 May the Convention debated how to consult the country on the next step, once the petition was rejected by Parliament. The Convention agreed a manifesto recommending specific ulterior measures, including the Sacred Month/General Strike, to be put to mass meetings planned for the Whitsun holiday. Bolton delegate William Carpenter moved that the people be asked a list of questions about possible options. Should they withdraw their labour in a General Strike? Refrain from purchase of excisable goods? Withhold rent and/or taxes? Make a run on the banks by withdrawing money? Exclusively deal with pro-Chartist shops and buy only pro-Chartist newspapers? Choose delegates at the hustings of the next general election and arm in readiness? But O'Connor opposed putting the ulterior measures before a show of hands, because this *"would only create a delusion throughout the land"* about a course of action that might not get enough mass support. O'Connor regarded the withdrawal of money from banks as *"the beginning of the battle, because it would be a war of capital against labour, and capitalists would soon find that labour was the only real capital in the world"*. He believed a run on the banks and the sources of taxation would precipitate an economic crisis, which would in turn lead to revolutionary change. Richard Marsden didn't buy O'Connor's first-things-first argument. Reminding delegates of the fate of unarmed people at the Peterloo Massacre of 1819, he called for arming at meetings and for ulterior measures to be brought in immediately if arrests of Convention delegates became general. This however, was rejected in favour of O'Connor's approach.

At no stage did O'Connor indicate that he favoured a revolutionary seizure of power. If he had come out definitively in favour of the General Strike, it would have been pointed out to him by pro-strike and anti-strike associates alike that the strike had an inexorable revolutionary logic: with no strike fund to draw on, the people would have to violate bourgeois property rights in order to eat. As William Benbow, the architect of the General Strike, had once put it, for subsistence the strikers would have to look to the *"sheep on a thousand hills"* and the grain stores for sustenance. Peter McDouall, who had been serving on a committee appointed by the Convention to evaluate ulterior measures, favoured getting the trade unions more involved with agitation for a General Strike. He argued for massive demonstrations in every area against the New Poor Law on the first day. Recalling that July for the French had been *"a celebrated month for revolutions"*, he and Dr Taylor called for a General Strike.

Harney, in discussing the possibility of a General Strike, had asked the readers of the *London Democrat*:

> how were the people to subsist during the 'sacred week' with wages for many as low as five shilling a week? For within a day would come the deadly conflict between those who had and those who had not the food. And what would this be but insurrection and civil war? I should not object to this plan, but those who have been its loudest advocates have, at the same time, denounced the arming of the people… These are not the times to be nice about mere words; the fact is, there is but one mode of obtaining the Charter, and that is by INSURRECTION![28]

The Convention, with the largest attendance of delegates (fifty-two) since it began in February, prevaricated, and decided that the matter was too important to be decided immediately. Harney agreed to this because he thought that the people weren't yet prepared for a General Strike, especially in the matter of self-defence. He argued that the Convention should move to Manchester where it would have the support of *"250,000 men who would be determined to defend their liberties"*. He expected the Government to commence the attack, so the Convention should be in a position to meet it.[29] Manchester was the heart of industrial England, and in the North as a whole the Convention would be in a far more secure position to coordinate ulterior measures. If the agitation in

28. *London Democrat*, 4 May 1839.
29. *Operative*, 5 May 1839.

the North continued to grow, it could be used as a launch pad for a million-strong march on London.

Bronterre O'Brien agreed on the proposed move. It would be safer, he suggested, *"under the guns of Manchester or Birmingham"*. Lovett and the moderates, on the other hand, were for staying in London: firstly to be near their Liberal friends in Parliament when the Commons got round to discussing the petition; and secondly because they could see the possibly dangerous consequences of the ulterior measures breaking out in the North and wished to avoid a direct clash with the authorities. But as was often the case in the Convention, a compromise was reached: Birmingham, now just a train ride away, was the chosen venue. The Convention voted to reconvene there on 14 May at the Lawrence Street chapel.

The large meeting held in Birmingham to welcome the Convention found the workers of that town in a militant mood. On 17 May the Convention adjourned to consult the public on ulterior measures. By this time the supposed lines between physical-force and remaining moral-force supporters were becoming blurred. For example, on 12 May the *Chartist* newspaper defended the right to use force *"in extreme cases"* against tyranny and pointed out that this was defended even by the *"most zealous Tory writers upon the Constitution of the country"*. The editorial went on to condemn the *"light and meaningless talk about physical force"* among men impelled by too much passion, who were *"fierce and destructive in proportion to their weakness"*; but in conclusion suggested to its readers, *"Retain your arms then… But use them not until the time comes"* and in the meantime *"pursue the course of peaceful agitation"*.[30]

Within hours of the adjournment of the Convention the new Birmingham leaders, Brown and Fussell, were arrested and a warrant was issued for Harney. Harney however, had just departed for Newcastle to report to his constituents. He was not immediately pursued, because since he was off the Birmingham magistrates' 'manor' he was not their problem; and Birmingham, with law and order breaking down by the day, was too short of police officers to spare one to chase after him.[31]

---

30. *Chartist*, 12 May 1839.
31. Schoyen, op. cit., p. 71.

According to the most optimistic Chartist estimates, at Whitsun weekend on 21 May 200,000 demonstrated in Glasgow, 80.000 in Newcastle, 200,000 in Birmingham, 300,000 in Manchester, 100,000 in both Bradford and Sheffield, at least 30,000 in Blackwood, South Wales, and lesser numbers in Bristol and London. At all of these meetings support was voiced for ulterior measures such as withdrawal of savings, abstention from taxable intoxicants, mass mobilisations to support Chartist candidates at the next general election, exclusive dealing, arming for self-defence and obeying the decisions of the Convention.

Before the Manchester meeting on Kersall Moor, General Napier called a secret meeting of Chartist leaders:

> *I understand you are to have a great meeting on Kersall Moor, with a view to laying your grievances before parliament: You are quite right to do so and I will take care that neither soldier or policeman shall be within sight to disturb you. But meet peaceably, for if there is the least disturbance I shall be amongst you and at the sacrifice of my life, if necessary, do my duty. Now go and do yours.*

After attending the Kersall Moor meeting himself, he reported to Colonel Wemyss, Commanding Officer for the Manchester district, that there were *"twenty-five thousand very innocent people, and ten thousand women and children"* present. He thought the crowd numbers *"worth recording as a testimony to the Chartist assertion that there were half a million"*. As far as he was concerned they were *"expressing orderly, legal political opinions, pretty much–don't tell this! very like my own…"*.[32] Napier reported that the local gentry had wanted the soldiers to *"make an example"*, but was pleased to hear that the troops had actually prevented a row between Chartists and 'respectables' developing into a riot. More disturbingly, he heard that Dr Taylor had travelled down from Glasgow to lead the Chartists at the event and that they still had five pieces of brass cannon concealed. He wasn't sure how good this information was but he decided to bring up the 10th Regiment from Liverpool by railway and, in a 'deception' manoeuvre, moved a troop of dragoons from

---

32. Dorothy Thompson, *Early Chartism* (London, 1971), pp. 24-26. Napier, II, pp. 40-69.

an outlying village on the morning of the meeting so as to give the impression that they might be the advance guard of much larger force.[33] Napier's sympathy for the Chartists did not sway him from drawing up contingency plans to meet them with armed force on the streets of Manchester; nor did it dissuade him from moving enough artillery to Nottingham Castle to turn back any Chartist army that attempted to march on London through Derbyshire.

On 25 May the petition was delivered to the doors of Parliament. Sheets of the petition had been added to the parent sheet on a specially built wooden rolling machine. A large frame made of two beams of wood supported a cup-like socket to hold the roll. Convention members and eighteen stonemasons who had volunteered to carry the load began the procession through the Old Bailey. Cheers went up as it was announced that they had 1,300,000 signatures to deliver. At a quarter past three a procession of several thousand set off. City and Metropolitan police were either friendly or indifferent, bystanders stood in awe and omnibus drivers, immobilised by the throng, shouted and cursed. The marchers passed through Fleet Street, The Strand, Charing Cross, Horseguards and finally reached Parliament House, at which point the cheering intensified, horses panicked, coaches crashed and the police ran to protect the entrance to the House. A message arrived for the petition to be delivered, and the stonemasons carried the load up the stairs past lines of MPs, finally rolling the massive document onto the floor of the lobby.[34] It would be another month and a half before the House of Commons deemed to consider it.

---

33. 'The Government and the Chartists', *Chartist Studies*, p. 380.
34. *Chartist and Republican Journal*, quoted in Ray Challinor, 'McDouall and Physical Force Chartism', *International Socialism* 2:12.

The July Riots
and the Debate on
the General Strike

The learning process is something you can incite, literally incite, like a riot.
Audre Lorde

Following the huge demonstrations at Whitsun time, most of the Convention members addressed public meetings throughout June, whilst a caretaker committee stayed in London to carry on with administration and publicity. Increasingly Chartist meetings were becoming fundraising events for the defence of the growing number of Chartists who were facing prosecution.

John Frost spoke at a number of meetings in South Wales, unaware that the Mayor of Newport, Thomas Phillips, had just filed charges against him for libel. Frost also travelled to Scotland for a meeting on 10 June at Glasgow. Addressing an estimated 150,000 people on Glasgow Green, he went so far as to advocate hostage-taking to secure the release of prisoners:

> *we seek for justice; in doing so we keep within the limits of the law. If others exceed the limits, if our leading men be imprisoned, no violence having been committed, why then we shall consider that a coal pit is quite as safe a place for a tyrannical persecutor as a gaol for an innocent Chartist.*[1]

Apart from prosecutions, the Convention was facing more resignations. By the time it reassembled in Birmingham on 1 July, with attendance down to thirty-two, several more delegates had resigned: Alexander Halley (Dunfermline); the aristocrat intellectual William Villiers Sankey (Edinburgh); and the middle-class

1. Williams, op. cit., p. 169.

delegates George Rogers (London), Benjamin Tight (Reading), James Whittle (Liverpool) and Hugh Craig (Ayrshire). Surprisingly William Rider (West Riding), a physical-force man, resigned as well, declaring that there were *"not eight honest members"* in the Convention.[2]

Charles Neesom, Richard Marsden and Dr Taylor proposed calling for the strike to start on 15 July. But William Lovett instead suggested that a new committee should be set up to plan it properly and test popular opinion on the matter. On 3 July a compromise was reached: to begin some ulterior measures immediately, such as arming for self-defence (though not bearing arms at meetings), withdrawing money from banks and abstaining from taxable commodities. It was also decided to postpone the decision on the date for a National Holiday until 12 July, when Parliament would consider the petition. This did not satisfy Manchester delegate R.J. Richardson. A firm physical-force advocate, he resigned in protest against prevarication.

The day after the Convention voted to inaugurate ulterior measures, Birmingham magistrate Dr Booth rode into the Bull Ring, in which an illegal meeting was taking place. His mission was to *"ascertain the state of the town"*, which he soon did when the large crowd greeted him with shouts of 'spy' and threw stones at him. He managed to leave unscathed, then rode off to report to Mayor Scholefield. Backed by a squad of Metropolitan Police 'loaned out' from London, Booth and Scholefield rode back to the Bull Ring, where they ordered the speakers to stand down and the crowd to disperse. Rashly the police, wanting to nab a 'ringleader', tried to snatch the speaker by wading into the crowd and wielding their batons, but they were violently beaten back by the angry crowd. A retreat was ordered and the Mayor and magistrate rode off to fetch the army. When they returned with troops the Bull Ring was still *"in a state of confusion"*, so Dr Booth placed himself under the Nelson Monument and read the Riot Act. In the face of the drawn sabres of the dragoons, the crowd withdrew into the surrounding streets and the troops were able to occupy the area. But the crowd remained on the streets and marched on the town after midnight, armed with clubs and iron railings torn from churches, and chant-

2. Kemnitz, op. cit., pp. 161-64.

ing 'Fall Tyrants Fall!' Convention delegates Doctors Taylor and McDouall addressed a large crowd in front of the Convention venue in Lawrence Street, urging them to disperse, and rescued two policemen from an angry mob that had surrounded them. Their efforts, however, were not appreciated. Taylor and McDouall were both arrested later in the night.[3]

Reporter John Hampden wrote:

> *Wanton outrages were perpetrated by the police sent down by Lord J. Russell, at the instigation of the Birmingham magistrates, not only upon the Chartists assembled in the Bull Ring, but also upon harmless and unoffending people in the streets… who ought to have been protected, instead of being maltreated. Arms-breaking and head-breaking, however, seem to have been practiced by way of diversion; it was, no doubt, fine fun to see a fellow go off with a fractured limb, and an exceedingly good joke to hear a woman beaten by the police ruffians, cry out against the brutality… it mattered little whether they were man, woman or child…* "Last night", *says a reporter, an eye witness at these scenes of terror,* "they shamefully abused a woman waiting for her husband", *and at a meeting of the Town Council, Mr Blaxland, a common councilman, exposed his arm, which was livid from the blows received from the police, while he was peacefully returning to his own house. Are not these circumstances calculated to rouse up all that is manly—all that is English—in our countrymen and produce a universal shout of execration against such tyranny and injustice?*[4]

Mayor Scholefield, observing the running battles in the streets, afterwards entertained serious doubts about the long-term ability of the troops to withstand the guerrilla-style hit-and-run tactics of the crowds.[5] The Convention met the next day, and on Lovett's initiative issued a proclamation condemning the magistrates and police for the previous night's action. Although all delegates were prepared to sign the proclamation, Lovett, in an act of heroic proportions, insisted that he alone would sign because, he declared,

---

3. *Northern Star*, 10 Aug 1839.
4. *The Planet*, 21 July 1839.
5. Schoyen, op. cit., p. 82. HO 40/50.

"the Convention cannot spare victims". The proclamation was plac-
arded all over Birmingham, and the authorities responded by arresting Lovett as signatory and Birmingham delegate John Collins
as publisher of the document. At the court hearing the *Birmingham Recorder* asked Lovett, *"Were you aware that certain members of
the police force were wounded dangerously by weapons?"* Lovett replied:

> I heard that several of them were wounded, and at the same time
> thought that the people were justified in repelling such despotic
> and bloodthirsty power by any and every means at their dispos-
> al, because I believe that the institution of a police force is an
> infringement on the constitution and liberties possessed by our
> ancestors; for if the people submit to one injustice after another,
> which self-constituted authorities impose upon them, they may be
> eventually ground to dust, without the means of any resistance.

The *Recorder* then turned to John Collins and asked if he was a
member of the 'National Convention'. Collins replied that he knew
of no such body, but there was the General Convention of the
Industrious Classes: *"I am a member of that, and was elected at the
same time as Mr Muntz"*. Mr Muntz was sitting in front of the accused on the magistrates' bench; he had indeed been elected to the
Convention in August 1838, having been sponsored by the BPU,
but he had never taken his seat. Bail was granted to both accused.[6]

The Convention adjourned again for a move back to London,
and reassembled there on 10 July at the Dr Johnson Tavern, Bolt
Court. By this time the Birmingham police had decided to execute
the arrest warrant issued for the absent George Julian Harney, and
sent an officer north to track him down. He was staying in the
Chartist stronghold of Bedlington, where he was recovering from
an illness brought on by an intensive speaking tour of Northumberland. When the Newcastle police discovered his whereabouts
they raided him at 2 a.m. accompanied by dragoons. He was handcuffed to a Birmingham constable, taken by hackney to Newcastle
and then by railway to Carlisle. When he and his guard arrived
at a Carlisle hotel, news of his presence leaked out. Soon a large
crowd gathered in front of the hotel, waiting for the mill-workers
to finish work and join them. Harney decided to try and prevent

6. Gammage, op. cit., pp. 133-34.

violence by arranging for a post-chaise to collect both him and his guard from the rear entrance of the building, and escape. They then took a stagecoach across Shap Fell to Preston and travelled on to Birmingham via the North Western Railway. Harney was released on 15 July after exercising his right to traverse until the Spring Assizes, and the Birmingham magistrates indicated that they saw little in the committal proceedings to suggest that he would be convicted. A London police officer had testified that during a speech in Birmingham on 14 May Harney had called on his audience to carry *"a musket in one hand and a petition in the other"*, but this allegation was not backed by any other witness or by any reports of the event in the press. Several witnesses stated that Harney had said *"biscuits"*, not *"muskets"*: he was apparently referring to provisions to be stored for the Sacred Month. Added to this, the guard who had brought him back testified that Harney had saved him from an angry mob of his own supporters. In the House of Lords the Duke of Wellington raised the case, fuming against the tolerance of radical subversion by the Birmingham magistrates.[7]

News of Harney's arrest in Newcastle coincided with a grand jury on 7 July which found true bills against Bronterre O'Brien, William Thomason, John Mason, James Ayr and Thomas Devyr for seditious speeches made at a meeting in the town. Troops were sent to guard the military stores at Walker, after magistrates received reports of a planned raid to seize gunpowder. *"The on-slaught in Birmingham"*, according to Thomas Devyr, *"set Newcastle aflame"*. Devyr put a motion to an NPU meeting, proposing *"That if the government attempted to put down dissent in Newcastle, the people would meet their illegal act by Constitutional resistance"*.

On 9 July in nearby Sunderland, the Durham County Chartist Association organised a meeting on the Town Moor, dispatching couriers to the collieries to call miners to the meeting. A thousand miners immediately travelled there from the eastern coalfield and caused a sensation by arriving on trains, having forced the locomotive engineers to carry them. This caused the authorities

---

7. Schoyen, op. cit., pp. 74-75. *Newcastle Weekly Chronicle*, 17 July 1890. HO 41/14.

to panic, and some of the miners were arrested for violating the property rights of the railway company.[8]

In Newcastle on 10 July a meeting on the Forth called for the National Convention to designate a day for the beginning of the Sacred Month. Two collieries immediately responded to this by coming out on strike in anticipation. With the rejection of the petition imminent in the House of Commons, attitudes were hardening—with talk of arming, stocking up food and withdrawing money from savings banks. According to a *Northern Liberator* report, at another meeting on the Forth on 14 July 40,000 pledged to support the Strike, while 20,000 took the same pledge in Sunderland.[9] The NPU voted to take on the role of coordinating strike action with the rest of the country on the favoured date of 22 July.[10] On 18 July 1839 William Byrne from Newcastle told a 5,000-strong audience at Stockton-on-Tees of the necessity to obtain arms and hide them, *"so as they can lay their hands upon them at a moment's notice".*[11]

In the second week of July, days before the House of Commons was to divide on the petition, the Convention sent out an address calling for ulterior measures to be put into effect:

> 1st. *That you individually and collectively Withdraw Moneys from Savings Banks as well as from all other bank and persons hostile to your just rights.*
> 2nd. *That you convert all your Paper Money into gold.*
> 3rd. *That you abstain from all excisable articles of luxury.*
> 4th. *That you commence at once an exclusive system of dealing, and deal only with those who are the advocates and supporters of your cause.*
> 5th. *That you exercise your ancient and constitutional right and provide yourselves with the Arms of Freemen.*

---

8. Maehl, op. cit., p. 395.

9. Ibid., pp. 402-3. *Northern Liberator*, 20 July 1839.

10. Maehl, op. cit., p. 399.

11. Malcolm Chase, 'Chartism 1838 to 1858: Responses in Two Teeside Towns', *The People's Charter*, ed. Stephen Roberts (London, 2003), pp. 152-75.

These means may not alone effect our object, but immediately af-ter the 12th inst., when we expect a division in the House of Com-mons on the National Petition, we shall proceed to name the day when the SACRED MONTH shall commence, unless the meas-ures of justice we are contending for have been previously conceded. WE REMAIN, BRETHREN, YOUR FAITHFUL SERV-ANTS,

The Members of the General Convention

W. G. Burns, *counties of Forfar and Aberdeen.*
T. R. Smart, *Leicester, Loughborough, Shilton and Hinkley.*
William Cardo, *Mary-le-Bone, London.*
John Warden, *Bolton-le-Moors.*
Christopher Dean, *Manchester.*
John Deegan, *Hyde, Staley Bridge etc.*
John Stowe, *Colne District etc.*
Peter Bussey, *West Riding of Yorkshire.*
P. M. McDouall, *Ashton-under-Lyne.*
John Taylor, *Renfrewshire and Northumberland.*
James Taylor, *Rochdale and Middleton.*
W. Lovett, *for London and its districts (except Mary-le-Bone).*
Feargus O'Connor, *for the West Riding of Yorkshire.*
John Frost, *for Monmouthshire.*
Matthew Fletcher, *for Bury and surrounding districts.*
L. Pitkeithly, *West Riding of the County of York.*
John Skevington, *Loughborough, Derby and Belper.*
John Collins, *for Birmingham.*
John Richards, *North Staffordshire and South Cheshire.*
James Woodhouse, *for Nottingham.*
Charles H. Neesom, *for Bristol.*
Robert Tilley, *for Lambeth.*
Robert Hartwell, *for the Tower Hamlets, London.*
James Moir, *for Glasgow and the County of Lanark.*
Richard Marsden, *for Preston.*
James Fenney, *for Wigan, Hindley and West Houghton.*
Joseph Hickin, *for Walsall etc. etc., etc. etc, etc.*

The Convention earnestly calls upon every Workingman's and Radical Association throughout the Kingdom to reprint, circu-

*late, and by all and every means give publicity to the decrees of
the Convention, to placard every House in every Village with
their recommendations as their local circumstances demand.*[12]

On 12 July the petition was presented to the House of Commons
by Thomas Attwood. His speech was dull and half-hearted. After
saying that he was convinced the petition should be granted, he
poured cold water on his own convictions by adding, *"I only wish I
was equally sure they will produce the fruits that are expected from them"*.
He added further confusion by going on to say that the important
issue for him was his scheme for a paper money currency, which
he said would be taken more seriously by a Parliament elected by
universal suffrage. Lord John Russell, who replied for the government, dismissed Attwood's paper money panaceas and argued
that there was no assurance of prosperity with universal suffrage,
as the country would always be subject to trade and manufacturing crises. He thought that the 700,000 people who had the vote
already were better judges than the 1,300,000 who had signed the
petition. He pointed out that Attwood's friends, the Chartists,
had been making speeches which seemed to him more violent and
atrocious than any heard *"during the worst times of the French Revolution"*. Russell also alleged that the petitioners were for an *"equal
division of property"*, and argued that monarchy and the peerage
would not be able to survive once there was universal suffrage.

Daniel O'Connell, the Irish nationalist MP, accused the Chartists
of treason in their advocation of physical force, and of alienating
the middle class, though he conceded that it would be unfair to
expect people to obey a legislature they had no role in electing.
The Tory Benjamin Disraeli made by far the most interesting con-
tribution, tracing the cause of Chartism to the invasion of people's
rights, in particular the enactment of the New Poor Law. But he
also pointed to a more fundamental cause: the empowerment of
the middle class by the Reform Act of 1832:[13]

*All would admit this: the old constitution had an intelligible prin-
ciple, which the present one has not. The former invested a small
portion of the nation with political rights. Those rights were en-*

12. H.O. 40/43 in Dorothy Thompson, *Early Chartism*, pp. 190-92.
13. Gammage, op. cit., pp. 138-44. Hovell, op. cit., pp. 160-63.

trusted to that small class on certain conditions—that they should guard the civil rights of the great multitude... They had transferred a great part of that political power to a new class whom they had not invested with those great public duties. Great duties could alone confer great station, and the new class, which had been invested with political station, has not been bound up with the great mass of the people by the exercise of social duties.

After the petition was rejected by the House of Commons by 235 votes to 46, MPs Attwood and Fielden suggested that the Convention should organise another one, with more signatures. When the Convention reconvened on 15 July this suggestion was immediately rejected, and a discussion ensued about the General Strike. James Taylor, a Unitarian minister from Rochdale, claimed that the masses were unprepared for a strike. Dr John Taylor disagreed: he claimed that in the northern manufacturing districts organisation and preparation were already going at full pace. Richard Marsden, the weaver, said that weavers were used to starving: for them a strike was *"nothing"*. Robert Lowery said that he had been in Scotland, Cumberland and Westmorland, where people thought that the best time to strike was in August, when the corn was ripe and the potatoes were in the ground. But to the Glasgow delegate James Moir it seemed sensible to delay until the harvest was in.

William Burns of Dundee pointed out that those who opposed the strike *"yet admitted that a bold step was necessary in order to avert revolution, while they abstained from suggesting anything relative to this bold step"*, seemed to be saying that *"if we go forward we are lost, and if we stand or retreat, we are lost"*. He could not see how the Convention *"could get out of the national holiday without covering itself with disgrace"*.

On 17 July the Convention finally voted to begin the strike on 12 August. But disagreements persisted. A letter arrived from R.J. Richardson, reporting that he regretted his haste in resigning from the Convention, but wanted them to know that in Lancashire the workers were quite unprepared for a strike because a lot of mills were at present on half-time working because of the economic downturn, and employers would actually favour a strike.

Returning from speaking engagements in the North, O'Connor said he favoured postponement. On 22 July he and O'Brien argued that the Convention could not take upon itself the responsibility of dictating the time or circumstances of such a strike. But this seemed to overturn the Convention's published manifesto which had promised, in the event of Parliament rejecting the petition, that *"we shall proceed to name the day when the Sacred Month shall commence, unless the measures of justice we are contending for have been previously conceded"*. So O'Connor, sensing that the Convention was in danger of losing what would remain of its leadership credibility, moved an amendment, calling all delegates back to London, *"prepared with the views of their constituents"*, so they could consider the *"most effectual means for carrying out the ulterior measures for the accomplishment of universal suffrage"*. The Convention voted 12 to 6 with 7 abstentions to postpone the strike.

But two days later, on 24 July, Neesom tried to revive the call for the strike by suggesting that far from leading to a bloody revolution, a strike would prevent one by creating a *"moral"* revolution: *"I am convinced that if the Convention does its duty to the people, they would do their duty to them. It is not that the Convention could stop the present movement, but they could stop the effusion of blood"*. He proposed an amendment to begin the strike on 5 August–earlier than first planned–and James Osbourne, the Brighton delegate, supported him. As for the problem of food supplies during the strike, Osbourne said: *"ten thousand fellows met together for breakfast would not endure a long fast... the cessation from labour would be the first step towards a revolution, but the result would not deter me. You have been coming to the point long enough"*. John Warden from Bolton said he did not believe the National Holiday would itself give rise to any disturbances. But Neesom's amendment was lost, receiving only five votes. At this point the tone of the debate became recriminatory. Warden reminded O'Connor that according to his own paper the *Northern Star "the whole country was organized and armed to the teeth"*. Warden said he was not *"at all sanguine as to the success of the National Holiday"*, but he believed it was *"the only means by which the real number of Chartists would be known, and their determination be put to the test"*. O'Connor retorted, *"There has never appeared in the*

columns of the Northern Star *a declaration that the people were armed,
but on the contrary a constant regret that the people were not armed".*

Bronterre O'Brien, who also voted against the amendment to begin the strike on 5 August, was attacked by Neesom for having
absented himself from Birmingham when the original decision to
strike had been voted on. He also pointed out that Harney was
on his way back from Newcastle and would report on the situation there. In the meantime he, Neesom, was opposed to postponement. O'Brien replied, alluding to Harney, who had also left
Birmingham:

> *Mr Neesom has said that I was not in my place at Birmingham
> at a time when I ought to have been. All I can say is that I was
> engaged elsewhere, doing the work of the Convention, but had
> I been in Birmingham, I would not have run away on the first
> symptom of danger, as some others had done. Perhaps those gen-
> tlemen thought discretion the better part of valour, and recollect-
> ing that; "He who fights and runs away, Will live to fight another
> day; but he who is in battle slain, Will never live to fight again".*

Neesom saw the allusion to Harney, and was furious. He said:
"I rise to order. I consider these observations are shameful". O'Brien
replied:

> *I hope Mr Neesom will not decompose himself, for I'll not pursue
> the subject further... I should not have mentioned it had he not
> said a great deal about timidity and cowardice... in reference to
> what had been said about the people being armed, that I believe
> that Mr O'Connor had never said that they were armed, but had
> always contended that until the people were armed throughout
> the country, they would never get Universal Suffrage; or that if
> they did get it, they would not be able to keep it.*

O'Connor proposed another compromise: the Sacred Holiday
should be regarded as "*on*" in a "*provisional*" sense for 12 August;
they should return to their localities and send reports back to a
central council of the Convention, which should remain in London
and direct the movement with a view to *"giving effect to such a plan
as the majority of the working classes shall decide upon".* Neesom seconded this resolution, as he believed that it would be the best way

under the circumstances to get the movement back on course and reverse the impression of a faltering leadership that would desert the people. McDouall also supported it, though he added, grimly, *"It is a curious coincidence that the holiday would take place on the same day that the aristocracy is going out on the moors to slaughter game"*. O'Brien argued that it was the people who should decide the fate of *"a movement which might be pregnant with great danger"*. Appealing for unity, he said:

> *It is only by showing a determined front that the people can succeed. The House of Commons, the Ministry, and the Queen are only the instruments of the middle classes. It is with the middle classes that the real battle must be fought… If we are not arrested there will still be the standard around which people will flock. If we are arrested there will still be the standard around which people will flock… and before the trials come up we will have two millions to support us.*

In Newcastle Thomas Ainge Devyr, news editor of the *Northern Liberator,* had been keeping an eye on the pike market that was held every Saturday above a shop on The Side. The pikes manufactured by the iron workers of Winlaton and Swalwell were selling for a reasonable 2s 6d each, and business was booming:

> *Enter three men into the Liberator office. One speaks:* "This youth needs a pike, and they're all sold. You must let him have yours that you bought last week". "What am I to do myself?…" "But you have a gun and a case of pistols, and with good use those will keep you busy".… *I cite this fact of throwing light on the condition of things. It is seen that the market was unusually good, the price unusually high, and the workmen unusually willing. At the time, as closely as we could calculate, we counted sixty thousand pikes—enough for every man, woman and child in the City of Newcastle.*[14]

On Tuesday 23 July the NPU began to hold nightly meetings on the Forth in support of William Burns, who had been arrested.[15] The next day Mayor Fife forbade public meetings. Fife who, like

---

14. Devyr, op. cit., pp. 178-79.
15. Gammage, op. cit., pp. 402-3.

his civic counterparts in Birmingham, had been something of a physical-force radical himself during the Reform Bill crisis in 1832, issued the following corporation placard:

> *Whereas.*
>
> *Certain ill-disposed persons are in the habit of meeting within the limits of this borough and using inflammatory and seditious language, calculated to make Her Majesty's subjects discontented with their condition and to produce terror in the minds of the population.*
>
> *This, therefore, is to give notice that these tumultuous assemblages will not be longer suffered to take place within the precincts of this borough.*
>
> **JOHN FIFE**, *Mayor*
> *In the name of the Corporation*
>
> *God save the Queen*

In response, the Chartists put up a counter-placard:

> *Whereas. Certain men calling themselves the Corporation of Newcastle-on-Tyne, have presumed to call in question the inalienable right of Englishmen to meet, discuss and petition the Queen and Parliament for a redress of their grievances... Now, therefore, we, the Council of the Northern Political Union, proclaim to the people of this Borough and surrounding neighbourhood, that it is their duty to meet for the exercise of the Constitutional right, and show the Corporation of Newcastle-upon-Tyne that this assumed power of theirs is held in contempt by all good Englishmen.*
>
> *God save the People.*
>
> *Postscript: A meeting will be held in the Forth every evening at half past six.*[16]

The NPU decided to get around the ban by using the well-tried tactic of being 'responsible' and asking the mayor to chair a meeting to discuss the prayer to the Queen–then holding the meeting anyway, whether the invitation was accepted or not. By the time the mayor's rejection of the request arrived on Monday 29 July

16. Devyr, op. cit., p. 180. Maehl, op. cit.

the Winlaton ironworkers, inspired by the NPU's proclamation, were arriving in Newcastle with their band, armed with staves and a number of guns (not primarily for offensive use but for the *"ceremonial salutes"* which were becoming commonplace). Grainger's stonemasons also downed tools and joined the large meeting on the Forth, chaired by the miners' leader, Thomas Hepburn. Thomas Devyr reported to the crowd that a similar meeting had gathered in Sunderland. John Rucastle denounced the *"shopocracy"*, and told people to arm and *"be ready to repel the hired assassins of the government"*.[17]

After the speeches several thousand of those assembled on the Forth headed up towards Westgate Road. Facing them was a combined force of about eight hundred police and troops. At the front were the special constables backed by the police; behind the police were the dragoons and behind them the infantry; and just in case that wasn't enough there was an artillery company further up the hill. Mayor Fife and his squire Mr Brown were both on horseback, urging the crowd to fall back when a man threatened them with a pistol–but didn't shoot. Elsewhere in the mêlée Devyr and some of the Political Union leaders were also shouting at the crowd, urging restraint.

When the crowd on the Westgate Road charged the police, the specials ran, taking cover among the tombstones of a nearby churchyard, but the police stood their ground and then rushed on the crowd, wielding swords and seizing banners. Several people were injured. That was as far as the fighting went. According to Devyr, *"Our people had been well taught that it was not riot we wanted, but revolution. So not a stone was thrown"*. Fifteen or twenty were arrested, but the police, in Devyr's opinion, *"acted with cool judgment"*, as they had seen the NPU leaders trying to get the crowd back. The dragoons who cleared the streets were *"good natured fellows, who laughed heartily as the women and girls ran screaming out of their way"*. Not so the specials: *"Gathering from their hiding places when they found there was no danger, they formed an awkward squad, and scouring through the public houses turned out the stragglers"*.

The mood of the North East was reported on by Harney when on 1 August he returned to the Convention, which had recon-

---

17. *Morning Herald*, 12 July 1839.

vened at the Arundel Coffee House on The Strand. Having addressed forty meetings in a month, he said:

> *I found the people often ready to slake themselves in blood rather than lose the Charter. If ever the Charter was won, it will by the men of the North, and if they are not prepared, they never will be... The Convention had begun in Birmingham to take steps which had excited the people that they would adopt energetic measures, But I'm sorry to be obliged to say that I believe the Convention, if it has not lost, is rapidly losing the confidence of the people, through its conduct on the subject of the sacred month... If the Convention is not prepared to meet the consequences of the struggle, let them resign their trusts and the people will elect another Convention.*

O'Connor replied:

> *I might have wished that the people had commenced the holiday when the convictions in Wales took place [Vincent and Edwards had just been convicted in Monmouth], but if they do not feel sufficient interest in it the Convention cannot excite them. I fear among the leaders of the people, not the traitor or the spy, but the fool. I do not mean to say Mr Harney is either, but this I know, the people will not be led by Mr Harney.*

The Convention council on the Sacred Holiday recommended holding a demonstration instead of a strike. On 6 August, after much debate, a resolution moved by O'Brien and seconded by O'Connor was passed, pronouncing that the people were not prepared to carry out the *"sacred Month"* on 12 August, and that as an alternative *"the great body of the working people, including most of the Trades, may be induced to cease work on the 12th instant, for two or three days"*, during which time they would hold meetings for *"deliberating on the present awful state of the country, and devising the best means of ending the hideous despotism with which the industrious orders are menaced by the murderous majority of the upper and middle classes, who prey upon their labour"*.[18] Lowery later recalled that this retreat was the *"finishing stroke"* to what remained of the Convention's prestige.

---

18. Epstein, op. cit., pp. 177-79. *Northern Star*, 10 Aug 1839.

The Collapse of the Convention

The thousand hills and the cattle thereon, are the Lord's, and what is the Lord's is the people's... I would not tell you to steal the cattle [but if the owners] will not lend you an ox or a sheep, borrow it yourself.

George Julian Harney, police evidence quoted in *The Charter*, **14 July 1839**

As August arrived, and the call went out for a general strike to begin on 12 August, Chartists throughout the country were attending church services. They would arrive before the regular congregation, pack the rented pews and submit suitable biblical texts to be read out. A contemporary drawing shows a group of working men slouching, smoking pipes and reading newspapers–all of them obviously bored with the sermon.[1] But many of the Chartists' activities extended far beyond going to church. For many of the Chartist leaders in the North, the alternative to the General Strike tactic was not retreat but armed rebellion. General Napier in Nottingham was so concerned by the reports he was receiving about the arming of the Chartists that he organised a display of modern artillery skills. He wrote of the would-be revolutionary army:

Armed, starving and interspersed with villains, they must commit horrid excesses... I would never allow them to charge me with their pikes, or even march ten miles, without mauling them with cannon and musketry and charging them with cavalry, when they dispersed to seek food; finally, that the country would rise on them and they would be destroyed in three days.

1. Eileen Yeo, 'Christianity in Chartist Struggle 1838-1842', *The People's Charter*, ed. Stephen Roberts, 74-75 (London, 2003). Stephen Roberts and Dorothy Thompson, 'Images of Chartism' 36 (London, 1998).

Napier, wanting to avoid any massacres, thought that pikemen could be easily routed by buckshot and the flash of bayonets:

> *if we deal with pikemen my intent is to put cavalry on their flanks, making my infantry retire as the pike men advance. If they halt to face the cavalry, the infantry shall resume fire, for if the cavalry charge pikemen in order the cavalry will be defeated; the pike must be opposed by the musket and the bayonet...*[2]

On 6 August he wrote:

> *The plot thickens. Meetings increase and are so violent, and arms so abound, I know not what to think. The Duke of Portland tells me there is no doubt of an intended general rising. Poor people! They will suffer. They have set all England against them and their physical force:—fools! We have the physical force, not they. They talk of their hundred thousands of men. Who is to move them when I am dancing round them with cavalry; and pelting them with cannonshot? What would their 100,000 men do with my 100 rockets wriggling their fiery tails among them, roaring, scorching, tearing, smashing all they came near? And when in desperation and despair they broke to fly, how would they bear five regiments of cavalry careering through them? Poor men! How little they know of physical force!*[3]

All the same he asked, "*What has made Englishman turn assassins?*"– answering: "*The new poor laws. Their resources have dried up but indirect taxes for the debt and the poor law throw them on a phantom, which it calls their resources—robbery follows, and a robber soon becomes a murderer*".[4]

When Napier heard that some of his infantry were Chartists, he wanted to send for their leader to explain that he agreed with the Chartists' aims but not their methods. He was, however, forbidden to do this by Lord Russell.[5] Napier encouraged his men to gather intelligence by drinking with Chartist ex-servicemen.[6]

---

2. Royle, op. cit., p. 186. Napier, II,p. 4.
3. Napier, II, pp.111-133.
4. Ward, op. cit., p. 128.
5. Ibid., p. 186. Napier, II, pp. 54-55.
6. Ward ibid. Napier, II, p.11.

From the beginning of August the West Riding Chartists were holding delegate meetings at Heckmondwike, at which they elected alternate Convention delegates to take over from those they expected to be arrested–rightly, as it would turn out.[7] In Bradford the Chartists took the call for a general strike very seriously: they began holding nightly meetings, forming gun clubs and canvassing shopkeepers in preparation for an exclusive dealing campaign.[8]

In Nottingham, on Sunday 11 August, a meeting to be addressed by the Convention delegate for Nottingham, James Woodhouse, was banned by magistrates. The crowd, of between 6,000 and 10,000, marched off to the Forest, a mile away. When Woodhouse began to speak, two magistrates approached on horseback and read the Riot Act. The crowd immediately began to stone the magistrates, who rode off for reinforcements. Woodhouse then adjourned the meeting, so that when the magistrates returned, with General Napier leading two troops of dragoons and two companies of riflemen, the crowd had dispersed.[9] Napier reported that in many areas Chartist supporters had only lacked *"the word from headquarters"* to begin revolutionary actions.[10] Clearly he thought the lack of firm leadership and direction from the Convention was a crucial factor in the failure of the strike.

In Manchester an anonymous letter had been sent to mill owners ordering them to close their mills on the 12th *"so that persons in your employ may observe the Sacred Month and thereby enable the Chartists to obtain their righteous objects. Those manufacturers who do not comply and aid such a righteous cause will be marked men"*.[11] At six in the morning of 12 August groups of Chartists rallied several thousand people to march on the mills. They succeeded in closing a dozen of them very quickly, at first swamping the police on duty. At Clark's Mill in Pollard Street, fifty-six police officers faced a crowd of several thousand, who unleashed a hail of stones and forced them to retreat. The police were soon joined

7. Epstein, op. cit., p. 175.
8. Peacock, op. cit., p. 22.
9. Ibid.
10. HO 40/53.
11. HO 44/32.

by a hundred others, and two companies of the 79th Highlanders and a troop of dragoons. The crowd was dispersed and twenty-three were arrested. In Bury the Riot Act was read at a meeting which then dispersed peacefully. In Bolton Chartists paraded the streets, gathering in strength through the day to a few thousand, until Convention delegate John Warden advised them to retire for the night. Warden and two local leaders were arrested when they turned up at the New Market the next morning. The Riot Act was read, and the crowd dispersed after they were warned that the dragoons were coming. Later that morning those arrested were taken to Liverpool by post-chaise, and the troops escorting them were heavily stoned. The crowd then attacked Bolton police station with bricks and proceeded to a number of mills, which they closed down. In the evening there were arson attacks in the town. When troops were sent in they confronted a large crowd, some of whom were armed with pikes and guns. After the troops were ordered to clear the town centre at bayonet point, a number of civilians were seriously wounded. According to one report two were killed, although this was not subsequently confirmed. The next day strikers marching on Rochdale were turned back by Colonel Wemyss's dragoons and Highlanders.[12]

In London on 12 August, an estimated 10,000 assembled on Kennington Common. On the 17th the Morning Herald alleged:

> *A meeting of Chartists took place last Saturday night, at which it was first agreed to commence insurrectionary acts on the following (Sunday) morning, but in consequence of a discovery having been made that spies were present at that meeting, the original intentions were abandoned, and the meeting was adjourned to Tuesday evening, when it was resolved, on account of the opposition of some influential members… to defer for the present any overt act or riot or insurrection.[13]*

A huge Chartist gathering was held at Dukestown, Monmouthshire on the 12 August at which Frost argued against the practicality of the Sacred Month and appealed to the better natures of the 'industrious' middle class. But, as we shall see, many of

---

12. *London Dispatch and Operative*, 18 Aug 1839.

13. *Morning Herald*, 17 Aug 1839.

his audience were considering 'practical' measures even less to his liking and were convinced that the appeal to the middle class was bound to fall on deaf ears.

On 14 August miners in the collieries in Northumberland and Durham miners came out on strike. Local Tory special constables sent a request for rifles to the Home Office, which was refused. Instead Napier's man in the North East, Lieutenant-Colonel Campbell, sent a force of troops to back the constables in an effort to disperse *"tumultuous and seditious"* gatherings. After police threatened to arrest leaders for breach of bond if they didn't go back to work, the strike faltered. The NPU, in calling the strike, had convened another big meeting on the Forth, but the decisive action by the troops and police against the strikers in the pit villages deterred people from turning out in force.[14]

By the time the Convention reconvened on 26 August, after a two-week adjournment, a third of the seventy-one delegates who had attended in the seven months of its existence were now either in prison or on bail. In August alone, Henry Vincent and William Edwards were sentenced at Monmouth to twelve months' and nine months' imprisonment respectively; Dr. Peter McDouall joined the Rev. J.R. Stephens in the gaol at Chester Castle to serve a one year sentence; John Collins and William Lovett got a year each for issuing the proclamation after the Bull Ring riot; and similar sentences were handed down to Edward Brown of Birmingham, William Carrier of Trowbridge and James Fenny of Wigan.[15] As the twenty-one Convention members in attendance had to carry out a post-mortem on their failed strategy and decide on what to do next, recriminations began to fly.

With the Convention in disarray, at the end of August John Frost, writing in the *Western Vindicator*, called for the organisation of Chartists in South Wales and western England into 'classes' of ten, ready for action at short notice *"to preserve the peace of the country"* from the likes of special constables, pointing out that this was already happening in other parts of the kingdom. In fact, as

14. Malcolm Chase, 'Chartism 1838 to 1858: Responses in Two Teeside Towns', *The People's Charter*, ed. Stephens. Maehl. pp. 409-12.
15. O.R. Ashton and P.A. Pickering, *Friends of the People, Uneasy Radicals in the Age of the Chartists*, pp. 7-22 (London, 2002).

Frost well knew, this was already happening in South Wales on a scale way greater than anywhere else. Frost was trying to assert his leadership over his radicalised 'constituents', but had only been able to so far because he had presented himself on occasion as an 'extremist', having argued months earlier that seizing magistrates and government officials as hostages would be a legitimate form of self-defence should ministers violate the liberties of the people's representatives–two of whom (Vincent and Edwards) were now languishing in Monmouth Gaol.

In South Wales the class captains had organised themselves into a semi-secret body known as the 'Directorate'. The authorities had become aware of this large organisation, but found the informer system largely ineffective because of the close-knit exclusivity of the work gangs in the mines and iron-works, and in the communities at large. According to a letter sent to Lord Russell on 2 August 1839 by 'An Old Soldier' in Merthyr, there were in the county of Glamorgan *"hundreds of thousands of miners and colliers, who are at this present time ripe for a general Revolution, and in the course of another fortnight"*. They were *"one, and all"* in favour of the strike and boldly asserted that they would *"not want for any good thing"* when it happened:

> *My Lord, where are our arms, where are our militias, whereunto we are to resort for sufficient force for order that we may thereby maintain peace and tranquillity at home? Our yeomanry cavalry is of no use whatever. They are a set of untrained and insufficient men. I therefore… entreat your Lordship to bring before the house the necessity of a reorganization of the Militias, and unless this is done–your Lordship may depend that there will be no sufficient power of earth to repel that force, which is now ready for combat.*[16]

Guns and pikes were being made at smithies, workshops and, according to some reports, caves in the hills. Mass meetings were being concluded to the sound of discharging muskets. The Abersychan Working Men's Association declared that *"if an attack were made on them as at Birmingham, they would repel force by force"*; and the Pontypool Association stressed their readiness to defend the

---

16. HO 44/32.

Convention with their lives: *"We must earnestly request all those who are able, to provide themselves with arms immediately"*. These statements were no more extreme than those coming from the physical-force tendency of the South Wales bourgeoisie. A leader in the Tory *Merthyr Guardian* on 27 July) had urged that, should there be opposition to the power of the military, *"it will be met with the word of command FIRE, and that word of command will neither convey the meaning that blank cartridges are to used, or that the firing is to be over the heads of the people but at the mob, and if possible, at those who are evidently leaders of the mob"*. [17]

In London, as August ended, O'Connor and Neesom argued at the Convention that the time had come to dissolve the organisation, as support for it seemed to be collapsing, and try a different strategy. Harney reported that he had been instructed by the Northern Political Union that it would send no more delegates and that monies being raised would go to support prisoners' families and not the 'National Rent' for the Convention. Harney argued that, with 60,000 colliers on strike in the North East in mid-August, surely Lancashire, Yorkshire and Birmingham would have followed if the Convention had exercised leadership; *"Even supposing the worst,"* he said, *"had the Convention stuck to the 12 August, the strike would have been universal in the northern counties—Northumberland, Durham, Cumberland, but the organization of two years the imbecility of the Convention had broken in two weeks"*. As far as he was concerned, he said, he had done his job, and he resented being slandered as a traitor and a spy for his troubles.

Dr Taylor was even more scathing of his fellow delegates, and drew consternation from Robert Lowery and Bronterre O'Brien when he complained that a large minority of them had been cowards, traitors or spies. Taylor called for the dissolution of the Convention but, in accepting O'Connor's argument that there still needed to be some guiding body, Taylor called for a new *"Provincial Convention"*. Finally, on 14 September, at the instigation of Taylor and Harney, and with the casting vote of John Frost, the Convention voted to dissolve itself by twelve votes to eleven.

---

17. Williams, op. cit., p. 171-72.

Secret Councils

Whether of open War or covert guile,
We now debate; who can advise, may speak.
John Milton, Paradise Lost

C olonel Francis Macerone's *Defensive Instructions for the Peo-*
ple was a popular pamphlet amongst Chartists in 1839.
Based on the colonel's own mercenary experience of street
fighting in Italy, it purported to show how a regular army of cavalry and artillery could be defeated by a massed attack of foot
soldiers armed with pikes. However, another former British Army
officer, Alexander Somerville, saw fit to warn of the dangers in
applying Macerone's theories to England. In a pamphlet entitled
Warnings to the People on Street Warfare, Somerville argued that no
force armed with pikes–or even muskets–could stand against the
cavalry and modern artillery of the British army.
  Somerville, a middle-class reformer, was also something of a
freelance spy. He later claimed that he had learned in early August
1839 that a secret council for organising armed force had been
formed within the Chartist National Convention, and that Dr
John Taylor, Peter McDouall and R.J. Richardson were its leading
members. Somerville claimed that these three men, along with the
Polish revolutionary Major Beniowski, made a reconnaissance of
Woolwich Arsenal to see how it might be captured. There is some
corroboration of this from the spy Edward Hancock, who reported to the Home Office (before the dissolution of the Convention
in September) that Beniowski was involved in an insurrectionary
conspiracy with members of the LDA, notably Joseph Goulding
and Joseph Williams. Another spy in the LDA, Joseph Bobiowski

Dr John Taylor, National Convention member

(also a Polish military exile), reported to the Home Office that a meeting of twenty-two members plus Dr Taylor had discussed secret preparations for arming a large number of men for an uprising in London.[1]

According to a memoir by Barnsley Chartist leader William Ashton, when the National Convention dissolved itself on 14 September a number of departing delegates held secret discussions about what to do next. He claimed that at one meeting John Frost, William Burns, Dr Taylor and Peter Bussey decided to support a

---

1. Bennett, op. cit., p. 99

rising in South Wales, which would begin on 3 November, and to organise similar actions in their own localities.[2]

Bussey, on returning to Yorkshire, attended a meeting at Heckmondwike on 30 September of forty delegates, mostly representing Chartist groups in Yorkshire, plus Convention members Cardo, Harney, and Dr Taylor.[3] This meeting was reported in the Chartist press as concerned mostly with prisoners' defence and routine matters. But behind the scenes the Heckmondwike delegates were operating as a secret council. William Lovett, who investigated these events after he had served his one-year prison sentence, claimed that the secret of the Heckmondwike meeting was Bussey and Ashton's presentation of the London resolution on the planned rising and its adoption by the delegates.[4]

It appears certain that Frost told departing National Convention delegates in mid-September that, following the prison sentences given to Vincent and Edwards in August, he didn't think he could hold back the people in the South Wales coalfield much longer; they were going to mobilise with or without him, and it would be an armed mobilisation. It seems there was a consensus amongst a number of delegates that they would follow the Welsh lead, whatever it turned out to be. But in reality Frost was trying to steer the South Wales Chartists away from armed confrontation towards a less drastic course of action. Frost, on returning to Wales, spent the latter part of September 1839 corresponding with the courts and the Home Office in the hope that they would grant some concessions regarding Henry Vincent's conditions of imprisonment at Monmouth. On 28 September he wrote to the Lord Lieutenant of Monmouthshire, claiming that *"the agitation has now subsided"* thanks to his assurances to the militants that he could get the middle classes to see reason. In reality, however, the valleys were in a state of near-insurrection. In their industrial heartland the working-class captains of the Chartist 'Directorate' had elected as leaders 'professional' men, committed to physical

---

2. Peacock, op. cit., pp. 29-32. William Ashton, *National Reformer*, 19 April 1845. *Northern Star*, 3, 10 ,17 May 1845.
3. According to the account Ashton gave to Lovett—though Taylor later denied being there.
4. William Lovett, *Life and Struggles*, pp. 238-41 (London, 1967).

force, such as Zephaniah Williams, William Lloyd Jones and Dr William Price. Dr Price, who travelled to Staffordshire in September on an arms procurement mission, was an Oxford graduate, surgeon, republican, freethinker, druid, nudist, vegetarian, anti-smoking campaigner and advocate of women's rights—in short, a man dangerously ahead of his time.[5] He was elected leader of the Pontypridd Chartists, who chose him because he was *"a good, staunch and independent brother"*. On assuming the leadership in Pontypridd, Price told his supporters:

> *we have tolerated the tyranny of those who oppose us—landlords, coal-owners and the clergy—too long. We must strike with all our might and power, and strike immediately. The time for hesitating is past and the day of reckoning is at hand. Let all cowards go their way, for they have no part to play in the great struggle. Men of the valleys, remember that the principle behind Chartism is the principle which acknowledges the right of every man who toils to the fruits of his labour. The points embodied in the Charter are our immediate demands, but ultimately we shall demand more. Oppression, injustice and the grinding poverty which burdens our lives must be abolished for all time… We are the descendants of valiant Welshmen and we must be worthy of the traditions which they have passed on to us. It is far better that we should die fighting for freedom, than live as slaves of greed and opulent wealth…*[6]

In South Wales the Directorate was organising volunteers. Each class of ten had a sergeant. The sergeants reported to section leaders who were in charge of five classes – fifty-five men in all. Three section leaders selected a captain to lead a company of 165 men, three companies formed a Brigade of 500, and three brigades formed a division of 1,500. It was calculated that such a force, within a 7 mile radius, could be assembled at two hours' notice on the order of the division chief.[7]

---

5. Jones, op. cit., p. 97.

6. Islwyn ap Nicholas, *A Welsh Heretic: Dr. William Price, Llantrisant*, pp. 25-26 (Aberystwyth, 1973, first published 1940).

7. Wilks, op. cit., p. 134. *Newport Examinations*, vol. VIII, doc. 830.

On 3 October at a public meeting in the yard of Zephaniah Williams's public house in Blaenau, John Frost addressed about 500 people, including leaders of the Directorate. Frost said that he had rushed to the valleys because there had been reports that thousands of men were already under arms and on their way to Monmouth Gaol to free Henry Vincent and the other prisoners. He told his audience to wait for orders from the top, to be issued as soon as other areas of Britain were ready to move. In fact Frost had just written an article, not yet published, for the *Western Vindicator*, which argued for a campaign to get him elected to Parliament as member for Monmouth at the next general election. His immediate problem was how to convince an audience, effectively organising itself as a revolutionary army, to become canvassers in a parliamentary election campaign. Frost told them that his election would be the first step, and only the first step, towards freeing the prisoners and winning the Charter—and of course his campaign needed to be backed up by thousands of disciplined men organised into sections of ten.[8]

William Jones arrived at the Blaenau meeting towards the end of Frost's speech. He missed the bit about electioneering but caught the closing words from Frost about the need for disciplined organisation into sections of ten. When he got up to speak he said that as far as he concerned preparations had to be made for a rising. Having returned from a missionary trip to the Forest of Dean in the east, he was convinced that the Foresters, despite harassment from anti-Chartist forces, were ready to help—as were other areas of England. If their enemies broke the peace that was going to be established, he said, *"their heads would be trampled under Chartist feet"*; and Frost, he was sure, would stand with them. Frost, sensing that he was in danger of losing control of the Directorate, said nothing to oppose Jones, and urged the audience to *"be ready at any time to meet me when called on"*. *"I will stand through and will head anything that will take place,"* he promised. But he also said that once he was elected to Parliament he would expect the Charter to be won in less than a month; if not, he would no longer urge restraint. Frost's final words were received rather coolly by his audience, which had just cheered the uncompromising speech of

8. *Western Vindicator*, 5 Oct 1839.

William Jones. At a secret meeting of the Directorate at Blaenau, probably later that same night or the night after, Frost repeated his call to *"be ready at any time to meet me when called on"*, and asked the delegates if they would obey. But this time he was challenged head-on by David Davies of Abersychan, a veteran of Waterloo who had served twenty-five years in the army and now commanded three Chartist brigades:

> *I will tell you, Mr Frost, the condition upon which my lodge will rise, and there is no other condition, as far as I am concerned. The Abersychan Lodge is 1,600 strong; 1,200 of them are old soldiers; the remaining 400 have never handled arms, but we can turn them into fighting men in no time. I have been sent here to tell you that we shall not rise until you give us a list of those we are to remove—to kill. I know what the English army is, and I know how to fight them, and the only way to success is to attack and remove those who command them—the officers and those who administer the law. We must be led as the children of Israel were led from Egypt through the Red Sea.*

According to Price, every other delegate spoke in similar terms. Frost didn't argue; in that way he appeared to accept their demands. He simply said he would lead them and he would 'call' them out.[9] Knowing that time was running out, Frost had to move fast. An engagement for 14 October in Bury, Lancashire, for a dinner in honour of Convention delegate Dr Matthew Fletcher, was cover for secret meetings with his English and Scottish contacts on the situation in South Wales. Frost announced in the *Western Vindicator* plans to visit Merthyr and Pontypool, so as to confuse the authorities, and headed north.[10] William Burns of Scotland attended Dr Fletcher's dinner in Bury, then went on to Newcastle, where he told Robert Lowery that the dinner had been a cover for some of them to *"concoct a rising"* of which he would hear *"bye-and-bye"*. He told Lowery that *"some of our leading men"* and a Welshman calling himself 'Mr Bately' had been present. Lowery recalled:

9. Wilks, op. cit., pp. 151-52. Jones, op. cit, pp. 101-2. *Ap id Anfryn, The Late Dr Price* (Cardiff, 1896). *Cardiff Times*, 26 May 1888.
10. Williams, op. cit., pp. 156-8. Wilks, op. cit., pp. 166-67. *Northern Star*, 19 Oct 1839.

I told him it would be madness to attempt such a thing. He dis-
sented and told me I did not know what he knew. I observed that
I supposed it was F. O'Connor's scheme, and that he would leave
them in the lurch. He answered, they had not let him into their
secret, for they did not think he was to be trusted.[11]

Frost, while in the North, sought to further confuse the authorities about his movements by getting the *Northern Star* and the
Northern Liberator to publish notices of lectures in various northern towns that he had no intention of turning up for. But sometime in the third week of October the discussions Frost was having in the North were brought to a close, when Charles Jones arrived from South Wales and informed him that the Directorate
had decided to call out the brigades in early November.[12] Frost
sent Jones to Bradford with a message for Peter Bussey and then,
instead of proceeding to Wales via Birmingham, took himself to
London to look for Dr Taylor. He hoped to find him through
Henry Hetherington, but Taylor was in hiding and Hetherington
did not know where he was. As Frost departed for Newport he
said to Hetherington, "*I am a doomed man*".[13]

 Apparently as a back-up measure, Frost had also assigned Charles
Jones to come down from Yorkshire and attempt to seek out Dr
Taylor through Hetherington before returning to Wales. Jones
took a steamship from Hull, but was shipwrecked and didn't arrive in London until Tuesday 29 October. He visited Hetherington, who by this time had found the doctor. Jones told Taylor that
the Rising was imminent, though he *"could give no precise details"*.
According to the spy Edwards, who worked in Hetherington's
bookshop, Taylor then left London for the North, after writing a
letter to Frost in which he expressed his alarm about the short notice, but assured Frost that he would be found at his 'post'. When
Taylor reached Yorkshire on or around the last day of October,
he learned that Bussey in Bradford had sent a courier to Newport to get the Rising postponed for ten days, as Yorkshire was

---

11. Lowery, op. cit., pp. 155.
12. Wilks, op. cit., pp. 167.
13. Ibid., pp. 168. Feargus O'Connor, *Northern Star*, 3 May 1845.

not yet 'ready'.[14] In Bradford, magistrates were telling the Lord Lieutenant that information about the Chartist movement was in short supply—because the Chartists were organising in groups of twelve and holding meetings in taverns, which excluded outsiders. Slightly bewildered, the magistrates reported that the Chartists had *"some way of communicating with each other not yet understood"*.[15]

A second delegate conference of the 'secret council' took place in Heckmondwike, Yorkshire, on 26 October. Bussey did not attend. The previous conference on 30 September had adopted the London resolution on the planned Rising, but had kept it secret from the press, including O'Connor's *Northern Star*. The *Northern Star* reported of the 26 October conference that delegates had decided that *"a copy of a resolution passed at the last delegate meeting [30 September] be transmitted to Mr Blakey [publisher of the Northern Liberator] of Newcastle"*. As historian A.J. Peacock says, this seems to indicate that a *"momentous decision"* had been made at Heckmondwike on 30 September, and that the secret was now to be shared with the comrades at the *Liberator*. It further indicates that on 26 October their decision to support a hypothetical rising in Wales was superseded by a decision to follow up the planned Rising with risings of their own.[16]

William Burns travelled to Scotland days before the Rising, and went to see Robert Lowery, who had a speaking engagement in Dundee. After the meeting Burns passed on an invitation from Dr Taylor to join the insurrectionaries of the secret council. According to Lowery:

> He [Burns] now informed me that the affair [the rising in South Wales] was still intended, and that he had received a letter from Dr Taylor, that he had come into the Newcastle district, intending to give lectures on Chemistry, explaining the nature of explosive forces, but that he could make nothing of them, and he wished me to go up and try as I was popular there. He knew something was up in Wales.

---

14. Wilks, op. cit., p. 172. Jones, op. cit., p. 103. HO40/44.
15. Peacock, op. cit., p. 29.
16. Ibid., p. 31.

Since Lowery wasn't a chemist, it was clear that it was his political and organisational skills that Taylor wanted for *"explosive"* purposes. Lowery replied:

> *If Dr Taylor makes bolts he may try and shoot them, but I am not such a fool as to try; but most likely he is at his usual lies, and this is a piece of his brag and mystery,—but it is too bad for such a fellow to send letters about at a time when we have every reason to suppose that the Post-office is tampered with, thus putting men's liberties in jeopardy…*[17]

Dr Taylor had been set on insurrection since the last day of the National Convention (14 September), when Bronterre O'Brien produced a draft document on constitutional rights as a final statement for publication. Taylor had drafted an alternative statement advocating *"resistance"*, which argued that *"all constitutional law is at an end… brute force is now the order of the day"*. O'Brien described this as a *"thoroughly illegal and dangerous document"*, and in the end no statement was agreed on.[18] After the collapse of the Convention, O'Brien had decided to withdraw from the movement on the grounds that he could not conscientiously take part in secret projects which would lead to partial outbreaks, as these would easily be crushed and lead to increased persecution of the Chartists. O'Brien believed that physical force *"should have no part unless it began with the oppressor, in which case, the oppressed would be bound (by the constitution itself), to resort to physical force in self-defence"*.[19]

O'Connor on the other hand, stayed half in and half out. He kept the *Northern Star* in circulation and planned a campaign to set up election clubs in preparation for a national Chartist challenge at the hustings in the next general election–which, as it was to turn out, was two years away. But suddenly he cancelled a tour of Lancashire in early October and took himself off to Ireland, where he remained until 2 November. There is no agreement amongst historians and the memoirs of Convention members about O'Connor's motives. Did he take flight in order to avoid responsibility for a

17. Lowery, op. cit., p. 155.
18. Fraser, op. cit., p. 30-31.
19. Epstein, op. cit., pp. 194-5. *Southern Star*, 26 Jan 1840.

dangerous situation that he himself had helped to bring about? In Lowery's view:

> [O'Connor] *undoubtedly knew what was soon to occur, and, through his newspaper and influence with the people, was the only man who could without much exposure have nipped the plot in the bud… But coward-like, he ran off to Ireland, under pretence of business in Cork, a soon as he knew that the explosion was to take place.*[20]

But Lowery himself recorded William Burns's assurance that O'Connor had not been let in on the secret, "*for they did not think he was to be trusted*". Others accepted that O'Connor had valid reasons for going to Ireland. Having been convicted in July, he was due to appear at the Queen's Bench on 7 November for sentencing–which involved a possible prison sentence. He later explained: "*as I had not been in Ireland since April 1836, it was not unnatural that I should wish to see my friends and arrange something about my property before I was incarcerated*". He also claimed that he had gone to get funding for the *Northern Star*, to hold meetings in Cork and set up Radical Associations, wishing to scotch Daniel O'Connell's assertion that he dared not set foot in Ireland (in Dublin that August, meetings organised for Robert Lowery had been physically broken up by O'Connell's thuggish supporters; and Lowery, who was too lame to fight or run, had only narrowly escaped injury).[21] In any case, whatever O'Connor's motivations for going to Ireland, events on the other side of the Irish Sea were about to spin out of his control.

William Ashton of Barnsley was convinced that the planned risings he had implicated himself in had no chance of success, not least because of leaders like Peter Bussey, whom he did not trust. Ashton decided to go to into exile, but before taking a steamer from Hull to France he visited William Hill, editor of the *Northern Star*, in Leeds. He warned him that Frost was involved in a dangerous enterprise, and was likely to be sold out by those who

20. Lowery, op. cit., pp. 157.

21. Epstein, op. cit.. 198-9. 'Democracy or Nationalism? The problems of the Chartist Press in Ireland', Michael O'Huggins, *Papers for the People*, pp. 129-45. Lowery, op. cit, pp. 144-48.

purporting to support him. Ashton urged Hill to send a warning to both O'Connor and Frost. But O'Connor was in Ireland and Hill didn't think the mail was safe enough to send such a message to Frost, so he did nothing.[22]

John Frost arrived back in Newport on about 20 October, to find his worst fears realised: the movement he had been leading was now preparing for insurrection. His immediate reaction was to sit down and write an address to *"the Farmers and Trades-men of Monmouth"* for the *Western Vindicator*. In this article he made one last appeal to middle-class opinion, pointing out that before the French Revolution the French people had been led by the *"most benevolent men in the world"*, and that the government's efforts to destroy them had produced *"leaders ten times more violent"*.[23]

On 26 October Frost sent a message to Dr William Price, requesting an urgent meeting. Price did not entirely trust him, and when he turned up the next day he even suspected that Frost had a listener hidden in the next room. Frost told him that the Rising was to take place one week later, but when Price asked to see the plan, he was told that it was in the office of Samuel Etheridge, a leader of the Working Men's Association. This was true, but the plans were concerned with the organising of men into groups of ten and not with the nuts and bolts of an armed uprising.[24] According to Price, Frost then made it clear that on 4 November he wanted to march solely on Newport, which he thought could be achieved without any violence being employed, as he believed the troops would lay down their arms. Price could not take this plan seriously. He angrily told Frost, *"You will not put a sword in my hand and a rope around my neck at the same time,"* and reminded him of the meeting of the Directorate at Blaenau three weeks earlier when, in response to the Waterloo veteran, he had promised not to call them out unless they were provided with a list of *"who to remove— to kill"*. Price's words horrified Frost, who exclaimed, *"What? Do you want us to kill the soldiers—kill a thousand of them in one night?"*

---

22. Peacock, op. cit., pp. 30-31. *Northern Star*, 10 May 1845.
23. *Western Vindicator*, 26 Oct 1839.
24. Williams, op. cit., p. 203.

Price replied, *"Yes, a hundred thousand if it is necessary"*. Frost said, *"Dear me. I cannot do it. I cannot do it"*.[25]

The next day, Monday 28 October, a delegate meeting of the Directorate took place at Dukestown, presided over by Zephaniah Williams and William Jones. Frost was absent. Reports on 'readiness' were mixed. Brigade leaders from Merthyr told the meeting that they had about 2,000 armed men at the ready, but representatives from Aberdare said that their own forces were not yet sufficient for commitment. The Directorate decided nevertheless to prepare for a mobilisation the following Tuesday, 5 November, the result of which would be to *"get the Charter within a month"*. The choice of Guy Fawkes Night was of a tactical rather than a symbolic significance, for the celebrations were often disorderly occasions (much decried by the respectable press), and therefore good cover for an insurrection. Zephaniah Williams said that the rank and file would be told that the aim was to destroy the workhouses and get universal suffrage and free trade, although they were not to be told what their destinations would be until the day. In the meantime the delegates were to hold nightly meetings and arm in self-defence.

According to Zephaniah Williams's later testimony, it was decided to occupy Abergavenny, Brecon, Newport and the left bank of the Usk simultaneously on Day One. These towns, which were defended by very few soldiers, would be infiltrated beforehand by armed detachments before the main assaults began. The Rising was to be a General Strike as well. The valleys were to be scoured for arms and conscripts, mines and works were to be closed and their managers arrested (there was common talk of making them work in the mines). Gunpowder stores and warehouses were to be taken and blast furnaces were to be used for weapons manufacture; magistrates' homes were to be attacked, and burned if necessary, and magistrates and selected aristocrats were to be imprisoned or executed; army officers and police were to be killed if they refused to surrender; the River Usk was to be blocked to shipping and resistance organised against troops sent by land. Looting of property and similar indiscipline would be punishable

---

25. Jones, op. cit., p. 104. Islwyn ap Nicholas, op. cit. *Cardiff Times*, 26 May 1888.

by death. Cardiff was to be taken once the initial targets had been achieved. This rising in South Wales was to signal similar events throughout the kingdom, and the mails were to be stopped to alert collaborators in other areas that the Rising had begun. Williams recalled, *"As soon as the day was agreed, and fixed upon for the attack, Messages were dispatched to the North of Wales with the information; also the North of England, from thence Dispatches were to be sent to Scotland".*[26]

The above account of the battle plan for the Rising relies on testimony given by Zephaniah Williams to a surgeon on a prison ship six months later, which was only discovered one hundred years after the event by Frost's biographer David Williams. The letter, discovered amongst the papers in Lord Tredegar's library in Newport, was marked 'copy', but there is little doubt as to its authenticity.[27] Historians of the Rising have disputed the extent to which the 'confession' should be taken seriously. David Jones thinks it should, as does Ivor Wilks, who points out that Zephaniah Williams had nothing to gain by making it, given that he was on board a prison ship heading for a life sentence. John Humphries and David Williams claim that Zephaniah's statement must have been made under duress and is therefore not believable. As we shall see, however, the veracity of the testimony regarding a kingdom-wide rebellion is born out by other accounts.

Humphries and Williams both assert that Frost was planning no more than a 'monster demonstration'. But in that case why did Frost tell Job Tovey, whose house-guest he was in the days before the Rising, that he would stop the mail for Birmingham, where the Chartists would take its non-arrival as a signal? Humphries points out that there wasn't actually a direct mail coach from Newport to Birmingham, but it seems reasonable to suppose that news of the stopping of all mails from Newport would reach Birmingham and other areas fairly quickly. Humphries thinks that Tovey may have been a spy (he turned Queen's evidence later, but in the end wasn't called as a witness), but Tovey's testimony is corroborated by William Davies, a shopkeeper's son, who testified that the final

26. Wilks, op. cit., pp. 137-38, 148, 157, 170-72.
27. Ibid, p. 152. National Library of Wales, Tredegar Park Muniments, box 40, doc. 2.

meeting in Blackwood before the Rising decided that the purpose of the march was to "*seize all authorities wherever they could be found, and stop the mails, so that people of the north would know they had succeeded*". Tovey also gave an accurate account of Frost's conviction that the soldiers at Newport would be disarmed without violence.[28] Frost told him that when the marchers reached the workhouse at the top of Stow Hill they would "*give three cheers which would so frighten the mayor that he would die in his bed and it would produce such an effect on the soldiers that they would throw down their arms*".[29] This was not totally wishful thinking, for of the 120 troops of the 29th Foot who had been sent to Newport in May thirteen had deserted, some under the influence of Chartist propaganda, and at least two army deserters helped to organise military drilling for the Rising; one, named Williams, would die in the assault on Newport.[30] The 29th, however, had now been replaced by a fresh and reputedly tougher regiment, the 45th–reputedly because in May the previous year the 45th had put down the revolt of agricultural labourers at Bossenden Wood in Kent, shooting ten men dead.

On Tuesday 29 October, the night after the Dukestown meeting, delegates from Pontypool district met at Pontnewynydd and the leaders adjourned to meet in secret.[31] Frost learned on Thursday what was on their minds, when leaders of the Directorate visited him in Newport and insisted that he prove his sincerity and commitment by coming to the hills to organise the rebellion. Frost later testified: "*What was I to do? I went up the mountains… the men surrounded me and said, 'Mr Frost, if you will not lead us, neither you or your family shall live in Newport; we are beginning to suspect you.'*"[32] So Frost went to Blackwood and spent the final days engaged in correspondence with the Welsh localities, London and other regions.

---

28. Humphries, op. cit., p. 132. Newport Public Library, *Chartist Trials and Miscellaneous Books and Pamphlets*, testimony of Job Tovey, Esther Pugh, Richard Pugh, William Davies. *Merthyr Guardian*, 1 Feb 1840.
29. Humphries, op. cit, p. 133.
30. Wilks, op. cit., p. 150.
31. Williams, op. cit., pp. 204-5.
32. Wilks, op. cit., p. 170. *Shrewsbury News*, 7 December 1839.

The final South Wales delegate meeting took place at the Coach and Horses in Blackwood on Friday 1 November, attended by representatives from the lodges of Dowlais, Rhymeny, Fleur de Lys, Maesycwmmer, Sirhowy, Argoed, Blackwood, Ebbw Vale, Victoria Ironworks, British Ironworks, Llanelly, Blaenau, Twyn y Star, Lanhilleth, Crumlin, Croespenmaen, Pontypool and Newport. Significantly this meeting was not attended by the Merthyr and Pontypridd delegates, who had another five brigades, totalling 2,500 men.

Frost realised that this was his final chance to reassert some control over events, and he took it, arguing for a modification of the plan adopted the previous Monday. He did not ask the directorate to abandon the plan for simultaneous occupation of the five towns on 5 November; rather he suggested that occupation of Newport should take place a day earlier, on Monday the 4th. His plan was for the two divisions led by Williams and himself to seize Newport, whilst the other divisions were brought out and held back until the outcome was known.[33] The success of the operation would quickly reach other regions, once Newport had fallen and the mail coaches been stopped. On the 3rd he would muster the Dukestown-Blackwood division and Zephaniah Williams would muster Ebbw Vale-Nantyglow, while William Jones's Pontypool-Abersychan-Blaenavon would mobilise as a reserve force. The three divisions would meet at Risca, just north of Newport, at midnight on Sunday to receive their orders and reach Newport by 2 a.m. Frost told them he thought bloodshed was unlikely, because he thought the soldiers wouldn't fight and that once the general Rising was underway the small detachments of soldiers in Brecon and Abergavenny would lay down their arms. Zephaniah Williams agreed, believing that the soldiers in Newport would be surprised and captured while drunk, after their usual Sunday night in the beerhouses.[34]

Dr Price was seen talking to Frost at the door of the meeting at the Coach and Horses in Blackwood on Friday 1 November, but he did not go into the meeting. The conversation could hardly have

33. Wilks, op. cit., p. 175. Williams, op. cit., p. 193.
34. Jones, op. cit., p. 113, Wilks, op. cit., p. 152, National Library of Wales, Tredegar Park Muniments, box 40, doc. 2.

been amicable.[35] If Frost had removed himself from the leadership of the Rising, William Price might well have filled his shoes. Although the doctor did not have the standing of the former mayor, he was at least of equal intellect, and unlike Frost he professed the physical courage and ruthlessness required for revolutionary leadership. Price, it was believed, had a number of cannon hidden away and ready to use, which might have proved useful on the day. But he would not be tested on the day as Frost would be.

The government intelligence apparatus in South Wales provided little of worth in the run-up to the Rising, apart from Superintendent William Homan of Tredegar's report on 29 October to the Marquis of Bute, which hinted at the plans of the secret council for a general uprising:

> *It is reported to me that they are to have a simultaneous rise throughout the kingdom this week and arms have been issued and pikes. The magistrates are undecided as what steps should be taken at present. I much fear things will not end as quietly as imagined. You shall hear from me as events occur.*[36]

The ulterior measures campaign had already intensified. Money was being withdrawn from the banks by friendly societies to buy arms. By this time it was becoming dangerous for people in some areas not to fork out 5d for a Chartist membership card when invited to join.[37] Although the level of Chartist press-gang intimidation in South Wales was later exaggerated in the ensuing trials by those who needed an explanation for their involvement in the Rising, it did happen and was widespread. Once the word was out that the Rising was on, potential 'conscripts' and their families fled the area or hid in barns, woods, caves and even down mines.

On Saturday 2 November the *Merlin*, the paper of the Whigs, carried an article headed 'The Extinction of Chartism', which echoed a speech by the Attorney-General, Sir John Campbell, claiming that because the Whigs had cleverly decided to imprison Chartist leaders rather than massacre their supporters, as the Tories

---

35. Williams, op. cit., p. 208.
36. Humphries, op. cit., p. 144. CCL Bute Papers, XX.30, Homan to Capt. Howells, 31 Oct 1839.
37. Jones op. cit., p. 104.

had done at Peterloo, the movement was rapidly being destroyed. But by the time this article appeared the valleys were already in the initial throes of a rising, the first sign of which was the sparse attendance at the Saturday markets. Later that day Frost was visited in Blackwood by a courier sent from Yorkshire (his identity is not certain; some historians think it was Charles Jones, the Convention member from North Wales, others that he was from Yorkshire). This courier relayed Bussey's urgent request for postponement, but Frost had to tell him that there was no going back. Neither Frost nor the messenger knew that by this time Bussey had sent his lieutenant, George White, around the West Riding of Yorkshire, ordering local militants to postpone all the actions that had being planned, on the grounds that he, Bussey, was too ill to lead them and needed more time.[38] But it wouldn't have made any difference if Frost had known. Frost told his messenger, *"I might as well blow my brains out as to try and oppose them or shrink back"*.[39] The Rising had begun.

38. Ibid., p. 114.
39. Lovett, *Life and Struggles*, p. 238.

Under Eastern Eyes–David Urquhart and the Chartists

When this Old Cap was New
O well I mind that when
Old England now so sad
Was merry England then
Her foes were in the mire
Her friends were leal and true
And blithe were England's songs
When this old cap was new
Thomas Doubleday

Most historians of Chartism who have covered the Newport Rising–which we return to in the next chapter–
take account of the claim by David Urquhart, a former
diplomat, that he almost managed to get it called off. The consensus is that Urquhart's account, though tantalising, is unreliable;
but there is no doubt that his intervention within Chartism was
significant and that it does cast some light on how the movement
in England was reacting to events in South Wales.[1]

In September 1839 George Fyler, a London barrister, gave a lecture on foreign policy and international trade at the Mechanics'
Institute in Marylebone, in which he expounded the controversial
views of his friend David Urquhart. The Institute was a regular meeting place of the West London Democratic Association,
whose members, such as the Polish democrat Major Beniowski
and National Convention delegate William Cardo, were leading
figures in London Chartism. Afterwards Fyler wrote to Urquhart,
"My speech has created a sensation among the Chartists… you and your
views have been the subject of discussion within the Convention…"[2] To

1. Thomas Doubleday quoted from Black and Metevier, eds, *The Harney Papers* (Amsterdam, 1969), p. 67.
2. Gertrude Robinson, *David Urquhart, Victorian Knight Errant* (London, 1921), p. 86.

understand how Urquhart, a prospective Tory candidate for Marylebone, could influence pro-physical-force Marylebone Chartists,
we must first outline his career and ideas.

Born in 1805 into an aristocratic Highland household in Cromarty, Urquhart was taken by his widowed mother at the age of eight
to be educated in France, Italy and Switzerland. In 1821 he went
to St John's College, Oxford, but left after a few months because
of ill health and returned to France. In 1827 he joined Lord
Cochrane's private naval expedition to fight for the Greeks in the
War of Independence, and was wounded in the sea battle that
destroyed a Turkish squadron in the Bay of Salon. Afterwards he
stayed in the Near East and travelled extensively.

The wisdom of the twice-born first came to Urquhart when a
Turkish soldier of the Greek War explained to him why he had ordered his company to give up a fortified position to the Russians
without firing a single shot. The Turk said that since war had not
been declared, to fight would have been murder: *"If I take this musket unblessed by God, then I take it of the Devil"*. Urquhart, who had
spilt Turkish blood in the war, felt an overwhelming sense of guilt
about the absence of 'Moral Law' on the side he had been fighting
for: *"I would gladly have given myself to justice had there been a tribunal
to deal with such cases"*, he recalled. Urquhart was possessed of a
Calvinist moral certainty and a Platonist passion for unveiling the
reality of the world and its affairs: *"Men of this corrupt age prefer
seeming right to being right. They are furious when they are shown to be
wrong; their self-love is hurt"*.

Urquhart came to believe that Russia rather than Turkey was
the real enemy of liberty in Europe and the Near East, including
Greece. He thought that Russia was in essence weak, but capable
of advancing her designs because the West did not grasp the un-
scrupulous guile of Russia's ministers and diplomats. In 1831 he
got the Foreign Office to send him to Turkey on a secret mission
to investigate the possibility of closer co-operation in trade and
commerce. On returning to England in 1833 he published *Turkey
and its Resources*, which advocated making the Ottoman Empire a
market for British produce. His next job was First Secretary at
the Embassy at Constantinople. Colleagues at the Porte muttered
that he had *"gone native"*, because he lived outside the compound,

wore Turkish clothes, employed Turkish servants, found Turkish friends, learned their language and manners, and ate their cuisine.

Urquhart was the first Briton to visit the Circassian tribes, who lived in the area between the Caucasian mountains, the Kuban River and the Black Sea. In 1829 Turkey had been forced to cede Circassia to Russia in a settlement fiercely resisted by these Muslim people. Urquhart got to know the Circassians so well that they honoured him with the name 'Daoud Bey' and asked him to stay and help them fight the Russians. He felt obliged to turn them down, but promised to help in other ways. His first effort was an attempt, in 1836, to break the Russian blockade of Circassian trading outlets by inducing a British merchant in Constantinople to sail to Circassia with a shipment of salt. When the ship was seized by the Russian navy, the owner, with Urquhart's support, claimed compensation through the British Foreign Office for violation of international law. But Lord Palmerston, the Foreign Secretary, refused to press the case and had Urquhart recalled. His Foreign Office career was over.

Urquhart now regarded Palmerston as effectively an 'agent' of the Tsar, who gave encouragement to Russian efforts to set European states against each other. Urquhart had some knowledge of Russian support for revolutionaries–mainly of the nationalist variety–in countries where a measure of de-stabilisation might be useful for political leverage, if not justification for Russian military intervention. The Greek War, Urquhart believed, was the most obvious example of this. The ultimate danger as he saw it was that Russian conquest of the Dardenelles would turn the Mediterranean into a Russian lake, and enable her to dominate south-eastern Europe and the Near East. Russia, having divided Europe from Asia, would then turn on British interests in India and the Far East. He believed that for over a century the British Foreign Office had encouraged Russia to become a dangerous power in Europe, and had allowed Russia to supplant Sweden as the main power in Baltic in the Great Northern War (1700–21). The main obstacle to Russian expansionism in the nineteenth century was now the Ottoman Empire, which was commonly regarded as the 'sick man of Europe'. Urquhart, however, was convinced that the Ottomans were strong enough to prevail and prosper, as long as other European powers did not assist or encourage the designs of the Czar.[3]

Furthermore, Urquhart regarded governance in the Muslim world as superior to the West in more ways than one:

> *The ordinary Englishman goes to the East convinced that he is a professor of political economy who has possession of the science of government, and that in all respects he is a free man of an understanding mind. He discovers that the Turk considers a public debt a bad thing. "The ignoramus!" he exclaims. That the Turk regards this debt as contrary to religion. "Ah! the fanatic!" He discovers again that the Turk has a repugnance to the idea of an Assembly which makes laws. "Ah! the slave!" That the Turk despises a representative chamber. "Ah! the tool of despotism!" and so on to the end of the chapter. But if the Turk were to reveal to him his own ideas of the duties of a sovereign and the obligation of dethroning him when he does not fulfill them, or the necessity for every civil and military subordinate to be sure of the legality of an order before executing it, the European would lose himself in conjectures and astonishment, and would exclaim, "These* Turks are revolutionists and communists". *He would be a hundred leagues from perceiving that science and liberty, as he understands them, are only perversions; arising from the impotence of past ages to resist the encroachments of authority, which has succeeded in subjugating the nations of Europe and putting them in handcuffs administrative, financial and intellectual.*[4]

In the East Urquhart had seen villages unspoiled by 'civilisation', unless civilisation meant *"the free right to property of every man, and the equality of all men before the law"* and the rule that every man had to *"either prove himself or admit he was wrong"*. In the Muslim world he had seen the codes of courtesy and respect that bound together master and servant, and brought up children to be neither timid nor unruly; and he had found standards of cleanliness unheard of in his homeland (Urquhart is credited for bringing the Turkish bath to England). He believed that class structure and

---

3. Ibid., chapter 1, p. 3.
4. 'Islam and the Constitutional System', *Diplomatic Review*, vol. xxiv, p. 178.

government in the East were based on the same Moral Law that had once ruled in Europe. Because of the universal religious duty of hospitality, pauperism–at least in the sense it was defined by the Poor Law Guardians–was unknown, just as, he believed, it had been unknown in European feudalism. Furthermore, the Eastern warlord, unlike his Norman counterparts in England, did not own any land: he was entitled to 10 per cent of its produce, but only if he protected the farmers, whose right of property was indefeasible and whose life and soul had as much value as his. In short, Urquhart, the Scottish clan leader, saw in the East a form of 'feudalism' still uncorrupted by bourgeois property rights. In contrast, England was becoming a 'nation of slaves'. The centralised state, with all its powers of taxation and war-making, had destroyed municipal self-government and had eroded people's sense of responsibility. The population no longer thought of affairs of state as their concern, and the very language of politics and civic life had been debased.

Following the meeting at the Marylebone Mechanics' Institute in September 1839 Urquhart's friend Fyler was approached by one of the Marylebone Chartists, called Westrup, who asked him to arrange a meeting between Urquhart and William Cardo and Bronterre O'Brien of the National Convention. Cardo and Westrup met Urquhart at the rooms of the Colonial Society, but O'Brien wasn't enthusiastic and didn't turn up. Urquhart laid out to the Chartists his analysis of international affairs and the state of the nation, in particular *"the injurious and deleterious effects of our boasted institutions"*. The only remedy for the *"evils under which the nations groaned"* lay in *"returning to the simple institutions of our forefathers"*. A decentralised state with proper local government, he said, would truly develop the powers of the human mind, and render such hated institutions as the county police, workhouses and customs-houses unnecessary.[5]

----

5. Robinson, op. cit., pp. 86-93. Mr Westrup, who is described by Urquhart as his first Chartist convert, is a mysterious figure, whose name is absent from the documentation of London Chartism. According to Robinson he sometimes signed himself as 'Westrop'. The only leading Chartist with a similar name was Charles Westerton, an Anglican churchwarden, supporter of William Lovett's Working

Having learnt his manners from his Cromarty clan and the Turks, Urquhart didn't patronise or look down his nose at his working-class listeners. Never having lived much in England, he was free from the affectations of bourgeois class prejudice and snobbery that the working-class Chartists were so used to in dealing with their 'betters'. *"My best converts,"* Urquhart claimed, *"apart from working men are men of genius and young girls"*. There was of course more to his appeal to Chartists than his personality. He was, according to his biographer, a precursor of 'guild socialism'. Certainly Urquhart's ideas on reversing the *"monstrous and unnatural division"* of agricultural and commercial/manufacturing interests could be seen as a 'feudal socialist' version of Thomas Spence's programme for the 'People's Farm' and a decentralised democratic republic. Urquhart's appeal to Chartists as an anti-capitalist visionary is also not so surprising considering that in years to come he had a certain influence on the greatest anti-capitalist of all time, Karl Marx.

Although Marx, who first met Urquhart in 1850, jokingly described him as *"a Scot by birth, a Turk by choice and a Circassian by nature"*, he took him seriously as a critic of bourgeois society. Writing on the division of labour in class society, he quoted Urquhart in support of his view that in manufacture the *"crippling of body and mind"* goes much further because it *"attacks the individual at the very roots of his life"*. Urquhart wrote: *"To subdivide a man is to execute him, if he deserves the sentence, to assassinate him if he does not… The subdivision of labour is the assassination of a people"*. Marx compared this view with Hegel's: *"Hegel held very heretical views on division of labour. In his 'Rechtsphilosophie' he says: 'By well educated men we understand in the first instance, those who can do everything that others do'"*.[6] Urquhart, in *Familiar Words as Affecting the Character of Englishmen*, wrote:

_____

Men's Association and firm opponent of physical force, whose election for the Convention had been thwarted by the London Democratic Association.

6. Karl Marx, *Capital*, vol. 1, chapter 14: Division of Labour and Manufacture, section 5, The Capitalistic Character of Manufacture. Footnote 51.

Before the sub-division of labour became known as a process of science... the people of England, the so-called 'merry', manufactured at home, in the intervals between field labour... England was consequently a self-subsisting country... [Then] the great idol, cheapness, was set up; distant lands adored, but the people at home were crushed. Civilisation draws everything to the towns and makes each family dependent on the factory... you divide the people into clownish boors and emasculated dwarfs... a nation divided into agricultural and commercial interests calling itself sane![7]

Marx quoted from this paragraph in his section in *Capital* on modern machinery and agriculture, and commented: "*This passage shows, at one and the same time, the strength and the weakness of that kind of criticism which knows how to judge and condemn the present, but not how to comprehend it*". This is footnoted to the following well-known paragraph by Marx on urbanisation:

Capitalist production, by collecting the population in great centres... on the one hand concentrates the historical motive power of society; on the other hand, it disturbs the circulation of matter between man and the soil, i.e., prevents the return to the soil of its elements consumed by man in the form of food and clothing; it therefore violates the conditions necessary to lasting fertility of the soil. By this action it destroys at the same time the health of the town labourer and the intellectual life of the rural labourer.[8]

Another important aspect to Urquhartism was 'internationalism', though this took a form quite different from what Bronterre O'Brien and George Julian Harney had been arguing for. Whereas to Harney the Greek and Polish rebels were comrades-in-arms in the cause of Jacobin internationalism, to Urquhart they were the playthings of much larger forces: the menacing Muscovites and their British collaborators in the Whig party. In Urquhart's view, the British government's imperialist adventures against Mexico and China, and its colonial oppression of Canada and Jamaica,

7. Robinson, op. cit., p. 75. *David Urquhart, Familiar Words as affecting the Character of Englishmen* (London, 1855), p. 119.
8. Karl Marx, *Capital*, Chapter 15, Machinery and Modern Industry, Section 10. Modern Industry and Agriculture. Footnote 244.

stemmed from its treacherous pro-Russian policy towards the Ottoman Empire. Furthermore this policy had produced a system of international relations in which trade and commerce were distorted at the expense of the British worker.

In the discussions between Urquhart and his Chartist contacts, William Cardo was converted to this view, as was fellow Convention delegate John Warden, who was on bail after being charged with possession of arms and riot after street-fighting in Bolton on 14 August. These, and others who fell under the spell of Urquhart in the coming months, seem to have discovered a new perspective on politics in which national schemes, however grand, were seen as at the mercy of a new and dangerous global politics, which required new universalist principles. William Cargill of Newcastle wrote:

> *I find in examining these topics that my mind is carried into the interior of a temple, of which I could form no conception, and I feel as if I could get introduced to very clime and hold intercourse with universal man. Party and its paltryisms are not worth notice when placed beside the rights of nations and the rights of man.*[9]

Lowery, who joined the Urquhartist cause some months later, recalled:

> *Hitherto I had simply applied my mind to forms of government and popular rights, thinking that if these were attained improvement would at once be achieved. One day I asked him [Urquhart] if he did not think that the working-classes had a right to the Charter. He replied, "You may as well ask me if they have a right to the air they breathe, but cannot you see that no institutional rights can give liberty unless the spirit is in the people? A nation may have these constitutional rights, and wanting that spirit be the slaves of faction. Greece and Rome did not fall because they had not the forms of liberty, but because the spirit of independence and patriotism had first died out…" His idea of efficiently improving the national mind was not by appealing to the masses from platforms, but by men of mind communing with each other… [until]*

---

9. Robinson, op. cit., p. 96.

the masses could be addressed with that oneness of mind which
rouses a nation.[10]

Sometime around late October 1839, according to Urquhart, a
group of Chartists (including Cardo) went to see him late at night.
They told him that, having been convinced by his speeches and
writings *"on the revolutionary actions of Russia, and the profit she made
by it"*, they had to tell him something, otherwise they would not
be able to sleep soundly. The failure of petitioning, they explained,
had left:

> *two million people, throughout the land, aroused and ready to*
> *accomplish their objects by national convulsion: all their numer-*
> *ous armies in the North and West, as well as in the South, had*
> *intended some day before the first of January to put themselves in*
> *motion. There were already shells and rockets which were explo-*
> *sive, spikes for the feet of cavalry horse, and other ammunitions*
> *of war prepared in secret in Birmingham.*

His Chartist visitors then laid bare an insurrectionary plan being
hatched by a nationally organised conspiracy: *"the government knew*
nothing of the organization. The chief was a secret agent of the London
Police. It was plain that the police were misled. It was revealed at 2 a.m.
by three of the five chiefs".[11]
   Urquhart claimed that he was told of the plan involving a force of
100,000 Chartists, organised from the bottom up in classes of ten,
into a pyramid that was controlled at the top by a central council
of five, which was to seize twenty towns. Urquhart perceived in
this the hand of Russia. Hadn't the Greek *Hetairia*, the Russian-
backed revolutionaries, organised in groups of ten? It was obvious, Urquhart told his Chartist listeners, *"You are in the hands of a*
Russian agent, who has been employed by the Hetairia or Greek insurrec-
tion". Urquhart became convinced that this *"Russian agent"*, *"mover*
and director of the whole plan", was the *"Pole, Beniowski, a Jew and a*
military surgeon"–Major Bartlomiej Beniowski was, like Cardo, a
member of the West London Democratic Association.[12] Born in

10. Lowery, op. cit., pp. 167-68.
11. Quoted in Robinson, op. cit., p. 88.
12. Schoyen, op. cit., p. 90. *Diplomatic Review*, July 1873. Gammage,
History of the Chartist Movement, p. 189.

1805, Beniowski served as a medical officer in the Russian army until the Polish insurrection of 1830, when he crossed over to the Polish forces and rose to the rank of major. As an exile in Paris he was active in the Paris-based Committee for the Emancipation of the Jews and studied military science. He also developed a system of learning languages and memorising words called 'phrenotypics', which might have had, if it worked, certain uses for military intelligence. Writing in Harney's *London Democrat* on military science, Beniowski argued that in freeing an enslaved people *"the science of killing and destroying is the most useful and necessary of all the sciences; it is in fact the only one which, if universally known by the people at large, could prevent homicide at all"*. Beniowski 'theorised' about an attack on London from the north and expounded on the science of fortification, explaining that *"this branch of military science teaches how to enable a comparatively small number of men occupying a town, village or any other place, to resist, for a certain period of time, the attacks of a more numerous enemy, and also how to direct systematically an attack upon a given fortified place"*. As a radical and a democrat, he found himself at odds with the Polish exile movement in Britain, which was still dominated by 'royalist' exiles who were hostile to republicanism and democracy. They were led by Prince Czartoryski, who in fact published Urquhart's writings in his diplomatic house journal, *The Portfolio*. Urquhart's belief that Beniowski was a Russia agent was almost certainly influenced by Czartoryski's views. The Portfolio described Beniowski as a *"man whose name has for some time been inseparable from every political row and disturbance"*. These Polish nobles had close access to Foreign Affairs luminaries in the Whig Parliament, such as Lord Dudley Stuart, and they had power over Polish exiles in London because of their veto over who qualified for monetary support from the Foreign Office. Beniowski's writings and activities did not go unnoticed: his allowance of £40 a year from the Whig government was withdrawn at the behest of the Polish nobles.[13] (Weeks later Beniowski, on hearing of Urquhart's accusations, attacked him outside his London club

13. Peter Brock, 'Polish Democrats and English Radicals 1832-1862: A Chapter in the History of Anglo-Polish Relations', *Journal of Modern History*, vol. 25, no. 2 (June 1953), pp. 139-56.
Robinson, op. cit., p. 27.

and had to be dragged off by onlookers. Urquhart claimed it was attempted murder by throttling, but was unable to get the courts to bring charges.)[14]

Urquhart told his Chartist informants that he thought Harney, Dr Taylor and similar pro-physical force elements to be only the apparent leaders of the insurrectionary movement, and quite unaware that they were being manipulated by a 'higher body', which Urquhart designated a 'Council of Five'. As well as Beniowski, he determined, this council included *"a secret agent of the London Police"*. In the latter case, Urquhart may have been referring to Thomas Ainge Devyr, who was a leader of the Chartist secret council in Newcastle and had been an officer in the Metropolitan Police. Devyr was an Irish revolutionary, and Urquhart might have been aware of secret Russian support for the Irish cause–which persisted for a good part of Victoria's reign.[15] But there is no evidence that Devyr really was a witting or unwitting agent of the Russians or Whigs. In any case, if his Chartist contacts were looking for justification to abandon a dangerous course of armed confrontation with the state, then a Russian-Whig plot scare might have seemed to them as an expedient way of pulling the plug on immediate plans for an uprising.

Fyler obtained for Urquhart a cryptic document sent from Birmingham. This was a copy of a letter, carried by a courier travelling between Newport and Yorkshire via Birmingham at the end of October. The letter requested a postponement of the Rising and said: *"I hunt in the mountains of Scotland on Sunday or Monday, but if the hounds won't hunt there I shall hunt on Monday or Tuesday in Yorkshire; and if the hounds shall fail me there, I shall proceed immediately to join your pack"*.[16] This could only mean that the writer was trying to find agreement with Chartist leaders in Scotland and Yorkshire to carry out armed actions in those areas, to support the planned South Wales rising, and would join Frost in South Wales if this couldn't be obtained. The author of the letter may have been Convention member William Burns, who was travelling

14. David Urquhart, *Diplomatic Review* (July 1872).
15. Christy Campbell, *Fenian Fire* (London, 2002).
16. Wilks, op. cit., p. 173. Crawshay, *Chartist Correspondence*. Quoted in Wilks, p. 173.

between Scotland and Yorkshire. Urquhart and his Chartist converts now determined that:

> In three days it [the Rising] was to have been put into execution. The three chiefs joined me and we set out at once for the points most menaced. Others joined in… Not an instant was lost. With the aid of these men and others which they brought, and collecting all my available friends, amounting to about twenty or thirty individuals in all, we proceeded to deal with the confederacy, now broken in London, throughout the provinces. I visited every district, saw every leader. There was no change in my language because of what I had learnt. The Charter was never mentioned from beginning to end. It was by showing another and a better way that doubts came over them as to the judiciousness of continuing in that in which they were engaged, and men in doubt do not risk property, liberty and life. Frost was missed by half an hour; otherwise this danger would have been averted without leaving a trace behind of its existence.[17]

Although it seems highly improbable that Urquhart *"visited every district"* before the Rising, he did have contacts in various parts of the country who might, if reached in time, have been able to warn off would-be Chartist insurrectionists in the light of his 'revelations'. In Birmingham, where the leak of secret communications about the impending Rising had occurred, Urquhart had a key supporter in Charles Attwood, brother of Thomas Attwood MP, founder of the BPU and co-author of *The People's Charter*. Some of the Birmingham magistrates were BPU supporters, and some of these had 'confidential' relationships with Convention delegates in Birmingham (indeed, some of them were Convention delegates who never turned up). They also handled reports by informers. One of these, William Tongue, was attending Chartist meetings and drilling parties in Birmingham and London between Octo-

---

17. David Urquhart, *Diplomatic Review* (July 1872). Fyler's memoranda on these matters, as published seventeen years later in Urquhart's *Free Press Serials* XIII (1856), are dated as 22 September 1839, a date which is unlikely considering Urquhart's statement about 'three days' before the rising.

ber and December 1839.[18] He reported that a Birmingham magistrate named Mr Clarke was regularly meeting Edward Brown,
one of the Chartist leaders, and warning him not to engage in
drilling or arms procurement because a spy in their midst was
reporting all talk of such activities to Birmingham Chief of Police
Redfern every morning. (Fortunately for Tongue, Clarke did not
tell Brown the name of the spy.) Tongue's statement about the
magistrate's secret warning is believable, because Redfern wrote
in a marginal note to the report: *"this Mr Clarke was one of the three
magistrates including the mayor with whom I thought it necessary to com-
municate. He has acted very unwisely and done much mischief by this
communication"*.[19]

Tongue's reports, however, give no indications that the Chartist
leaders in Birmingham were made aware of Urquhart's 'revelations'. In Newcastle, if Urquhart's warning arrived at all (and there
is no evidence that it did) it was ignored. In Bradford, at the very
last moment, Peter Bussey was calling off a rising, but there is no
evidence that Urquhart influenced him either.

It is possible that Urquhart's fantasy of a 'Russia-Palmerston
Plot' behind Chartism may have been stimulated by his partaking
of one Eastern delight too many. In Harney's copy of Urquhart's
book *Reflections*, which has survived, there is an enclosed note by a
person called Searle, describing Urquhart as:

> a strange, erratic, often wild and half mad man in his conduct,
> and in his bearing to visitors. I believe he ate opium regularly…
> A man of real genius, a Scholar, a good resolver of political and
> philosophical and historical questions, he was nevertheless not a
> good speaker—but diffuse and at times, utterly incomprehensible,
> owing to some confusion of the intellect consequent upon his opi-
> um habit as I suppose…

Harney, in his copy of another Urquhart book, *Spirit of the East*,
wrote:

> He was a man of genius and his capacity was fully equalled by
> laborious activity… an original but strange character. It is be-
> lieved that he was much under the influence of opium—cause suf-

18. 'T' Report, 23 Nov 1839 HO 40/50.
19. Dorothy Thomson (ed.), op. cit., p. 242.

*ficient for his fantastic aberrations… He was in many respects an
enigma of the most sphinx-like proportions.*[20]

To these statements we might add the observation that the following extract from a letter of Urquhart's recalls certain passages in De Quincey's *Confessions of an English Opium Eater*, as well as Coleridge's account of his opiated creation of *Kubla Khan*, if not the poem itself:

> *In my dreams, I am a being of a higher order than in my waking state, for I can not only imagine what is beyond my power to imagine when I am awake, but also can represent those imagined things to the senses as if real. I see the landscape and its colours. I see the endless vistas of statues never seen with the waking eyes, and groves of bas-reliefs of the most exquisite beauty. I see the most intricate designs, endless, never, never the same, and as entirely original in conception as they are perfect in execution. They convey the most exquisite enjoyment, and to that extent, that when my waking eye takes in an object with pleasure, it seems but the faint reflection of memory of what I have enjoyed in sleep… I labour more, I never rest, I see more, understand more, enjoy more and suffer more… If then, in another state I can accomplish what I cannot in this, there needs must be a faculty in the mind higher than its own powers of apprehension. It is in me all the time, only latent at some time, and that sometime is our normal state when awake.*[21]

But while the 'Russian Plot' may have been drug-fuelled fantasy, the plans for uprisings were real enough, and in South Wales the plans had passed the point of no return.

20. Margaret Hambrich, A Chartist's Library (London and New York, 1986). A compilation of the literary and historical works, 1,634 titles, owned by G.J. Harney and deposited in the Vanderbilt Library, Nashville, Tennessee.
21. Robinson, op. cit., p. 37.

Insurrection

The deathshot hissing from afar –
The shock, the shout, the groan of war
Reverberate along the vale
More suited to the shepherd's tale
Byron, 'The Giaour'

T.E. Lawrence formulated six principles of guerrilla warfare, based on his own Arabian campaign against the Turks during the First World War.[1]

One: the guerrillas must have a secure geographical base, defendable against both armed assault and propaganda.

Henry Vincent observed in the spring of 1839, during a visit to Blackwood: *"Fine fertile hills rising in all directions. I could not help thinking of the defensible nature of the country in the case of foreign invasion! A few thousands of armed men on the hills could successfully defend them. Wales would make an excellent republic!"*[2] Monmouthshire was surrounded by areas in which there was strong Chartist support: to the east the Forest of Dean; to the north the Montgomeryshire wool-towns; to the west the rest of the coalfield. The propaganda of the Radicals had so far been effective.

Two: the enemy must be dependent on its military technology, communications and logistics–and vulnerable for that reason.

In Lancashire, during 1839, the military authorities had been able to move troops very quickly to disturbed areas by means of the new railways. But for the whole of the country there was less than 1,000 miles of track, and in South Wales the railways still

---

1. T.E. Lawrence, *Seven Pillars of Wisdom*, chapter 33, also 'The Evolution of a Revolt', *Army Quarterly and Defence Journal* (Autumn 1920).
2. *Western Vindicator*, 6 Apr 1839.

barely existed. The canal and tramway networks of the area were vulnerable to attack, as had been shown in the Merthyr Rebellion of 1831. The Royal Navy was a powerful mobile force, but the insurrectionists in Monmouthshire had in mind the seizure and blockade of Newport, the major seaport of the area.

Three: the enemy must lack the numbers of troops and fortifications necessary to occupy the disputed territory.

General Napier wrote in April 1839:

> I lay down as an axiom, and our first great principle, that the queen's troops must not be overthrown anywhere, because the effect on the three kingdoms would be fearful... The disaffected, in moral exaltation of victory, would be in arms. This is more especially to be apprehended in Ireland, where rivers of blood would flow.[3]

The South Wales authorities were short of troops and dependent on untrained and poorly armed special constables. On a national scale there were never enough troops during 1839 to keep order in the event of widespread disturbances. As historian Edward Royle has pointed out, Napier's strategy was *"based on a successfully maintained illusion"*. General Napier also knew that many servicemen sympathised with the Chartist cause, and that the morale and loyalty of the British armed forces was so far untested.

Four: the guerrillas must have the support of the populace, even if this support is largely passive.

The local working-class population supported the rebels, either passively or actively; and those who didn't were intimidated enough to lie low or flee.

Five: the guerrilla force must have presence, mobility, endurance and logistical independence.

The fighters were mobile, familiar with the territory and had a fifty-year tradition of physical-force resistance and secret organisation to draw on–although their capacity for endurance was untested. The rebels had logistical independence, inasmuch as logistics is the science of planning, implementation and coordination.

Six: the guerrilla force must have the weaponry to hit the enemy's vulnerabilities.

---

3. Royle, op. cit., pp. 182-83. Napier, II, pp. 13-14.

By November 1839 there was extensive arming amongst the South Wales Chartists and, as Zephaniah Williams said, there were *"a great number of Arms and Warehouses which contained powder magazines"* which could be requisitioned once the rebels had established control of the area. Williams also expected the ironworks to be used for production of cannon and small arms.[4]

On the strength of the six principles, as applied to South Wales, it might be argued that the 'objective' conditions for revolution existed in November 1839. Individual human subjects are, however, part of those conditions.

At dawn on Sunday 3 November William Lloyd Jones mounted his horse and set off from Pontypool on a round trip to Abersychan, Blaenau, Tredegar, Blackwood and Crumlin. His assignment was to co-ordinate the mustering of the three divisions which were to march on Newport that night: one starting from Pontypool, led by himself; one from Ebbw Vale, led by Zephaniah Williams; and one from Blackwood, led by John Frost.

As Jones proceeded through his own area he told the men assembling at the beerhouses to set off at 2 p.m. for the race-course, a mile south of Pontypool, and 'scour' for recruits and arms in the meantime. He also assured them that Williams would be bringing a good supply of guns from Ebbw Vale. According to one witness, he told the men that posters had been printed in Newport that announced the formation of *"the executive government of England"* and were signed by 'John Frost, President'.[5]

As Williams Jones was approaching Blackwood he met an advance column of armed men from Tredegar, travelling south on horse trams. They were led by John Rees, a stone mason, known as 'Jack the Fifer'. Rees probably got his nickname during service as a youth in the British Army. In New Orleans, in 1835, he had joined an international regiment called the New Orleans Greys to fight in the Texas War of Independence against the Mexicans. These volunteers had been promised citizenship in a new Republic of

4. Wilks, op. cit., p. 158. Zepahiah Williams letter to Dr McKechnie (25 May 1840), National Library of Wales, Tredegar Park Muniments, box 40, doc 2.

5. Williams, op. cit., pp. 212, 218-19. Wilks, op. cit., p. 186. *Chartist Trials*, testimony of J. Emery.

Texas, plus a few hundred acres of land. Rees was part of the force that captured the famous Alamo near San Antonio de Bexar in December 1835. Months later he was captured after the siege of Goliad, and was one of twenty-eight who managed to survive a massacre of 360 prisoners by the Mexican Army.[6] Presumably because of his experience in storming buildings, Rees was chosen to lead the assault group at Newport. One of his lieutenants, known as Williams, was a deserter from the 29th Regiment, which had been garrisoned at Newport. Another was David Jones (alias 'Dai the Tinker'), who was left to complete the Tredegar muster as Rees went down to Blackwood.

William Jones arrived at the Blackwood Coach and Horses rendezvous at about 6 p.m. Jones didn't get to see Frost, as he hadn't yet turned up. But the muster for the division to be led by Frost was well under way, so Jones, satisfied with the proceedings so far, rode back to Pontypool, arriving at 10 p.m. By this time 2,000 men had gathered at the racecourse. Already the scouring parties had raided the houses of managers and clerks—most of whom had fled—for weapons and conscripts, and had begun to shut off the ironworks' furnaces.[7]

By the time the Tredegar men led by Jack the Fifer arrived at Blackwood, at around 6.30 p.m., Frost was there to meet them. By this time it was raining heavily and Frost waited to see if it would stop before proceeding further. By 7 p.m. the rain showed no sign of letting up, so Frost led his men off. He and Jack the Fifer led the column south towards Newbridge and Abercarn by the route of the Sirhowy tramway, so as not to be noticed on the roads; while John Reynolds, 'The Preacher', of Gelligroes, led a contingent south to Pontllanfraith. As the brigades proceeded,

---

6. Humphries, op. cit., pp. 78, 84-88. Wilks, op. cit., pp. 186-87. Ivor Wilks, 'Insurrections in Texas and Wales: the Careers of John Rees', *Welsh Historical Review* (11/1, 1982). Although the Texas People's Army was a democratic body, with election of officers from the bottom up and fighting against a corrupt Mexican regime, those who stood to gain from independence were the slave-owning 'Anglos' of the territory, who tended to see the poorer elements and the foreign adventurers as cannon fodder.

7. Jones, op. cit., pp. 138-39.

parties were assigned to scour for more recruits and arms. The main bodies of the march were guarded side and rear, to discourage would-be deserters.

At 11 a.m. on Sunday morning, at his pub, the Royal Oak in Blaenau, Zephaniah Williams had told the 200 organisers present to go home and collect an extra shirt and some food, then rally the rank and file for a 'great meeting' on the mountain at Mynydd Carn-cefn, between Ebbw Vale and Nantyglo. He did not tell the organisers where they would be going next. By 6 p.m. the crowd at the Royal Oak had swelled and was moved off on a 2-mile march to the mountain, where Williams was waiting for the arrival of all the contingents from the Heads of the Valleys. Many of these took some time to arrive because of time spent dragging unwilling recruits from the arms of wailing wives and children.[8] At a divine service early that evening in Beaufort, the reverend was telling his congregation that that they were all born to die, when a gang of Chartists broke in on his sermon with the words, *"Yes, some of you sooner than you think!"* The reverend escaped conscription by blowing out his candle and hiding under the stairs.[268] As the evening wore on thousands of men were left standing on the rain-swept mountain until finally, at about 10 p.m., Williams told his men that they were marching to Risca, 5 miles north of Newport, where John Frost would be waiting to issue further orders. Williams told his men that he was sure they would meet no armed resistance. If they did encounter troops, he said vaguely that they should *"do the best they can"*. He watched with some satisfaction as the furnaces at the Victoria Ironworks were shut off and ordered his sodden forces to proceed.[9]

According to the plan, all of the columns were to meet up at Cefn, on the north-eastern outskirts of Newport. But during the day the rendezvous had been changed to one slightly further north, the Welsh Oak beerhouse in Ty'n-y-coed, just south of Risca, to avoid alerting scouts from the Crown forces in Newport. At 10 p.m. an advance party of the Frost/Rees contingent arrived there to ensure that all columns heading for Newport stopped and waited. A section of this party was sent south to Cefn, but half-way

8. Ibid., pp. 127-28.
9. Williams, op. cit., pp. 216-17.

there, sure enough, they were surprised by two of Mayor Phillips's scouts, who rode straight past them. The scouts nearly ran into the column headed by Frost at Risca, but stopped in their tracks when they heard bursts of gunfire and loud cheers ahead of them. The guns were being fired into the air to greet the arrival at Risca of a column from Argoes and Croespenmaena.[10] The two scouts beat a hasty retreat, but this time the men they had ridden through minutes before recognised them as the 'enemy' and tried to stop them. One of the scouts was stabbed in the leg, but they both escaped and headed back to Newport to warn Mayor Phillips of the impending invasion.[11]

A few miles north-east of Risca, Reynolds's column arrived at Gelligroes. Noticing that one of the men assembled there was unarmed, Reynolds slapped his face and shouted, *"You have nothing in your hand. You ought to be hanged"*.[12] Heading on for Risca, at about 10 p.m., Reynolds's men met another column coming from Nelson and Fleur-de-lis, led by Thomas Llewellyn, at Nine Miles Point. Reynolds and his men continued their scouring until 'Williams the Deserter' arrived from Welsh Oak on horseback and urged them to move on. He told Reynolds that Frost was ailing, owing to exhaustion, but he had a horse for him and hoped to find a saddle.

By 1 a.m. the main force at the Welsh Oak had swollen to about 2,000, but there was still no sign of Zephaniah Williams's contingent from the Heads of the Valleys.[13] Frost then decided to go to Cefn and see if he could make contact with Jones's Pontypool contingent. In fact Frost was prevaricating. He had argued at the Friday delegate meeting that his and Zephaniah Williams's divisions would be able to take the town through one of the three turnpike entrances and that the Pontypool division would be expected to contribute at most only a couple of 165-man companies to the attack on Newport, and for the most part would be held in

---

10. Wilks, op. cit., p. 195.

11. Ibid., pp. 186-90.

12. Williams, op. cit., p. 201.

13. Wilks, op. cit., p. 189. NE XIV, doc. 566: evidence of Thomas Morgan.

reserve.[14] Much of the force mustered by Jones in Pontypool and points north would have been required for the next stage of the rebellion, which was to seize Brecon and Abergavenny, and to free Vincent from Monmouth gaol.[15]

At 11 p.m. William Lloyd Jones had set off from Pontypool with the first contingent, guns to the front, many in disguise. At 1 a.m. they reached the Marshes turnpike on the northern outskirts of Newport, about 3 miles east of where Frost was waiting for them.[16] It is likely that Jones had expected a message from Frost which never came, as it wasn't until 3.30 a.m. that Jones ordered a contingent of his men at the Marshes to move towards Cefn and took himself back up the road towards Pontypool in search of a second column he was expecting. Jones's men proceeded cautiously towards Cefn and didn't finally make contact with Frost until about 5 a.m.[17] Zephaniah Williams, having procured a horse and two trams at Lanhilley, arrived at the Welsh Oak between 3 and 4 a.m., where he discovered that Frost had gone in search of Jones's columns from Pontypool. When Frost eventually got back to Welsh Oak at 6 a.m. he decided not to go through Cefn but to take a 'safer' route through Pye Corner, just north of Tredegar Park.

The Chartist forces in Newport town had expected the main assault to be made via Cefin, High Cross Road and the Stow Hill workhouse, in which troops were garrisoned. They had waited at 1 a.m. for the incoming columns from the hills to announce their arrival with rockets, which would also have been a signal for the Newport men to take magistrates hostage and seize a gunpowder warehouse on the docks.[18] But the rockets did not appear.

By 7 a.m. Frost had gathered at least 5,000 men and he could no longer delay, even though he knew that facing the armed force of the state in broad daylight was not what had been planned. Dr William Price, whom Frost had effectively ousted as leader

---

14. Wilks, op. cit., p. 190
15. Jones, op. cit., pp. 139-40.
16. Ibid., pp. 142-43.
17. Williams, op. cit., p. 133. Wilks, op. cit., p. 197.
18. Jones, op. cit., pp. 133-35. Wilks, op. cit., p. 198. *Chartist Trials*, testimony of Simon Simmons.

of the South Wales Directorate, would later claim that by this time Frost had lost his nerve. But perhaps he could never accept the possibility that such nerve would be required. He had been hoping all night for news from friendly forces in Newport that the troops had surrendered or deserted. Finally, once he realised these hopes were in vain, he was ready for (or rather resigned to) the final stage. The pikemen and musketeers were rallied, and men who had sheltered in barns and cowsheds were dragged out. Frost ordered Jack the Fifer's Tredegar column to the front, and an estimated 5,000 marched to Pye Corner and then along the tramway through Tredegar Park. The rain had stopped and it was now daylight.[19]

Although the authorities' knowledge of what had been going on in the valleys over the weekend was sparse, the mayor of New-

Armed Chartists arrive at the Westgate Hotel in Newport

port, Thomas Phillips, had known by the previous Thursday that Chartists from the coalfield had been visiting their comrades in the town and discussing arms procurement. He also knew that Newport Chartists were planning to be at strategic points on the outskirts, preparing to meet the incoming marchers. On Saturday Phillips had warned Captain Stack, who had seventy troops

19. Wilks, op. cit., p. 197.

of the 45th Infantry garrisoned in the Stowe Hill workhouse, to be ready for an attack, and ordered the police superintendent to round up 150 specials for immediate duty. On Sunday terrified middle-class refugees arrived from the valleys, bringing news that others were fleeing in all directions. When the scouts who had narrowly escaped with their lives from the columns at Risca got back to Newport and reported to Mayor Phillips, he sent urgent messages to Bristol and London asking for help, and sent a warning to Monmouth and other towns of the imminent danger. He ordered reinforcements for the constables guarding the Westgate Hotel and sent officers to round up the 500 specials who had signed up during the last few months. Phillips also sent a company to guard the bridge over the River Usk.[20]

During the night patrols of specials arrested isolated armed men on the outskirts of the town, and took them to the Westgate Hotel or to the workhouse at the top of Stowe Hill. Captain Stack was told to keep his men at the workhouse out of sight. At daybreak the mayor was told that there were 5,000 or 6,000 Chartists approaching on the outskirts of Newport. Fearing for the safety of the Westgate, he requested that troops be sent there from the workhouse. Thirty-one troops, commanded by Captain Basil Gray, arrived at the Westgate shortly before 8.30 a.m. and stood guard in front of the hotel.[21]

Frost was leading a column a mile long by the time it reached the Cwrt-y-bella weighing machine, a mile from the centre of Newport. At this place two boys coming from the town were asked where the soldiers were, and they said some had gone to the Westgate Hotel. A Chartist joked that it wasn't the Westgate he wanted but a waistcoat, as he was damned wet.[22] But the time for joking was long gone. Frost decided that the hotel and not the workhouse garrison was the immediate object. At the Waterloo beerhouse, near the bank of the River Usk, Jack the Fifer ordered the marchers to halt. He called for those carrying guns to step forward, and carefully organised the columns of pike-men six abreast, with a gunman at the end of each rank. He then ex-

20. Jones, op. cit., pp. 135, 145-46.
21. Ibid., pp. 146-148.
22. Williams, op. cit., p. 224.

changed his pike for the pub owner's gun, which hung over the fireplace.[23]

Muskets were fired simultaneously to make sure the rain hadn't dampened the powder and then Jack the Fifer then gave the order to 'March!' to 5,000 or 6,000 men, of whom about one in ten was armed with muskets or pistols. They proceeded to the

The Chartists forced entry at the Westgate

turnpike gate on Stowe Hill, where 200 yards to the left was the workhouse. Here there were thirty troops under the command of Captain Richard Stack, and a cache of arms. The Chartist leaders had to resist arguments from the rank and file to attack both the workhouse and the house of magistrate Lewis Edwards, which was nearby, and directed the main body of the march down Stowe

23. Humphries, op. cit., p. 142. PRO TS 11/502.1650.

Hill towards the Westgate. Frost called out, *"Let us go towards the town, and show ourselves to the town"*–a rather ironic statement, considering that the whole point of the operation had been to take the town under cover of darkness.[24]

The gun battle at the Westgate begins. Note the special constables fleeing the scene, left and right

At 9.20 a.m. the marchers came down Stowe Hill, some firing weapons into the air and others shouting. The troops at the front of the Westgate were called into the building, where they were joined by sixty-odd specials. As the noise of the approaching Chartists grew louder, Mayor Phillips ordered the troops in the walled yard at the back of the Westgate to come inside as well.

The developing confrontation was now beyond the control of the three 'Generals' of the Rising. Zephaniah Williams was 600 yards away at the top of Stowe Hill, rallying stragglers; William Jones was miles away on the road from Pontypool; and John Frost's whereabouts were uncertain. Frost was certainly in the close vicinity of the Westgate, but when the shout went up from the men near the front steps, *"Mr Frost, appearance to the front,"* he was nowhere to be seen.[25]

At the front of the Westgate marchers stormed up the steps, where a scuffle broke out. Each side grabbed at the other's weapons, and the pikemen stabbed at the shutters of the hotel's front

24. Jones, op. cit., p. 148. Wilks, op. cit., p. 198.
25. Wilks, op. cit., p. 198.

windows. At this point, according to the testimony of Henry Evans, who owned a saddler's opposite the Westgate Hotel, Jack the Fifer, waving a sword, appeared at the front and someone shouted the order, "*In my boys!*"[26] Another witness, Edward Patton, said, "*I was distant from the door of the Westgate twenty-five yards… I could not say where the firing began. No man could judge. You nor I could not tell. Saw no smoke outside. It is likely enough the firing began from the Westgate inn*".[27] However, a special constable claimed that as he slammed the door it caught a Chartist gun, which went off. This may have been the first shot. Captain Gray of the 45th Infantry saw assailants form from column into line, assisted by 'powder monkeys' carrying bags of powder and ammunition. According to his testimony, the rush to the door coincided with small-arms fire striking the windows. It was at this point that Gray ordered his men to load their rifles with ball cartridge, while he and Mayor Phillips threw open the shutters to give the soldiers a clear shot at the marchers.[28] The immediate effect of throwing open the windows may have been to make those inside more vulnerable to incoming fire. Mayor Thomas Phillips and Sergeants Daily and Armstrong were hit and wounded, as were two of the special constables in the hall. Shots were also fired in the entrance hallway. Some of the specials fled further into the building or up the stairs, while others, including the superintendent, jumped over the back wall and headed for home. Those fleeing may have only survived because the Chartist gunmen could not get a clear shot at them, since there were so many people on the streets.

Gray ordered his soldiers to open fire. The first volley was directed at the crowd in front of the hotel. As the musket balls slammed into the crowd with devastating effect, someone shouted the order 'Fall off,' and the crowd ran for cover. Then came a second volley from the troops directed at those who could still

---

26. Humphries, op. cit., pp. 148-49.

27. F.C. Mather, *Chartism and Society* (London, 1980) Documents 96-97. *Annual Register*, 1840 (Appendix to the Chronicle, Law Cases, &c), pp. 215-16.

28. Wilks, op. cit., p. 199. E. Dowling, *The Rise and Fall of Chartism in Monmouthshire* (London, 1840).

be seen at the front, some of whom had continued fighting.[29] The Westgate was also being assaulted from the rear: an armed group had entered the back of the hotel through the yard. Inside, the soldiers, no longer taking fire from the front, opened the door leading to the passage way and rear door, fired a third volley of shots and then fired intermittently. At first the invaders pressed their attack under cover of the gunsmoke, but faltered when they saw the bodies of their comrades and were hit themselves. When the smoke cleared, according to one of the specials, *"there was a scene, dreadful beyond expression—the groans of the dying—the shrieks of the wounded, the pallid ghostly countenances and the bloodshot eyes of the dead, in addition to the shattered windows, and passages ankle deep in gore"*.[30]

By this time there were more than twenty men either dead or mortally wounded. There were five dead in the hotel and four in the street in front of it, with others in the surrounding area. Some of the wounded, who were carried away by comrades, died later. Edward Dowling, owner of the *Monmouthshire Merlin*, reported:

> *Many who suffered in the fight crawled away; some exhibiting frightful wounds, and glaring eyes, wildly crying for mercy, and seeking a shelter from the charitable; others, desperately maimed, were carried in the arms of the humane for medical aid; and a few of the miserable objects that were helplessly and mortally wounded, continued to writhe in torture, crying for water.*[31]

Jack the Fifer and Dai the Tinker were next seen retreating towards the Waterloo beerhouse and the Cardiff road. The Fifer reportedly told a local man that the marchers had taken *"one pop at them"* and *"got a few"* with *"no loss to us"*—not an accurate assessment, but he might have thought, in the confusion and lack of visibility caused by the smoke, that the Chartists had inflicted more casualties than they had taken. The Fifer is reported to have said to another witness, *"We made retreat, then went back for another*

29. Jones, op. cit., pp. 151-53. Humphries, op. cit., pp. 146-47.

30. Jones, op. cit., p. 153.

31. *Monmouthshire Merlin*, 7 Nov 1839.

volley".[32] As Zephaniah Williams finally approached with his division there were thousands fleeing in the opposite direction. Frost was seen heading through Tredegar Park, broken and sobbing. Later he reportedly said, "*I was not the man for such an undertaking, for the moment I saw blood I became terrified and fled*".[33] The attack

Drawing by military artist of the scene at the Westgate, just after the battle, showing dead bodies and weapons on the ground

had become a rout.

Ten minutes after the fighting had started Captain Gray had ordered a ceasefire. In the streets surrounding the Westgate 150 weapons were recovered.

On 7 November the ten bodies from the Westgate were taken and buried in unmarked graves in the cemetery of St Woolos's Cathedral, Newport: William Evans, Reece Meredith and David Morgan from Tredegar; David Davies from Brynmawr; David Davies's son (first name unknown) from Waunhelygen; John Jonathan and Abraham Thomas from Blaenau; Isaac Thomas and John the Roller from Nantyglo; and William Williams of Cwmtillery. Of the others who died the following ten names have been recorded: John Codd from Pembrokeshire; Evan Davies, collier, home unknown; John Davis, carpenter; William Farriday of Blackwood; William Griffiths, Merthyr; Robert Lansdown, occupation and home unknown; John Morris, miner; George Shell, carpenter,

32. Jones, op. cit., p. 155. Humphries, op. cit., p. 150. *Chartist Trials*, testimony of T. Pritchard and S. Smith.
33. Jones, op. cit., p. 213.

Pontypool; Williams the Deserter; William Aberdare, occupation and home unknown. The known death toll, then, is twenty, but there were probably others whose names were never recorded. Estimates varied at the time between twenty-two and thirty. On the other side there were under ten wounded, all of whom survived.[34]

The Valleys remained in a state of disturbance for some days afterwards, with middle-class residents still fleeing the area. Within days troops at Abergavenny, Brecon and Bristol were being re-

The treason trial at Newport.
In the dock on the right (l to r) Frost, Jones and Williams

inforced. A troop of the 10th Hussars arrived from Bristol at Newport by steamer, and several companies of infantry marched to Newport from Bristol.[35]

Frost fled Newport through Tredegar Park and headed in the direction of Cardiff. Near Castleton he hid himself inside a coal tram. When he emerged after eight hours the first thing he saw was a bill offering £100 reward for the capture of himself, Zephaniah Williams, William Jones, Jack the Fifer and Dai the Tinker. Frost decided to return to Newport, say farewell to his family and

---

34. Wilks, op. cit., appendix 1.
35. Jones, op. cit., p. 167.

then attempt to flee the country. On arriving in Newport he called on his friend Partridge, the printer, whose house had a garden through which Frost could access the back door of his own home. But shortly after he arrived, Mayor Thomas Phillips and a squad of constables broke down Partridge's door: they had come looking for Partridge, and were amazed to find Frost. Frost was armed with pistols but went quietly. William Lloyd Jones was caught after a brief struggle at Crumlin. Zephaniah Williams almost escaped into exile: he was caught on the merchant ship Vintage at Cardiff just before it sailed for Portugal. Jack the Fifer, who was reportedly shot through the hand at the Westgate, made it into exile and rejoined the Army of Texas. Dai the Tinker was never caught.[36] Dr William Price took a boat to Cardiff disguised as a woman. With his shoulder-length hair he evidently fooled a police inspector, who gallantly helped the 'lady' to board the ship. When the ship called at Milford Haven, Price changed into male dress and went ashore for a few drinks. The captain of the ship had by this time discovered the true identity of this passenger, and sent out an urgent request for an arrest warrant. While awaiting its arrival the captain bought Price a few drinks at the Nelson Tavern to put him off his guard. But the warrant did not arrive in time and the captain had to set sail in order not to miss the tide. Price somehow got wind of the captain's ruse and told him he was a traitor to all *"true Welshmen"*: *"You are nothing less than a grovelling worm… if I ever meet you on shore I will whip the life out of you"*. From Liverpool, Price travelled by railway to London, where, still in disguise, he saw 'dead or alive' wanted posters for himself and other Welsh leaders. Next he took a steamer to Le Havre and then on to Paris, his place of exile, where he would enjoy the friendship of another exile: the German poet Heinrich Heine. The authorities in Wales searched in vain for his legendary cache of seven pieces of cannon.[37]

A hundred and fifty were arrested in South Wales in the weeks following the Rising. Twenty-one of them were indicted for high treason. By the end of 1840 there were 140 serving prison sentences in Monmouth gaol alone. The *Western Vindicator*, after a

---

36. Williams, op. cit., pp. 231-34.
37. Islwyn ap Nicholas, op. cit., pp. 19-21.

witch-hunting campaign by *The Times*, was suppressed by approval of the Home Secretary Lord Normanby.[38] At the trial of the Newport men, which began within weeks, the evidence presented by the prosecution to convict the defendants of sedition was so paltry that had the jury not been stacked with men of the ruling orders, many with personal axes to grind, the trial might well have ended differently. In fact, in his summing up the trial judge, Lord Chief Justice Tindal, tried to steer the jury towards acquittal. The prosecution could get very few credible witnesses to testify, either because those who had seen and heard what went on were loyal to the defendants or because they were intimidated within their tightly knit communities.[39] Another factor was that the Whig legal establishment believed that the insurgents had come quite close to overwhelming the authorities: questions in Parliament about a 'riot' were easier to fend off than one about a seditious plot that came close to full-scale insurrection.

As a general, John Frost had been ineffective. Firstly, he had underestimated the morale and discipline of the troops guarding Newport. Secondly, by leaving the Glamorgan columns out of the operation at the last moment he had divided and confused his forces. Thirdly, he had failed to properly utilise the forces at his disposal: he marched all of them into the town, when he could have used the best-armed and most serious fighters for the assault and kept the rest back for later support.

Certainly there were weaknesses in the rebellion which Frost had little control over. Of those thousands who set off for Newport we can speak of four kinds of participants. Firstly, there were the idealists and freedom fighters, prepared to kill and die for a noble cause, such as nineteen-year-old George Shell, who fell at Newport, after writing to his parents, *"I shall this night be engaged in a struggle for freedom, and if it should please God to spare my life, I shall see you soon; but if not, grieve not for me. I shall fall to a noble cause"*.[40] Secondly, there were those less militant—like Frost—who naïvely hoped that the town would fall without a shot being fired. Thirdly, there were those who had been coerced and feared

38. Wilks, op. cit., p. 31.
39. Humphries, op. cit., pp. 156-65, Jones, op. cit., pp. 169-95.
40. Williams, op. cit., p. 230.

for their lives if they refused to participate. Fourthly, there were those for whom the Rising was an adventure of vandalism and score-settling (drunkenness, contrary to legend, does not seem to have been a serious problem). There were probably at least 1,000 in the first category–the freedom fighters–who, if they had been unburdened by the less-committed and been better led, might have arrived as planned at 1 a.m. and taken the town. Of the others, it turned out that they lacked endurance and nerve. The conscripting of the unwilling may have been effective as a means of establishing a sans-culottist 'revolutionary terror' in the valleys, but a large presence of such men in the final assault meant that as soon as the going got rough they were going to become the vanguard of a rout.

Frost had been spoken of by his supporters as the 'Lord Protector of South Wales'. But unlike Cromwell, he couldn't conceive of leading a real army because he couldn't accept the need for real violence. He wrote later: "*so far from leading the working men of South Wales, it was they who led me, they asked me to go with them, and I was not disposed to throw them aside*".[41]

As George Julian Harney would reflect a few years later in a letter to Friedrich Engels, "*A popular leader should possess great animal courage, contempt of pain and death, and be not altogether ignorant of arms and military science. No chief or leader that has hitherto appeared in the English movement has these qualifications*".[42]

---

41. Jones op. cit., pp. 210, 213.
42. George Julian Harney to Friedrich Engels, 1846: Harney Papers 141.

The Final Conflicts

'God pity him' we said and 'God bless him,
He died well fighting in the open day' –
Yea such one was happy I may think,
Now all has come to stabbing in the dark.

William Morris, 'Scenes from the Fall of Troy'

Before the outcome of the Newport Rising of 4 November was known, one of the local worthies who fled the area managed to inform *The Times* in London that John Frost had led an attack on Newport with several thousand armed men. This story went out in the stop press of the final edition of 5 November:

> *The Chartists have almost entire possession of the town. 7,000 or 8,000 have marched in from the hills, and attacked the Westgate Inn, where the magistrates are sitting. I have heard 30 or 40 shots fired, and learn that several of the Chartists as well as the soldiers are killed. What the end will be God only knows; they are firing now.*

In Newcastle on 5 November, before any news of Newport arrived, Dr John Taylor told a large audience of the NPU that he looked forward to a Republican form of government, which would abolish rented property and make small tenant farmers the proprietors of the land they worked. Having secret foreknowledge of the Newport Rising, he counselled his listeners *"to be quiet and orderly and wait the time till a merciful providence would make them free"*. The next day he travelled west to Cumberland, calling at Carlisle, Wigton and Dalston.[1] According to a memoir by a Carl-

---

1. Fraser, op. cit., pp. 70-71. *Northern Liberator*, 8 Nov 1839. *Northern Star*, 16 Nov 1839.

isle handloom weaver named William Farish, the events in Wales *"were certainly well known beforehand in Carlisle, and if successful might have been imitated in a fashion there, but more extensively on the Banks of the Tyne and Wear"*.[2] Robert Lowery believed that *"undoubtedly there would have been an insurrection in the Newcastle district"* had August Beaumont, the American founder of the *Northern Liberator* and one-time revolutionary fighter in Belgium, still been around (he had died in 1838).[3]

Thomas Devyr, the *Northern Liberator* political editor, recalled that the inconclusive report in *The Times*, which would have reached the North East by the morning of Wednesday 6 November, immediately scared the Newcastle police into easing their clampdown on street meetings and bill-posting. Chartist placards were pasted up, optimistically declaring that *"The hour of British Freedom has struck! John Frost is in possession of South Wales at the head of 30,000 men"*. Devyr, himself a former police officer, wrote: *"Past these placards the policemen quietly walked. The fact will bear one explanation. In revolutions a large portion of the people are passive, and readily obey the stronger side, and our policemen, it seems, were among this number"*.[4]

Devyr has left us with a remarkable description of a meeting of Chartist delegates on Wednesday evening, 6 November, at a secret location in Newcastle. He estimated that about sixty-five localities—in Northumberland, Durham and possibly Cumberland— could be called on and only needed a signal to mobilise. Upstairs was a large room full of *"the earnest and. gloomy chiefs of the insurrection"* (he did not name any names). Downstairs Devyr beheld *"numbers of unthinking, good natured men, staging and playing music,*

---

2. Fraser, op. cit., p. 69. *Autobiography of William Farish* (private circulation, 1889).

3. Lowery, op. cit., p. 123.

4. Devyr's account in this chapter is taken from his *Odd Book of the Nineteenth Century*, pp. 195-211. Written more than forty years after the event, it has been treated with some scepticism by historians. At the turn of the century W.E. Adams wrote, *"It is a story I have heard old Chartists dispute, and other old Chartists say they believe"*. W.E. Adams, *Memoirs of a Social Atom* (chapter XVII. http://www.gerald-Massey.org. uk/adams/c_autobiog04.htm).

General Sir Charles Napier, commander of the Northern army

*even with their wives and daughters among them, waiting for the signal…
Here they were in midnight muster, waiting the signal to grasp the pike
and level the musket–to give or receive death…"* At midnight he went
back upstairs. Soon they would know the fate of the Newport
Rising, for the mailcoach from London, carrying the first editions
of Wednesday's newspapers, would be in by 2 a.m. He didn't have
to wait that long. There was a rap on the door and a messenger
from the *Northern Liberator* office on The Side delivered a letter
which had arrived from Sunderland by express, having been sent

to Chartists there by a friend who resided in Newport: *"Three days'
storm in the hills, only about 1,000 of the first division reach Newport,
tired, drenched, at 8 a.m. instead. The soldiers under cover, the rebels in
the streets. The slaughter all the one side. Frost prisoner"*. Devyr felt as
if his heart had been struck by *"an exceedingly sharp instrument made
of ice"*. He turned to his hushed comrades: *"There has been no 'overt
act'. Every man to his home, as if this night and its resolve had never had
an existence"*.

In Bradford, as we have seen, the Chartist leader Peter Bussey
did not wait for news from Newport to renege on his commitment to start the Rising in Bradford. He called it off just before
the weekend preceding the Rising, claiming that he was too ill to
lead it. Despite Bussey's decision, according to a police informer
the Chartists in Bradford spent the first weekend of November
casting bullets for their muskets. *"Had not Bussey been taken badly,"* the informer said, *"they would have commenced the same day that
Frost did"*. As soon as the first inconclusive news about Newport
came through, the other Bradford Chartist leaders went looking
for Bussey at his beerhouse. Despite his wife's assurances that he
wasn't at home they insisted on searching the house, but didn't
find him. Bussey's small son gave the game away some days later,
when he told them, *"Ah, you could not find my father the other day,
but I knew he was there all the time; he was up in the cock-loft behind the
flour sacks"*. But by that time Bussey was on the run and heading
for exile in New York. His former followers denounced him as a
coward, turncoat and embezzler.[5]

General Napier at the Northern Command in Nottingham was
unimpressed by the Chartist effort at Newport. He wrote,
*"The Chartists swear they will not let the ball drop. I believe them, but
they must show more pluck to make anything of it; they seem to have
shown none at Newport…"*[6]

The authorities were now placing greater reliance on informers,
but in some areas the informers were finding it difficult to gain
access to the secret bodies of decision-making. In Manchester, so
unsuccessful were the authorities' efforts to penetrate Chartist

5. Peacock, op. cit., p. 33.
6. Jones, op. cit., p. 157.

ranks that Chief of Police Sir Charles Shaw had to ask the land-lady of the premises used by the local Chartist leadership to allow him and his men to eavesdrop on the proceedings from an adjoining room.[7]

In a report on Chartist organisational tactics in Bradford, Magistrate Matthew Thompson likened the mood to a deadly plague:

> *the Chartists now meet in sections at each other's Houses under the pretence of prayer Meetings and commence by Singing Hymns and prayers The lower orders continue in a very feverish state which is continually increased by a want of employment. Typhus Fever and the Small Pox are prevelent* [sic] *and fatal in many instances.*[8]

That the 'religious' tactic had become widespread is confirmed by Devyr, who recalled: *"The scriptures afforded us no scarcity of Reform texts, and we improved them to the edification of the policemen, who always attended to take note of our proceedings"*. He noted how the mood changed in the days and weeks after the Newport Rising. To many of the Chartists it now seemed that the government was invincible, and that retreat had become an unpalatable necessity. Others found it impossible to accept defeat: *"Men were now growing more desperate, the spirit of forbearance and humanity that actuated the former movement (under Frost) was disappearing. Respect for either life or property would no longer be permitted to stand in the way of success"*.

Robert Lowery observed that Chartist opinion on the Welsh action in the North and Scotland was divided between those who were annoyed at such a miserable effort (*"When they determined to start, what for did they no tak t' th' hills and stand it out like men"*) and those who thought it was ill-advised and counter-productive. In any case, he wrote: *"A new danger arose from the state of mind among the people of England. The physical force feeling had not evaporated–it was aroused now on behalf of Frost. 'Were they to let Frost hang?' 'No; never.'"* He also noticed that *"In a very large number of people at that time there was a sort of double-mindedness. The one mind, which was ex-*

---

7. F.C. Mather, *Public Order in the Age of Chartists* (London, 1959), p. 216.
8. Peacock, op. cit., p. 29.

pressed, arose from the idea of the force of their numbers; the other, which was private, held convictions of the impracticability of such schemes".[9]

Dr Taylor, for his part, was utterly single-minded. Taylor, whom Napier regarded as the most dangerous of the Chartist leaders, claimed to have several hundred armed fighters under his command in the Cumberland and North West Border district. Taylor wrote:

> *at least half a dozen emissaries have been sent to see what state the North of England was in and the universal feeling is that there is no country like… [illegible], this is partly to be attributed to the vast extent of moorland which has generated a race of hardy Poachers all well armed… this together with the number of Weavers necessarily in want has made a population ripe for action and its Neighbourhood to the Scottish border, with the facilities for a guerrilla warfare, are said to have… [illegible] to make it the Headquarters for a winter campaign.*[10]

This letter was written by Taylor to Mary Ann Groves, a leading member of the Female Political Union in Birmingham. Taylor regarded her as his *"confidante"*, but it seems that she was passing this correspondence on to David Urquhart, her political confidant.[11] Mary Ann was probably the author of a letter to Taylor, beginning *"Dearest"*, that was sent on 13 November and clearly intended to obtain information about the good doctor's house calls. She wrote: *"our house has been besieged by persons enquiring for you—and they all express their surprise that your name was not prominently forward in the late movement [the Newport Rising]"*. She also seemed to be probing Taylor for intelligence about Beniowski, who was accused by Urquhart of working for the Russians. Major Beniowski, she wrote, was *"anxious to know your movements"* and *"to know when his services would be required"* in the North.[12] Some days before

---

9. Lowery, op. cit., pp. 156-60.

10. Fraser, op. cit., p.76. The letter originally appeared in David Urquhart's *Chartist Correspondence*.

11. Fraser, op. cit., p. 84. *Northern Star*, 29 Feb 1849.

12. Enclosed in letter from John Grey of Dislton to Lord Howing, 20 November. Papers of 3rd Earl Grey, Durham University Library, GRE/B102/7/4, 5, reprinted in full in Fraser, p. 93.

the Rising, Urquhart claimed, he met Dr Taylor: *"[I] never so shook any man. He seemed tortured, struggling between responsibility, sham and failure brought home, and self-love and pride... I must add that Dr T repeatedly asserted that bloodshed and convulsion were inevitable. The die was cast"*.[13]

In Newcastle Taylor had been quick to exploit the widespread disillusionment over O'Connor's mishandling of the General Strike. During the secret preparations for the Rising, Taylor had called for a second National Convention to be set up under new leadership. The NPU immediately agreed to his proposal and contacted other areas, urging support.[14] At the beginning of December a Newcastle meeting of delegates from the North East, Yorkshire, Wales and Edinburgh called for the second Convention to assemble in London on 19 December.[15]

Further south, in Dewsbury, on 12 December nineteen West Riding localities were represented at a meeting which chose delegates to send to London. In Manchester a similar gathering was held on 10 December, attended by Dr Taylor. General Napier learned of this meeting and reported, *"Dr Taylor told the meeting to be ready with their arms; that he had seen two revolutions, one in Greece and one in France, and he hoped to see one in England. This was received with loud cheers of 'we are ready'".*[16]

Police informer James Harrison reported he had heard from Bradford Chartist John Hodgson that *"Dr Taylor had volunteered to stay at home amongst his own men in Carlisle district, or he would come to Yorkshire to head and assist them, or he would go to Wales... He said that Dr Taylor had 900 men ready to rise well armed..."*[17] As Taylor's recent biographer Hamish Fraser has noted, *"How far Taylor was carried away by his always fertile romantic imagination and how far it was the demon drink to which he was succumbing is far from clear"*. But the authorities were sufficiently alarmed to get Home Secretary

13. Robinson, op. cit., p. 101.
14. Epstein, op. cit., p. 203.
15. Epstein, op. cit., p. 204.
16. Fraser, op. cit., p. 76. Napier, II, p. 98. Taylor had spent time in France, but as Fraser points out there is no evidence to back up Taylor's claim about Greece.
17. Fraser, op. cit.

Normanby to issue a warrant on 21 December to open Taylor's mail to Carlisle.[18]

Feargus O'Connor was in principle in favour of the new Convention; he had called for it back in September, as soon as the previous one had collapsed. But his conception of it was different from Dr Taylor's.[19] With Frost and his colleagues now facing likely execution, O'Connor wanted the new Convention first of all to establish a national campaign to save them by legal and peaceful means.[20]

The new Convention duly assembled in London on 19 December at the Arundel Coffee House on The Strand. This time there was no artist to depict the opening, no welcoming rally on Clerkenwell Green and no radical press corps to record the debates. The consensus amongst those who had elected it was that, unlike the first Convention, the delegates would be directly answerable to their local organisations. The new Convention was to meet for only two or three weeks, do what it had to do and then disband. In any case the real power base was the Dewsbury council of organisers, who were actively and secretly preparing for insurrections in their localities.

The London Convention was attended by delegates from Bradford, Sheffield and Dewsbury in the West Riding and from Newcastle, Hull, Bolton, Nottingham, Surrey and London. Because of the secrecy we can only compile a short list of delegates who are known to have attended. These are Major Beniowski, the Tower Hamlets delegate; William Ashton of Barnsley, who later wrote an account of the affair; a Mr Law from the West Riding, who acted as courier; and Robert Lowery, who represented the Dundee Chartist Committee. It is also likely that members of the LDA such as Joseph Williams, Richard Spurr and Charles Neesom participated (though not Harney, who was in the North). O'Connor was elected at a Dewsbury meeting in his absence as one of the town's delegates to the Convention, but he didn't attend any of its

18. Ibid., p. 77.
19. *Northern Star*, 23 Nov 1839.
20. Epstein, op. cit., pp. 202-3.

meetings because, he said, he was too busy campaigning for Frost. Dr Taylor remained in the North waiting for instructions.[21]

On arriving at the Arundel Coffee-House, Lowery found the atmosphere tense and secretive. If anyone entered the private room in which the delegates were meeting they changed the subject until the intruder left. Lowery, who had just published a pamphlet calling for non-violent ulterior measures such as abstention from taxable goods, was disturbed to find delegates discussing *"wild and dangerous topics as to what the people could do if roused to insurrection"*, including the blowing up of gasworks. He claimed that when this second Convention ended, departing delegates suggested to Beniowski that *"now was the time for him to be useful"* and that he should take command. The Polish major replied that he would need £50 to buy a chronometer and maps. But by this time suspicions about Beniowski being spread by the Urquhart camp were damaging his credibility.[22]

The delegates sent a deputation from Arundel Street to see O'Connor at the Tavistock Hotel and, according to William Ashton, he assured them that he would *"place himself at the head of the people of England, and have a bloody revolution to save Frost"*. The courier from the West Riding, Mr Law, was informed of O'Connor's 'pledge' and took this information back to Dewsbury. The council in Dewsbury then resolved that between 12 and 14 January a number of northern towns should rise simultaneously, although local leaders would be left to decide what action should be taken. Classes of ten was the chosen form of organisation. Each would elect its own captain; and although these captains would know each other for purposes of consultation, they would know nothing of the personnel of any other classes, except their numbers and state of preparedness. Also, for the first time, it was deemed necessary by leaders in some areas to make all participants swear an oath of absolute secrecy, obedience of orders and a readiness *"to hold their lives of no account in the attainment of their object and to execute death upon any one who might be found to betray information of our action to the governing authorities"*.[23]

---

21. Ibid, p. 205.
22. Lowery, op. cit., pp. 157-59, 167-68.
23. Peacock, op. cit., p. 37. HO 40/57.

On Sunday 5 January Samuel Holberry, a former soldier, returned to Sheffield from the Dewsbury conference and told the
Sheffield council of class-leaders of the date set for the Rising.
He explained that for purposes of secrecy the delegates would
share this information with only two class-leaders of their own
towns. Law was immediately sent as a courier back to London,
while Holberry departed for Nottingham to inform the class-
leaders there of the decision.[24]

According to Lowery, around 7 January courier Law arrived in
London with the news that the council in Dewsbury had decided
on an insurrection to begin in the middle of the month. The council was now certain that, with the end of the Frost trial now imminent, the time was right for simultaneous risings.[25] Law then
headed back up north and on 9 January met Holberry, who had
been joined by Barnsley delegate William Ashton.[26]

Despite the secrecy, news of the council meeting in Dewsbury
soon began to leak out. The Newcastle Courant reported, "*It
was known... that a committee of delegates from various towns were
assembled in Dewsbury... their proceedings however were ordered to
be kept a profound secret, and not a whisper was heard of their future
movements*".[27]

Dewsbury magistrates said that their town had been selected as
the place "*where a rising might be hazarded with the best chance off success and the greatest prospect of impunity in case of failure*".[28] General
Napier, on hearing of it, reflected:

> *Dewsbury—A curious place. Cavalry could not be here. The town
> is in a hollow, bounded on one side by the river Calder, it has*

24. Peacock, op. cit.

25. According to William Ashton, the decision on the rising was
taken in London, whereas Lowery says it was taken in Dewsbury.
Lowery seems to be right, because his version is corroborated by other
sources—see Peacock, op. cit.

26. Gammage, op. cit., p. 173. Mark Hovell, *The Chartist Movement*
(London, 1918), p. 186, Depositions by Samuel Foxhall and Samuel
Powell Thompson. TS 11/816/2688, in Thompson, *The Early Chartists*,
pp. 264-79.

27. Peacock, op. cit., p. 37.

28. Ibid., p. 37. HO 40/57.

Mr John Frost, condemned to death for high treason, Jan 8th 1840

> three entrances, each through a pass, and no messenger could
> get out of the town save through them, so that cavalry might be
> blocked up.[29]

The Dewsbury council, having notified the London Convention
delegates of the date of the Rising, had advised them to get back
to their localities. But the Convention delegates could not leave
without paying the rent on their meeting rooms and obtaining
travel expenses. They dispatched an emissary to Newport to see
O'Connor, who had taken charge of the £200 in funds left over
from the previous Convention. O'Connor at first demurred, but
when the messenger told him that those he represented would
damn his newspaper if he didn't pay up he handed over the sum
demanded. According to Ashton, the messenger also informed
O'Connor of the decision on the impending Rising in the North.[30]
But O'Connor, true to form, after promising *"a bloody revolution to
save Frost"*, tried to scotch the planned Rising by publishing, on 4
January, a *Northern Star* editorial which said *"We hear of secret meetings"*, while cautiously adding *"but… know not whether any such have
been held"*. The article went on to warn of *"ill-advised individuals"*
who were contemplating an *"emeute"* to save Frost. And in case
that wasn't enough, on 12 January, the very day the risings were
to begin, the *Star* warned against *"any outbreak of physical violence…
by such means that are common in the neighbouring country of France;
that is by emeutes and risings"*. [31]

O'Connor's 4 January editorial must have added to the intelligence being accumulated by General Napier, who, on 6 January
1840 summarised it as follows:

> The Chartists have what they call rockets, which they believe will,
> if thrust into a window, blow the roof off a house. Their arms are
> chiefly pistols and they have cast a vast quantity of balls. Their
> plan is to attack the middle classes and reduce them to the same
> state of poverty with themselves. They have no fear of the soldiers,
> because they mean to go about in small parties of fives and sixes
> according to their classes and sections, with their arms hidden

29. Quoted in Peacock, op. cit., p. 36. Letter of 17 Jan 1840.
30. Dorothy Thompson, *Early Chartism*, pp. 205   6.
31. Peacock, op. cit., p. 37.

and so as not to attract attention by their numbers… The moment any Chartist is convicted, whether it be Frost or any other, this warfare is to begin and all labour instantly to cease…[32]

In Newcastle, according to Devyr, a *"fierce and even vindictive element"* of the insurrectionists was held in check by *"the coolness and humanity"* of their *"leading spirits"*. When one delegate on the secret council urged that all the corporation police should be slain on their beats he got no support. It was decided instead that no injury should be inflicted on the police and that it would be better to capture the station houses and lock the officers in the cells. It was also decided to confine the mayor and other officials of the town to their own houses. The main problem on Tyneside would be the military. The Duke of Northumberland had just stationed a sloop and a contingent of marines on the Tyne, as he had done during the disturbances of 1832.[33] Devyr was aware of a force of 800 infantry, two companies of dragoons, and two companies of artillery: *"And we purposed to meet it with every appliance within our reach"*.

On Sunday 7 January Devyr walked in the noonday sun past the Forth and turned left into the Scotswood Road, which, he recalled, sparkled in the frost and snow. He was thinking of all the *"sordid and inhuman men whose rapacity to the millions had turned all this brightness and beauty into a darkness and a curse"* when he saw a familiar figure:

> "And here is one of those sordid men," *I exclaimed, as Alderman Potter met me, astride on a saddle returning to town. We understand each other. He is one of the respectable, loyal, 'law-and-order' starvation men. I am one of the turbulent and disloyal crowd. But he does not know that I am unthinking of the day and its worship—that my path is across that picturesque bridge to the iron villages beyond, or for what purpose?… But I am nearing Scotswood Bridge, on my way to Swalwell and Winlaton, and not at all on a message of peace.*

---

32. Ibid.
33. Maehl, op. cit., pp. 414 (footnote) Northumberland to Lord Russell, 14 Dec 1839. HO 40/46.

At his destination in Winlaton the tables were covered with maps of the Newcastle and Sunderland barracks and Tynemouth Castle, identifying the officers' quarters which were to receive the first blows. The conspirators thought that with officers *hors de combat* the troops would come over. Devyr, as an Irishman, had some confidence that the mainly Irish infantry would turn, as they had shown indications of their good will towards him and other Irish in the Tyneside area. General Napier wouldn't have agreed with him, for when he requested reinforcements to be sent over from Ireland he had specified that those regiments with the highest proportion of Irish Catholics should be sent. *"The difference of religion and of country form additional barriers around the fidelity of the soldier,"* he wrote.[34]

In Winlaton, Devyr and his men assessed the logistics. In the Newcastle area there was plenty of gunpowder, which was used for blasting in the mines. Devyr was told that some old cast-iron cannon were available, though no one seemed to know how many. The plotters did have some 4½in grenades and some 13in shells. They computed that the shells could blow down an ordinary brick wall or shatter a 2in wooden gate, but they would have to be discharged by graduated fuses. Skilled workers in Newcastle were to make up the fuses and construct models of the missiles, which would then be cast by moulders. The Winlaton and Swalwell foundrymen were to gain access to at least one blast furnace to complete the job in less than a week. Devyr walked home in the moonlight, pleased with his mission.

In the days that followed, men from every trade pitched in. In the rooms adjoining the *Northern Liberator* office a small fuse factory was turning out five-second and half-minute fuses. This was an unfamiliar trade to those working there, and fingers were burnt before it was sufficiently mastered. Cartridges were made up with buckshot. Three cannon moulds were made, one of 13in and two of 4½in diameter, but the Winlaton men were unable to erect a furnace because no ground was safe from the prying eyes of the local Whigs.

Nemesis arrived on the Saturday night, when only seventy men assembled out of the secret enrolment of seven hundred. Some

---

34. Schoyen, op. cit., p. 82. HO 40/53, 29 July.

reacted to this setback by arguing for arson attacks as a means of precipitating a rush to arms.[35] Devyr only persuaded them to drop this idea with great difficulty, recommending that in the event of Chartists in any other town rising, barricades would be thrown up to prevent the troops on the Tyne and Wear from marching against them. No one argued against this and Devyr left the meeting. When he arrived back home at The Side, his wife anxiously grilled him on the decisions that had been taken, asking him, *"Have they separated?"* He replied, *"They agreed and were preparing to do so when I left"*. She was not convinced and told him, *"Throw on your cloak, and back as fast as ever you can. They will revert to their first opinion and use the torch. Those men are desperate enough to do anything"*. Devyr hurried back to Sandgate, where he found the men formed into four parties, just about to leave on *"their most desperate, and, indeed, mad mission"*. One of Devyr's most trusted friends, the printer John Mason, appeared to be in charge and told him, *"We have resolved to do it. We must rouse the people by some desperate action, and the torch is to be the action"*. *"Over my dead body first,"* Devyr said, *"if you don't allow me five minutes to speak"*. A man from Blaydon pointed a gun at Devyr's head and yelled *"Not one minute. You're a traitor"*. Fortunately Mason wrenched it from the man's hand and shouted, *"Who are you, whom we didn't know a week ago, that dares to confront a man who has been acting vigorously with us from the first?"* Devyr insisted on speaking:

> *Friends, brothers!… how will it be with the multitude, even of your own friends, when dawn rises over the smoking ruins that once was Newcastle?… What a change will that morning bring*

35. John Humphries, in arguing that *"the case for the [Newport] Uprising being part of a general insurrection throughout Britain is poor"*, says, *"When the night arrived and only 70 Chartists resolved for action in Newcastle, it was decided that rather than rise they would burn the town to the ground. Then the news came about the defeat at Newport and the Newcastle Chartists resolved to await developments"*. (*The Man From the Alamo* , p. 307.) Humphries has confused the 6 November incident in Newcastle with this later event at Newcastle in mid-January 1840, at which, according to Devyr, only seventy turned out. Humphries seems to have been misinformed here by W.E. Adams (op. cit.), who makes the same error in reading Devyr's account.

> *forth! Magistrates, Military, Police, Middlemen, all sweeping through the streets, and you crouching, hiding among the ruins in vain from their just vengeance... You condemned this proceeding not an hour ago, and now you adopt it. How can you rely on your judgment, such a judgment as this? This step would be utter, total, irretrievable ruin!*

He added that he was still convinced that associates in other towns would make a start that night, and that the plan to throw up barricades in Newcastle to prevent movement of troops was still viable. When he called for a vote to support his view the only dissenter was the gun-wielding newcomer. But the next evening Devyr learned that the men had reassembled, so he rushed off once again—only to find that they had already gone out. He spent a sleepless night, but when day broke it soon became clear that no fires had been started. Devyr would eventually determine that the gun-wielding newcomer was an agent provocateur.

Devyr and John Rucastle, a local pharmacist engaged in the making up of explosives, were sought out by Robert Peddie, a Scottish staymaker and poet who had been active in the North East. Peddie demanded a horse and carriage of them so he could seize Alnwick Castle. Peddie threatened to turn them in to the authorities if they refused, but they chose the lesser risk. Peddie did not turn them in, but Devyr soon received intelligence at the *Liberator* offices that local magistrates had learned the details of the 'nightly muster' of insurrectionists, although no written testimony had been obtained from witnesses that would justify arresting anyone. Then, days after the aborted rising, the printing supervisor of the *Northern Liberator*, Mr Bell, pulled Devyr aside:

> *Mr --- [naming an official] sends yon word that the magistrates have information of two assemblings in arms on Saturday night in ---- Street. The Information is vague, not sworn to, and therefore no warrants issued. If it be true, and if you were present, he desires to warn you.*

Devyr pretended not to be bothered, and his colleague said, "*Well, then, let me have some copy*". But Bell would get no more copy from Thomas Ainge Devyr. His time in England was spent. He sought out John Rucastle and together they fled.

Twenty minutes before I started for America, I had not the re-motest idea of ever crossing the Atlantic. Mr Rucastle and myself crossed the Tyne bridge to Gateshead, as if to take a customary walk up the river bank. But crossing the hills to Chesterlee Street, my companion cast his last longing look at that river.

At Liverpool Devyr and Rucastle met two other fugitives from Newcastle, who were sailing the next morning on the Independence, a liner bound for the United States. Devyr and Rucastle decided to join them and got on board just before cast-off. At that moment Home Office men reached the pier head in hot pursuit. Devyr had unwisely entered his real name at the shipping agent's office and the pursuers had discovered it. As the steam tug was casting loose from the ship, the fugitives could hear the Home Office men shouting, *"Where to the Independence?"* and being told, *"Yonder, under a press of sail"*. Devyr and Rucastle thus escaped into exile.

In Dewsbury on 12 January the Chartists assembled and made signal by firing guns and launching fire balloons. These were answered in kind from Birstall and Heckmondwike. But that was as far as it went. According to the Home Office reports, *"the non-appearance of leaders from Bradford as had been arranged caused the design to be abandoned yet so bent were the people that numbers from Earlsheaton took leave of their wives and set out in search of leaders"*. Troops were sent into the town and arrests were made.[36]

In Bradford on 12 January Chartists in Queenshead, Clayton and Horton signalled by firing guns off in the air. The spy James Harrison had been reporting on the activities of the Bradford Chartist movement since September, having been discharged from his previous job as a gaol-keeper at Preston for drunkenness and neglect of prisoners. In late December he had reported that Bradford Chartist leaders reckoned to have 250 'well armed' men ready to rise; and that Bradford leader John Hodgson had been in consultation with Convention leaders in London.[37] In Bradford centre, where constables were guarding the joint stock bank, an armed group stormed a police station and took officers away as hostages,

36. Peacock, op. cit., p. 38. HO 40/57.
37. Quoted in Peacock, op. cit., p. 38. *Yorkshireman*, 18 Jan 1840.

but this group was later intercepted by a larger force of police, and eight of them were arrested and committed to York assizes.[38]

In Nottingham General Napier patrolled the town all night. He reported and reflected:

> saw the Chartist sentinels in the streets; we knew they were armed with pistols, but I advised the magistrates not to meddle with them. Seizing these men could do no good; it would not stop Chartism if they were all hanged; and as they offered no violence, why starve their wretched families and worry them with a long imprisonment? I repeat it, Chartism cannot be stopped. God forbid that it should: what we want is to stop them letting loose a large body of armed cut-throats upon the public.[39]

In Sheffield on Friday 19 January Samuel Holberry met eight of his class-leaders to plan for a rising the following night. They ascertained that as many as 500 men would come out. They also knew that only a few dozen would be armed with guns, which would leave the majority having to make do with knives, swords, grenades and fireballs. Holberry told the class-leaders to order every man to wear warm clothing, carry concealed arms and be ready at 10 p.m. the next day.

On Saturday 20 January, at the Reuben's Head public house in Lambert Street, Holberry told the class leaders that the men would form two separate forces, which were to capture the Town Hall and the Tontine simultaneously. Other men would be sent to take up positions on the outskirts of town, to wait for more classes coming from Rotherham and Attercliffe. The classes were to arrive at their allotted targets in and around Sheffield at 2 a.m. on Sunday, having calculated how long it would take to get there from their rendezvous so as to arrive at the same time. So as not to attract suspicion, they were to approach in pairs and walking some distance apart, but always in sight of each other. The meeting also decided, against Holberry's advice, to send some of the men to raid three local gun shops for arms.

Unfortunately for Holberry, the landlord of the Station Inn (a Chartist meeting place in Rotherham) was an informer, and had

38. Gammage, op. cit., pp. 173-76. *National Labour Biography*, p. 155.
39. Napier, op. cit.

reported the plans to the police; while one of Holberry's most trusted lieutenants, Samuel Thompson, was another informer. When Thompson assembled his classes at a house in Forge Street on Saturday night he told them they had to stay put because troops were out on the streets. He then went off to find other

In August 1839 Chartists marched to parish churches and held 'sit-ins' to get around restrictions on assembly. Drawing shows distinct lack of enthusiasm for the service

class-leaders in the Reuben's Head, and tried to persuade them to 'Moscow', i.e. burn, the town centre. Next he returned to his men, brought them out, ostensibly to link up with the other classes, and promptly deserted them. Soon the classes, wandering the streets in an uncoordinated manner, effectively leaderless, were being rounded up by the police. The police staged an 'arrest' of Thompson at dawn, in order to provide him with cover.[40]

At about midnight Holberry was arrested at his home, in possession of grenades and guns, just as he was about to leave for the rendezvous. His wife, Mary, who was pregnant at the time,

40. Gammage, op. cit., p. 173. Hovell, op. cit, p. 186.

was also arrested. Kept without food for eighteen hours, she was threatened by the magistrates with prosecution for high treason if she refused to give evidence against those held in custody. She held out, and was discharged owing to insufficient evidence. Her husband, sentenced to four years' imprisonment, was to die of tuberculosis in prison after two years on the treadmill.[41]

The last gasp of insurrection came the following weekend. Robert Peddie, having failed to muster an attack on Alnwick Castle, turned up in Leeds on 22 January and then proceeded to Bradford to address a meeting for John Frost on Monday 27 January. On Saturday Peddie was visited at his lodgings by four armed men. They told him that they were to go out with a large force that night to capture Bradford, take over the iron-works and march to Dewsbury. Peddie agreed, but unfortunately for him the leader of this delegation was Harrison, the spy and agent provocateur. Some time after midnight Peddie found himself leading a small group of armed men to the market, where they took two watchmen prisoner. But the large force that Harrison had promised did not materialise, and those who had turned out were being arrested, so Peddie fled the scene. One of those arrested, woolcomber Emanuel Hutton, later told his captors:

> I was called up at night and when I came down a gun was put
> into my hands. I don't know who gave it to me. I wish I did...
> I went down stairs and saw a man who told me to follow him—I
> did so for 200 yards and there I saw a lot of men who bade me go
> into the market place with them. I asked several questions—there
> seemed no one appointed to lead. We went into the market place
> and as soon as I saw the Constables I set off—but I was caught.[42]

On 31 January Harrison found Peddie in Leeds, and tried to involve him and local Chartist James Marsden in yet another adventure. This time Harrison claimed that there were 800 men wait-

41. Schwarzkopf, op. cit., p. 143. Samuel Holberry, *Sheffield's Revolutionary Democrat* (Holberry Society Publications, Sheffield, 1978). Jools Duggleby, 'A Mind of No Mean Order', *Undertakings* (newsletter of Sheffield General Cemetery).

42. Royle, op. cit. HO 20/10. *Report of Inspector of Prisons*, W.J. Williams, on an interview with Emanuel Hutton.

ing in Bradford *"for another brush of it"*. Peddie, no longer trusting Harrison, refused to join them, but soon after the meeting ended he was arrested by police and charged with riot and conspiracy with regard to the events of 12 January. He was later sentenced to three years' imprisonment. Eight others received similar sentences.[43]

E vents in London during the months following the Newport Rising were less violent but equally full of intrigue, if not more so. In mid-November 1839 Home Secretary Lord Normanby received a Metropolitan Police report on *"a deep and dangerous conspiracy against both life and property"* involving a *"council of three generals connected with the Chartists"*. The report was based on the testimony of spies, including some in the LDA.[44] One William Tongue, a 'professional' spy who had also worked in Birmingham, reported on the organisation:

> *Received this information upon Sunday 10th [November 1839] and Monday 11th at their Smithfield meetings for defence. Their aim is to fire property. The shipping in the River and Docks. To Kid Nap the principal men of the State. They have several thousands of fire arms to the account of Fergus O'Connor. The Democratic Association meet nightly at Mr [Joseph] Williams's bakery, Brick Lane, Spitalfields, where they receive daily communications for Major Beniowski. There is to be a general rise the day before the execution of Mr Frost should this take place. There is to be arises in Manchester and Newcastle upon the same day. The money raised is to be given as reward for the capture of the hostages and for the men slain in battle, providing for the orphans and widows.*[45]

Tongue then went on to claim that the plot extended to members of the armed forces:

---

43. Peacock, op. cit., pp. 39-53. Report from the spy James Harrison to Bradford Police, from Harewood Papers and prosecution statements by Harrison and John Ashton, TS 11/814/2618, in Thompson, *Early Chartism*, pp. 280-86.
44. Bennett, op. cit., pp. 100-2, Schoyen, op. cit., pp. 63-64.
45. 'T ' Report 23 November 1839 HO 40/44(973).

Four soldiers who were present at the last meeting were deserters going to Wails [sic]. They were according to the subscriptions list 18 thousand strong by the enrolled bodies. They have been cautioned not to take arms. They do not mean to stand before the soldiery but to intimidate and defeat the police force. They are meditating the destruction of the shipping on the river with the full expectation of getting the sailors to lead the van. The main body is to leave London and go down into Kent while a few incendiaries are to remain in London agitating, and nothing else but assassinating their enemies. Be prepared for there is a black cloud hovering not far from the city, even covering the whole town. They received some imported dispatches last night not yet come to light. I expect they will not be disclosed till Tuesday evening. There was a delegate from all the associations for securing the intelligence and mature plans for Tuesday night.

A few days later he suggested that owing to police preparedness, the revolutionists were now in such a state that they had decided on incendiarism:

Dear Sir, I have just returned from Mr Williams, Brick Lane and I am happy to inform you they are in a lamentable panick [sic] about the preparedness of the police and the report that the military men within the hospital prepared to advance if called upon… I would recommend a good lookout upon the River and Docks as I assure you they have well matured plans for to destroy the property of the mid-class and commercial world by firing the shipping with Balls of Hay saturated with different combustible matters. There are to be ignited spirits of wine and lucifer matches to be thrown into windows, warehouses, even in the churches, on the tops of houses and in fact wherever it will injure the property of what they call the aristocracy and middle classes… We were able to meet this evening again. The Shoreditch association has boys making the destructive fireballs. I have seen this morning one of their hand grenaids [sic], which has been tried and found to their satisfaction.

He could find out more, he explained, if the revolutionists trusted him more, which they might if he had some money to give them:

I am still treeted [sic] *as a strange member not as a tried friend.
I hope I have had sufficient scope of their intending to put the
publick* [sic] *on their guard against any outbreak which is certain from their present position. I have been obliged to subscribe
at their meetings and still I cannot be admitted as an actual
member till I pay all arrears. And not till then will they give
to me that knowledge I want of the manufactory and magazine
stores. I hope this will suffice till I call tomorrow as I am on the
scent with a view of their Body.*[46]

Another spy reported, perhaps not surprisingly, that he thought
Tongue was one of the most dangerous trouble makers.[47] The authorities clearly did not take Tongue's reports seriously enough to
act on them immediately. But two months later, during the days
of the attempted risings in Yorkshire, Home Secretary Normanby wrote to the Lord Mayor, "*I have received information that some
evil disposed persons contemplate disturbing the Metropolis in the course
of this night*". Troops were marched from Hounslow to the City;
police and fire stations put on alert; the Tower reinforced with
troops; and marine fire engines stationed on the Thames.[48]

As it turned out, the only LDA 'mobilisation' was on 16 January for the weekly meeting at the Trades Hall, attended as usual
by about 700 people. Neesom was presiding and Richard Spurr
was speaking when police rushed in. The police allowed a number
of people to leave, before seizing several people who had arms
in their possession. The police apparently knew exactly who to
go for; and others who were bearing arms were allowed to leave,
which suggests that they were *provocateurs*. Neesom, Spurr, Williams and four others were charged with seditious speaking at an
illegal meeting, and five men were charged with arms possession.[49]

---

46. HO 40/44.
47. Hovell 178. Reports by Birmingham Police spy, William Tongue.
HO 40/50, in Thompson, *Early Chartism*, pp. 241-48. W.C. Alston to
Home Office, 31 Aug 1839, HO 40/50. *Public Order in The Age of the
Chartists*, p. 204.
48. Bennett, op. cit., p. 100.
49. Gammage, op. cit., pp. 172-73. HO 40/44, HO 41/15, HO 61/25.
Bennett, op. cit., pp. 100-1, 117.

The same day as the London police raid, John Frost, Zephaniah Williams and William Lloyd Jones, along with five other Chartists, were sentenced to be hanged, drawn and quartered. On 24 January 1840 Home Secretary Normanby wrote to the Duke of Wellington, thanking him for providing information *"as to the unprotected state of the depot belonging to the Honourable Artillery Company"* in Hatton Gardens and assured him, *"I have lost no time in communicating to the proper authorities on the subject"*. Lord Normanby had just sent a missive to the lieutenant colonel at the depot, informing him that the *"depot belonging to the Honourable Artillery Company (which is said to contain arms and ammunition) is in a very unprotected state"* and ordering him to take measures *"to place the arms and ammunition in a secure position"*. Normanby had also been contacted by the deputy governor of the Bank of England, who was concerned about reports about dangerous *"proceedings after dark"* which might threaten the bank—although whether these reports came from scare stories in the press or from elsewhere is not known. Normanby replied:

> the report to which you allude to has reached me. I have taken every precaution in my power and have written to the Lord Mayor, acquainting him to have the police of the city in readiness to quell any disturbance of the public peace… It will be prudent to direct a strict guard to be kept at the bank.[50]

The available evidence points to a strange twist in this story of fantastic schemes hatched by insurrectionists and panicky reactions by the London authorities. The informers' tales about plans to fire the ships on the Thames, assassinate politicians and raid the arsenals were actually reminiscent of the plans of the Cato Street Conspirators of 1821—plans which had been 'encouraged' by spies and *provocateurs*. Tongue and other informers may simply have been overhearing conversations of the old 'Cato Street men' in the LDA about past misadventures. But there is also the possibility, suggested by historian Jennifer Bennett, that the wily Chartists recognised the spies for what they were and fed them outlandishly false information in order to pull the wool over the eyes of the authorities. That this was the case was strongly hinted at ten

---

50. HO 41/26 Disturbances, London.

years after the events by Edmund Smallwood, in a speech he made at Joseph Williams's funeral. Smallwood said that through their 'shrewdness' Williams, Neesom, Beniowski and fellow leaders had *"defeated the wily craft dealing of the Whig spies and saved the people from the arms of the police and soldiery"*. The elders of the LDA, such as Neesom, Davenport, Preston and Waddington, had suffered informers throughout their political lives and could probably sniff them out better than the spies could sniff out any real conspiracy. The LDA leaders knew that no serious revolutionary actions were possible in London; but they knew full well that insurrections were being planned in other parts of the country–and by fooling the authorities they might have helped to tie down Crown forces in the capital which might otherwise have been sent elsewhere. As no real insurrection actually occurred in London, anti-government newspapers reporting on the visible military mobilisations accused the government of anti-Chartist hysteria.[51]

As the lawyers acting for Frost, Williams and Jones tried to get their death sentences commuted, a petition campaign for reprieve got under way. Many in the establishment, including General Charles Napier, favoured this, because it was thought that this would relieve the tension and anger that were still widespread and prevent further disturbances. One alternative to execution was transportation. In 1838 a House of Commons Committee had recommended that transportation be abolished because the penal colonies were in a state of vicious depravity, with brutal punishments, starvation, disease and systematised child-prostitution all taking place, but the government remained unconvinced. On 1 February the sentences passed on Frost, Williams and Jones were commuted to transportation for life; and after a spell on a prison hulk at Portsmouth they were shipped out to Van Dieman's Land on 24 February.[52] That same month prison sentences of between nine and eighteen months were passed on former Convention delegates R.J. Richardson, Bronterre O'Brien and Feargus O'Connor.[53] So ended the first phase of the Chartist movement.

---

51. Bennett, op. cit., p. 101.
52. See Humphries's chapters on the Welsh prisoners' treatment in *The Man from the Alamo*.
53. Kemnitz, op. cit., pp. 161-64.

Loss Assessment

When I look back upon the past, when I remember the wrongs and sufferings of the working classes, far from being able to reproach myself with 'violence' I am astonished by my moderation; considering as I do that the wrongs referred to would have satisfied a degree of 'violence' far beyond anything my recollection enables me to charge for my own account.

George Julian Harney, 'Reply to William Lovett',
Newcastle Weekly Chronicle, 2 December 1876

As the year ended George Julian Harney hiked across the border into Scotland. Having spent the last weeks of 1839 in Cumberland under the watchful eyes of police spies and envelope-steamers, he now extended his lecture tour to southwest Scotland and Ayrshire. Enjoying New Year's Eve in the company of the Chartists of Dumfries, Harney was entertained by Robert Burns, son of the bard. Not all the Scottish Chartists rolled out the red carpet for Harney. The *True Scotsman*, a Chartist paper that opposed ulterior measures, inhospitably called on him to go back whence he had come. More welcoming was the *Scottish Vindicator*, voice of the Glasgow Democratic Club, whose Jacobin leadership included Thomas Gillespie and Allan Pinkerton (future founder of the famous American detective agency). Another Chartist paper, the *Scottish Patriot*, though no firm advocate of physical force, reported Harney's speeches favourably.[1]

Harney's contact with the Scots was the catalyst for a major rethink of his position regarding the future of Chartism. Compared with the English movement Scottish Chartism, divisions notwithstanding, was much better organised: with centralised county-

---

1. W. Hamish Fraser, 'The Chartist Press in Scotland', *Papers for the People*, op. cit., pp. 88-89. Alex Wilson, 'Chartism in Glasgow', *Chartist Studies*, op. cit., pp. 266-67. Schoyen, op. cit., pp. 94-95. *Scottish Patriot*, 9 Nov 1839

wide Chartist Associations, Chartist Sunday Schools and properly organised finances. Harney opined in the Scottish Patriot:

> *Organisation is the next thing to be looked to. Without it you are powerless. What folly is 'physical force' while you are disunited... I still believe in physical force, or the fear of it, to which in the end we shall be compelled to resort... it is but a question of time. In the meantime... if we cannot do what we would, let us do what we can.*

With the Chartist associations united into a national body, he argued, "*There will be no need to discuss the question of moral versus physical force. A people thus combined will be capable of effecting anything. To my English friends I say 'go ye and do likewise'*".[2]

Harney remained in Scotland until March, when he returned to London to prepare for his trial at the spring assizes in Birmingham for seditious speaking. As it turned out the prosecution had no evidence to offer against him, and he was released.[3] Many others did not have such a good day in court. By the end of June 1840 at least 500 Chartists were serving, or had served, prison sentences. Peter McDouall, who was to stay in prison until 1841, echoed Harney's organisational conclusions: "*Centralisation and organisation are weapons of the government, and until you can successfully imitate their tactics, you never can reduce their power*".[4]

Chartism never did achieve such organisation. Helen Macfarlane, the Scottish-born Chartist-Marxist, complained in 1850: "*Frenchmen have the instinct of military discipline. We, on the other hand, carry the Saxon principle of the local management and the infinitesimal division of interests, too far. Absolutely this will not do in fighting a battle*".[5]

Harney, writing to Engels in 1846, expressed his conviction that, although the English people would not adopt "*slavish notions about peace and non-resistance*", neither would they act upon the "*opposite*", i.e. armed insurrection, as a "*doctrine*": "*they applaud it at public meetings, but that is all*". He observed:

---

2. *Scottish Patriot*, 21 March 1840.

3. Schoyen, op. cit., p. 96.

4. Peter McDouall, *Chartism and Republican Journal*, 24 April 1841.

5. David Black, *Helen Macfarlane: a Feminist, Revolutionary Journalist and Philosopher in Mid Nineteenth Century England* (Lanham, 2004).

Notwithstanding all the talk in 1839 about 'arming', the people did not arm, and they will not arm. A long immunity from the presence of war in their own country and the long suspension of the militia has created a general distaste for arms, which year by year is becoming more extensive and more intense. The body of the English people, without becoming a slavish people, are becoming an eminently pacific people. I do not say that our fighting propensities are gone, on the contrary I believe that the trained English soldiery is the most powerful soldiery in the world, that is, that a given number will, ninety times out of a hundred, vanquish a similar number of the trained troops of any nation in the world (I hope I shall not offend your Prussian nationality). Wanting, however, military training, the English people are the most unmilitary, indeed, most anti-military people on the face of the earth. To attempt a 'physical force' agitation at the present time would be productive of no good but on the contrary of some evil—the evil of exciting suspicion against the agitators. I do not suppose that the great changes which will come in this country will come altogether without violence, but organized combats such as we may look for in France, Germany, Italy and Spain, cannot take place in this country.[6]

But there was another process already in motion in 1840 which would mould the future *"fighting propensities"* of the English. In the Victorian era the 'workshop of the world', with its 'labour-aristocracy' epitomised by the Tory-voting 'Birmingham Man', would be fed by imperialist plunder and exploitation. In contrast, the Chartists of 1839 regarded their cause as both 'patriotic' and anti-Imperialist. When in June 1839 the Qing dynasty blockaded the British opium-smuggling quarter of Kwangchow and seized over 2 million pounds of opium, the *Northern Star* supported the measures of the Chinese. When, in reaction, the Royal Navy started the First Opium War by firing on Chinese ships at Kowloon, the *Northern Star* condemned the action, arguing that the opium trade was pernicious and only benefited the British middle class.[7] When, in 1840, conflicts in the East brought Anglo-French rivalry

6. Harney Papers, 240.
7. Shijie Guan, 'Chartism and the First Opium War', *History Workshop Journal* 57 (Autumn 1987). *Northern Star*, Nov 1839.

to the brink of war, Harney linked the threat to the attack on China and warned:

> *We are in all probability, on the eve of a general war, and if the plunderers cannot carry on a Peace without fresh loans, and attempting to levy new taxes, how in the name of common sense can they carry on a War? The contest now raging in Central Asia, and commenced with China, is pregnant with the most ruinous consequences (and that ruin is our salvation) to the miscreants, who in this country have erected a system more hideous and damnable than the most atrocious despotism that ever cursed Eastern slaves.*[8]

But there was no stopping imperialist expansion. General Napier, having saved the British ruling classes from the Chartists, once again put all his radical opinions in his blue-coat pocket when he took a commission from the East India Company in 1841 to conquer the province of Sind. He did so in one of the bloodiest campaigns in British colonial history, and was rewarded with £60,000 in silver rupees by the company.

Despite the setbacks of 1839 the Chartist movement had another decade and a half ahead of it as a force to be reckoned with. The second phase of Chartism began in late 1840 with the founding of the National Charter Association. Another petition–this time with over 3 million signatures–was presented to the House of Commons in 1842. This time the rejection of the petition by Parliament did result in a general strike; but the strike (which was not successful) was initiated by the trades unions, not the National Charter Association–and in fact Feargus O'Connor denounced the strike as a plot by the Anti-Corn Law liberals.

In the mid-1840s many thousands of people bought into Feargus O'Connor's grandiose and impractical scheme to provide smallholding farms for 'Chartist communities'. In the end the scheme was a failure, but it helped him to get middle-class support for his election as Member of Parliament for Nottingham in 1847.[9] In 1852 O'Connor, suffering mental damage from syphilis and

---

8. *Scottish Patriot*, 21 March 1840.

9. After the third Chartist petition in 1848 Harney, breaking with O'Connor, came out clearly once again in on favour of a revolutionary

facing the collapse of his Land Scheme, was forcibly removed from the House of Commons by the Sergeant at Arms after being declared insane. Chartism, by then reduced to an organisational rump, staggered on until 1858, when its remaining leaders formed an alliance for electoral reform with the Liberals and formally buried the movement.

The Fabian founders of Labour history in the 1890s did not so much break with the Whig historians idea of 'progress' as develop a socialist version of it: working-class history was seen as the forward march of social and political reformers, trade unions and co-operative and self-help societies towards unity under a state-socialist parliamentary 'Labour' party. According to Sidney and Beatrice Webb's *History of Trade Unionism*, the Chartist leaders, with the exception of a few moderates like William Lovett, were *"pretentious and incompetent"* extremists, who preached *"political and economic quackery"*, *"disgraced"* the cause of progress, and alienated respectable opinion.[10] George Julian Harney would not have agreed with the Webbs.[11] When Keir Hardie was elected to Parliament as a Labour candidate, with trade union support, in 1892, the ageing Friedrich Engels wrote to his old comrade Harney, expressing the hope that a mass socialist movement was finally being built by the *"grandchildren of the Old Chartists"*. But Harney, who saw the trade union leaders as just as *"greedy"* and *"selfish"* as the capitalist class, replied: *"You are the Prince of Optimists… My sight is not so good, nor my hope so sanguine. Least of all have I any belief in the Trades Union chiefs and Labour leaders. To not one of them at present before the public would I give a vote…"*[12]

course of action and tried unsuccessfully to transform the National Charter Association into a socialist party.

10. Quoted in John Strachey, *Theory and Practice of Socialism* (London: Left Book Club, 1936), pp. 349-50.

11. In a memoir published in the *Newcastle Weekly Chronicle* in 1888 Harney explained that for him in 1839 Revolution had meant *"the enactment of the Charter wrung from the 'three Estates' either by force, or fear of force - as had been the case with the Reform Bill".*

12. Harney to Engels 14 July 1892. *Marx-Engels Archives*, International Instituut voor Sociale Geschiedenis, (Amsterdam) L I V 237; published in *The Harney Papers*, ed. Frank Gees Black and Renee Metevier Black

Since the 1970s, Left historians have debated whether Chartism was a forerunner of working-class socialism or merely the tail end of the bourgeois popular radicalism espoused by Thomas Paine and William Cobbett. Gareth Stedman-Jones, in arguing the latter position, has criticised some Marxist-inclined historians for essentially taking the same ground as the Whig theory of history—equating history with 'progress'. Stedman-Jones says that *"as a coherent political language and a believable political vision"* Chartism really disintegrated in the early 1840s, not the early 1850s.[13] But Stedman-Jones reduces the entire history of Chartism to an ideology of 'popular radicalism' held together from the 1770s to the 1860s by the grievance that too much power lay in too few hands. Stedman-Jones' Althusserian post-structuralism prevents him from understanding Chartism as a response to capitalist crisis, something Ricardo predicted would bring social development to a standstill. Post-structuralist 'fear of agency' cannot recognise Chartism for what it was: a conscious attempt by working-class insurgents to resolve this crisis by breaking forever the power of 'Old Corruption'.

In our view what existed in 1839—and ceased thereafter—was a mass working-class democratic movement, with revolutionary and socialist tendencies. As we have seen, by the summer of 1839 the middle-class moderates of the movement had jumped ship, and all the subsequent defining events of that year—the street fights against the police, the exclusive dealing, the strikes, the campaigns for prisoners, the plots, illegal arming and insurrection—were exclusively working-class struggles. In this first phase of Chartism there was a widely held belief that the capitalists and aristocracy were bringing in a system of tyranny and mass pauperism; and this belief was crucial to holding Chartism together as a mass movement. After 1839 never again would the working class, in a huge swathe of territory stretching from South Wales to the North East coalfield, be as united and armed in the cause of democracy as it was that year; and never again would the ruling

(Amsterdam: ISH, 1969). See also Peter Cadogan, 'Harney and Engels,' in *International Review of Social History*, X, 1965, pp. 66-104.

13. Gareth Stedman-Jones, 'The Language of Chartism', *The Chartist Experience*, pp. 3-57.

class and its army and police be so unprepared for insurrection. In 1839 the ideas of Thomas Paine stood in dialogue with the socialistic ideas of Thomas Spence, Robert Owen, Bronterre O'Brien and Gracchus Babeuf. After the defeat of the General Strike in 1842 Chartism became a fractious coalition of groups such as Teetotal Chartism, Free Trade Chartism, Co-operative Chartism, Land Scheme Chartism, and Christian Chartism. However, the movement undoubtedly did have revolutionary and socialist tendencies, which persisted and developed well into the 1850s–and were only wilfully 'forgotten' by the Fabian founders of Labourism in the 1880s and '90s.

In 1842 Engels, just before he made the acquaintance of Harney, reported to the *Rheinische Zeitung* on the second phase of Chartism, in which both petitioning and industrial action again failed to win the Charter. Engels, who was not yet a Marxist, wrote that whereas on the Continent the revolution was talked about as almost inevitable, in England popular wisdom held that *"even the lowest class of the nation is well aware that it only stands to lose by a revolution, since every disturbance of the public order can only result in a slowdown in business and hence general unemployment and starvation".* This *"national English standpoint of the most immediate practice, of material interests"* stood in contrast to the German Hegelian philosophy, which sought the *"motivating idea"* behind political phenomena and held that *"the so-called material interests can never operate in history as independent, guiding aims, but always, consciously or unconsciously, serve a principle which controls the threads of historical progress".* Engels concluded that, although he thought revolution was *"inevitable"* for England, he was convinced that *"as in everything that happens there, it will be interests and not principles that will begin and carry through the revolution; principles can develop only from interests, that is to say, the revolution will be social, not political".* [14]

Certainly the Chartist socialist radicals believed that *"immediate practice and material interests"* made revolution rational and necessary rather than foolish and impossible. The Chartist leaders of 1839 told their supporters that the Charter would be won in a very short space of time, and that the practical, immediate issues–

---

14. *Rheinische Zeitung* nos 343 and 344, 9 and 10 December 1842. MECW vol. 2.

the Ten Hour Day, the Poor Law, bread prices, land monopoly–
would be immediately addressed. But as Engels's future friend
Marx would argue, the *"threads of historical progress"* were under-
pinned by the dialectic of labour and capital, which had its own
'principle' of development in the absence of a credible alternative
and a revolutionary subject to implement it–as it still does. In
1839 capital was still in the phase of 'formal domination', in which
the workshop owner could be seen as a 'middleman' standing between the workers and the 'moneyocracy'–and indeed oppressed
by the latter through rent, interest and tax. By the time Chartism
had run its course in the 1850s the relation between capital and
labour was becoming 'socialised' into the totalising form of 'real
domination', which *"transforms the situations of the various agents of
production"* and *"revolutionises their actual mode of labour and the real
nature of the labour process as a whole".*[15]

Finally, we might consider to what extent the significance of
the movement that disintegrated in 1839–40 lay in the world-
historical importance it might have had if it had been victorious.[16]
Had the assault on Newport been successful, other towns such
as Monmouth, Abergavenny, Brecon and even Cardiff might have
succumbed as well. The great danger, which Prime Minister Lord
Melbourne was very relieved to see averted, was of an armed uprising setting off a chain reaction through the Midlands and the
North. The result of such a conflict could well have been bloody
repression of the democratic forces. But another possible outcome
could have been either a democratic republic or a compromise that
circumvented civil war with some major reform, such as universal
male suffrage–the main plank of the Charter.

If a democratic regime had been established in Britain, the cause
of democracy might have taken hold on the Continent earlier than
it did. The *anciens régimes* of Europe that were shaken in 1848
might have been finished off for good even earlier, and would
not have been around to plunge their subject peoples into world
war in 1914. Rather than upbraid our 'democratical' ancestors of

---

15. Karl Marx, *Capital*, vol 1, p. 1021.
16. For further critique of Stedman-Jones see Black, op. cit., chapters
1-3.

1839 for violence and extremism, we can only salute them–and try and understand why they lost.

Appendices

George Julian Harney: The Tremendous Uprising

The following text was published by the *Newcastle Weekly Chronicle* in three parts (22 and 29 December 1888, and 5 January 1889) to mark the fiftieth anniversary of the birth of the Chartist movement.

'Tis Fifty Years Since

Round the people's bright banner are gathering fast
The good, and the true, and the brave;
And he who would shrink from so holy a cause -
Is a traitor, a coward, a slave!

Part I

Old Coaching Days

When the Rev. James Murray, Minister of the High Bridge Meeting House, Newcastle-on-Tyne, author of *Sermons to Asses*—what an extended field, how abundant the texts, for such sermons now!—when Mr. Murray made his pilgrimage from Newcastle to London in 1771-72, the date is uncertain, and paid £3 8s 6d, presumably for an 'inside seat', his first experience was well calculated to damp the ardour of any intending traveller. He found nearly an hour consumed in crossing from the northern to the southern side of the Tyne: an hour (!) in which now the traveller finds himself well on the way to York! There was no bridge crossing the Tyne at the date of Mr. Murray's expedition. There had been one but like the mythical 'London Bridge' of children's rhymes, it had 'broken down' . (curious that

I have heard those ancient rhymes chanted in the streets of Boston, New England.) Waiting the erection of a temporary bridge, a ferry boat ran from the Swirle, Sandgate, by which coaches and other vehicles, as well as individuals, were conveyed to the Gateshead side. This Noah's Ark had no power of self propulsion, but was dragged across the river by four rowers in a small boat! No wonder the rev.gentleman nearly lost his temper, and wrote and preached *Sermons to Asses!*

 I was more fortunate when, in the early morning of a winters day, late in December, anno domini 1838, our coach from London was driven at a rattling pace down Gateshead's steep descent, and over the substantial–and, if memory serves, handsome–stone bridge which then spanned the Tyne; and toiling up the steep ascent from the 'The Side', landed its living and other freight at the Turf Hotel, Collingwood Street, where I was more than glad to find a bed after the long and exhausting ride from London. We had left London at 8 o'clock the preceding evening but one. Our route omitting mention of minor places not to be remembered after so long a time, had been through Grantham, Newark, Doncaster, Selby, York, Northallerton, Darling, and Durham. Imagine, gentle reader, you who can speed from Newcastle to London , by the Flying Scotchman in some six hours; imagine yourself five times that number of hours on top of a stage coach, first in darkness, unless there happened to be moonlight, for twelve hours; imagine the raw morning, from two until about half past seven, when stopping at Grantham, I think for breakfast. Then the long cold day, perhaps now snow falling, without any protection, save one's overcoat–an umbrella being an unmitigated nuisance–and the cold leather apron buckled across the knees of the travellers. There may have been lunch at Doncaster, and a late dinner at York, about 5 o'clock, for those who could afford it I say nothing about the changes of coachmen and guards, and the extortionate taxing of the passengers. Then through the darkness again, benumbed with cold. It has been said that the inspirations of patriotism, even on the plain of Marathon, the scared soil of Runnymede, and the battle field of Naseby, would be lost of upon a man suffering from toothache. And on such a ride of thirty hours one must have been more than mortal if one had cared for the magnificent spire of

Grantham, the pleasant streets of Newark, and the racing record of Doncaster, the glories of York and of Durham–the last shrouded in midnight darkness. These were to the travellers–like the States of Connecticut and New Jersey–good places to get away from. The torture of cold feet was something indescribable. The traveller felt his legs were encased in ice, and his pedal sufferings gave him a deadly-lively appreciation, though not much comfort from the philosophy, of *Locke on the Understanding*.

As we neared Gateshead our driver indulged in an extra whip-up–to time his time. Hazlitt's bones had long since fallen from their gibbet-chains, as seen hanging by Mr. Murray, and we were in no mood to look around for his ghost. As before said, we entered Newcastle at a rattling pace, and I was thankful to find myself safe sound; the traveller incurring no small risk, overpowered by somnolency and benumbed into helplessness of pitching headlong from his seat and breaking his neck. It was about 2 in the morning. We were due at Newcastle at 50 minutes past 1 am. 'Something hot' and a chamber candlestick, concluded the thirty hours journey, 278 miles from London.

I doubt if I remained in bed, like Lord Tomnoddy, until half-past two, but I could not that morning been accused of early rising. Some two or three members of the Political Union, whose names I cannot recall, induced me to expedite my breakfast, and them I was taken to the office of the *Northern Liberator*, in 'the Side' where I first made personal acquaintance with several of the local leaders, and members of the *Liberator*'s staff, including Devyr, who after more than fifty years absence, made his appearance again in Newcastle a few years ago.

Newcastle's Renaissance

After obtaining information as to the arrangements in connection with the forthcoming great meeting, I took a stroll through the principal streets of the town. Naturally attracted by Grey's Monument, I made my way in that direction. I was astonished by what I saw. At that period London was but little removed from the meanest aspect it had worn all its history. Its antique quaintness and beauty had largely perished in the Great Fire; and the

greed of its citizens, and the imbecility of it and England's rul-
ers, had rejected the plans of Sir Christopher Wren, which would
have made modern London one of the handsomest of European
capitals. The era of Georgian ugliness and meanness succeeded,
and perhaps, Harley Street, Baker Street of today, offer examples
of what our great (or great, great but not very great) grandfa-
thers conceived was becoming for the capital of Britain. Moreover
I knew the London of the people rather than that of the Aristocracy, and though it had happened that, as a boy, I had been
frequently to Park Lane, and remembered seeing Pall Mall when
newly lighted with gas, my intimate acquaintance was rather with
the 'City', the East End, and the South East. Hence the stone built
streets of that portion of Newcastle which probably, the Yankees
would have termed 'Graingerville' struck me with admiration. It
is not often it occurs that after so long a term as fifty years Time
confirms first impressions; but when I was recently in Newcastle I
was delighted to find my earliest impressions more than fully confirmed. Setting aside the best of London, wonderfully changed
(not in every instance improved) within the last fifty years–setting
aside Bath, Chelthenham, Leamington, and other show places; also
places of antiquarian interest, like York, Canterbury and other Cathedral cities, I know not so pleasant a place as Newcastle. As an
industrial and commercial centre, it, to my mind, is far handsomer
and cheerier than larger manufacturing towns and cites would be
invidious to name. Frankly, I don't like large towns; but all large
towns in England I have any knowledge of, commend me to canny
Newcastle.

The Cause and Rise of the Chartist Movement

The bitter disappointment and brooding anger of the unenfran-
chised, consequent on finding themselves defrauded by 'the Bill,
the whole Bill, and nothing but the Bill' had culminated in a new
movement almost wholly restricted to the working classes, having for object of attainment Universal Suffrage and accompani-
ments to secure its verity: the old principles enunciated by Cobbett, Cartwright and Hunt; but which now took more elaborately

defined shape and form in the famous document known as *The People's Charter*. I stay not to speak of the inception and preparation of that document, soon to be the watchword of millions. The new movement had received strong impetus from the Birmingham Political Union, the council of which after some dallying with 'Household' had come out 'squarely' for Universal Suffrage. But the London Workingmen's Association and the Birmingham Political Union combined could never have produced a tremendous uprising as the Chartist movement became in consequence of another contributory force, that of the impassioned masses of Lancashire, Cheshire, and Yorkshire, to which should be added those of Northumberland, Durham, and, in Cumberland, Carlisle and its neighbourhood. The cruel evils inflicted by the unreformed factory system, and the inhumanity with which the New Poor Law was introduced , had goaded the masses of the first three named counties especially, well nigh to desperation. And when the flame of combustible mass was fanned by such a preacher as Rev. J.R. Stephens (to say nothing of Richard Oastler, Feargus O'Connor, and others), the present day reader may have some faint idea of the kind of movement which set aside the academically teachings of the London Working Men's Association and the stereotyped political guidance of the Birmingham Council. The adhesions of Lancashire, Cheshire and Yorkshire was a source, at once of present strength and future weakness. A campaign for the Charter such as these counties demanded could have but one of two issues—revolution, or disastrous failure. Let it be understood by revolution I do not mean a French revolution, or general capsize, but the enactment of the Charter wrung from the 'three Estates' either by force, or fear of force—as had been the case with the Reform Bill.

The People's Charter was first published on the 8th of May, 1838, and in a few weeks the Chartist movement had assumed formidable proportions. People of the present day associate the name of Chartism with the fiasco of 1848. The Chartist movement of the European Revolutionary Year was but a remnant of the grand uprising ten years earlier. The Council of the Birmingham Political Union had formulated a National Petition embodying the points of the Charter. Generally at all the meetings the petition was adopted, a resolution was passed approving the Charter as that of the People, and in the more important districts the meetings elected delegates to a 'General Convention of the Industrious Classes' (commonly termed the National Convention) to watch over the presentation of the petition and to take measures toward obtaining the reform prayed for. The Convention like the Petition, and what was termed the 'National Rent' to supply the Convention with necessary funds for general, not individual expenses, had been suggested by the Birmingham Council.

Rapid Progress of the Movement

To the honour of Scotland, Glasgow led in the Series of popular gatherings of enormous magnitude which marked the year 1838. It is on the record that two hundred thousand working men of Glasgow and adjacent towns within a circle of from ten to twenty miles, with forty bands of music, and banners innumerable, gathered on the 21st of May to meet, welcome and listen to strong delegation from the Birmingham Council, in addition to their own local orators. It is only just to add that with the workers was associated a fair sprinkling of Glasgow men of the middle class, at the head of whom was James Moir, elected delegate to the Convention. Birmingham followed on the 6th of August with an enormous assemblage at Holloway Heath, said to number two hundred and fifty thousand. On 17th September the Petition and the Charter were adopted and the London delegation was elected at a meeting in Palace Yard, Westminster presided over by the High Bailiff. In point of numbers his was far inferior to the meetings in the North of England and Scotland. But London can only be moved in sections; even fifty years ago it was too vast to be moved as a whole. But all preceding gatherings were eclipsed in numbers, and perhaps enthusiasm, by the great Lancashire demonstration on Kersal Moor. The Chartists claimed three to four hundred thousand. Some speakers I suppose determined 'not to put too fine a point upon it' talked of half a million! Probably an exaggeration. But that the assemblage was enormous may be inferred from the fact that the Annual Register, an unfriendly authority, admitted or spoke of two hundred thousand. The Yorkshire demonstration on Peep Green, was hardly second in numbers and not at all in enthusiasm.

It is almost superfluous to say that smaller, but usually very numerously attended meetings, indoors and out of doors, were almost nightly in nearly all parts of the country; but especially in the Midlands, a considerable portion of the West of England, and all of the North from Macclesfield to Carlisle, from Leeds to Berwick-on-Tweed; and in Scotland from Dumfries and Hawick to Aberdeen.

As the year advanced, and open air evening meetings became inconvenient from want of daylight, torch-light meetings became into vogue. The ruling Whigs became alarmed, or affected to feel alarmed. That kind of illumination was indeed throwing too much light upon the subject; after some hesitancy; the Home Office issued a proclamation forbidding said meetings. As the leaders had no wish to bring on a collision, submission was counselled. But the prohibition furnished a text for bitter declamation against the Whigs in power, contrasted with their seditious incitements when appealing to the masses to overthrow the Tory aristocracy during the Reform Bill agitation.

The reader may suppose Newcastle was somewhat laggard. Not so. The *Northern Liberator*, established by Augustus Beaumont, who died too soon, now 1838; in the hands of Thomas Doubleday, Robert Blakey of Morpeth and other able writers fed the growing flame of popular enthusiasm, and the Northern Political Union was indefatigable in making converts and enrolling members. I had been admitted a member before I had ever seen Newcastle, or had been asked to allow myself to be nominated as a delegate. Well I remember the Unions card of membership–at least the striking and significant inscription from Byron:

> *But the heart and the mind,*
> *And the voice of mankind,*
> *Shall arise in communion,*
> *And who shall resist that proud union!*
> *The time is past when swords subdued–*
> *Man may die–the soul's renew'd:*
> *Even in this low worlds of care*
> *Freedom ne'er shall want an heir:*

Millions breathe but to inherit.
Her for ever bounding spirit—
When once more her hosts assemble,
Tyrants shall believe and tremble.

Whether the card also contained the two concluding lines of the quotation, I am not sure:

Smile they at this idle threat?
Crimson tears will follow yet.

A long inscription for a card; but if any old Chartist has preserved one; it will be found as I have stated.

And now—to bring these remarks to a conclusion for this week—it was Newcastle's turn to take from a sister hand the Torch of Liberty, passing it on until the whole island should be ablaze with the fire of a holy enthusiasm for Freedom.

Part II

Lo! We ANSWER! See! We come!
Quick at Freedom's holy call:
We come! We come! We come!
To free our Native Land from thrall.
And hark! We raise from sea to sea,
The glorious watchword—LIBERTY!

The above, or similar lines—with a stanza or two more—were, I believe, chorused at some meetings of the Birmingham Political Union, when—throughout the land—public enthusiasm was used and abused to give place to the Whigs and make the Middle Class the ascendant power in the State. But those lines were much more applicable in the earnest uprising of the 'masses' in 1838-39.

Strange to say, Newcastle had seemed to outsiders somewhat laggard in demonstrating its attachment to the Chartist cause; but, in reality, there had been for some months a strong and unceasing agitation. A considerable time before the meeting of which I propose to speak, there had been a great demonstration on the Town Moor—at which, I think Feargus O'Connor spoke—called to express sympathy with the Lancashire and Yorkshire warfare against the New Poor Law. On that occasion the town authorities had, either timorously, or wickedly, made obtrusively offensive military preparations to quell a riot, or an insurrection, which there was not the slightest reason to apprehend. Worse still some military officers thrust themselves man and horse, into the midst of the meeting, as if brutally desirous of provoking a riot. A rankling of the circumstances named contributed not a little to the fiery character and violent tone of the speeches at

The Meeting in 'The North'

A meeting on the bleak Town Moor at Christmas was out of the question. 'The Forth' offered some degree of shelter. If memory serves, that place either surrounded, or, in part, fringed with trees; were they poplars? The morning of Christmas Day 1838, broke fresh and fair. It was cold, but crisp cold, such as sets the blood dancing in the veins. And most of us were then young, or men in the prime of their strength. The elderly mature were few, though there were not wanting veteran Radicals who, nineteen years before had attended a great meeting on the Town Moor to protest against the 'Manchester massacre', and to hold up its authors, abettors and approvers–from Fum the Fourth (then Prince Regent) down to the despicable Manchester magistrates–to public execration, pillorying their names to 'fester in the infamy of the years'. In the assembly gathering on Christmas morning (1838) were also most of the numerous signers of the patriotic address presented to the great William Cobbett on the occasion of his visit to Newcastle some five years earlier. In 1838 Newcastle was 'full' (so to speak) of stone masons, for the Grainer renaissance was not yet perfected. A fine body of working men they were: cleanly, healthy, handsome, eager, full of enthusiasm; any man might have been proud of such a constituency. Of other trades and callings in Newcastle and Gateshead there were abundant representatives bodies; whilst South Shields, North Shields, and smaller towns and villages, including Winlanton, Swalwell and Blayden sent innumerable contingents–the majority composed of the delvers in mines, with the sons of Tubal Cain. Indeed, numbers attended from as far east as Blyth, and as far west as Hexham; and Carlisle sent a representative speaker. Ah! The men of Winlaton of that day! Can I ever forget them? Never!–whilst memory holds her seat: how single minded, how pure hearted, and warm-hearted, too; generous, hospitable, and inspired by an enthusiasm which left no room for doubt or misgiving as to the early attainment of the grand object they sought. Hotspur was not more confident:–

> *By Heaven! Methinks it were an easy leap,*
> *To pluck bright honour from the pale-faced moon.*

I make special mention of the Winlatonians, not because they were specially exceptional, but because they were representative of the best of the Tynesiders.

The man who was asked if he could play the fiddle, answered he did not know he had never tried. I never tried to commit to memory Homers list of ships that carried the Greeks to the Trojan shore; and it would be vain for me now to try to recollect the designations of the political and trades organisations and friendly societies constituting the procession that with bands playing and colours flying, having paraded the principal streets of the town proceeded to the announced places of rendezvous–'The Forth'. Of the flags and the banners it is not difficult to summon up an imperfect recollection. Their figurative adornments and mottoes showed the still surviving influence of the great French Revolution–'Liberty, Equality, and Fraternity', 'The Rights of Man' &c; whilst the old Cromwellian spirit found utterances in Biblical denunciations of the Oppressors of the Poor, and such appeals as 'To your Tents! O'Israel!' There may also, I am not sure, have been an inscription which had already done duty at the Lancashire and Yorkshire demonstrations: 'He that hath no sword, let him sell his garment and buy one!'.

The Chairman and the Speakers

At that time, Newcastle was well provided with public speakers. Unfortunately, the most eloquent of the Tyneside orators, Charles Larkin, held himself aloof from the movement. I will not say that the fire of his patriotism which had so blazed in the time of the Reform Bill agitation, had died out; but for some unexplained, if not inexplicable reason, he chose, like Achilles in his tent, to stand apart, to the movements serious loss. Not so his lifelong friend Thomas Doubleday, who, though as a speaker as inferior to Charles Larkin as we may assume Caesar was inferior as an orator to Cicero, yet–military genius excepted–had much of the great Roman's versatility of talent. Philosopher and pet, political economist and novelist, his most prominent trait and crowning glory was his intense sympathy with human suffering, and his righteous anger against wrong-doers, oppressors and selfish and blundering statesman and legislators. It was this noble son of Newcastle who was unanimously elected to preside over the meeting.

If memory serves, Mr. Doubleday, then entering upon middle-age, was medium height, 'well built' fair complexion, blue eyed, a mellow and kindly voice, and so sweet an expression of countenance that many fair lady might have envied him the possession. That expression was the index to his good heart and highly cultivated mind. The people of Newcastle owe a debt of gratitude to Thomas Doubleday, of which, I suspect, those who at the present day call themselves 'Reformers' and 'Liberals' have no conception.

The Chairman's opening speech, necessarily restricted in length, was to the point (and indeed, to the 'six points'), and was loudly applauded. The meeting being held in the open air, and as far into the winter as on Christmas Day, the chilliness, which had not much affected the processionists as long as they were 'on the move', forbade long speeches. But what was wanting atmospheric warmth was amply made up for by the more than mere warmth of the sentiments uttered by al the speakers.

The movement had now so far advanced, and the meeting of the General Convention was so near, that there was little for the meeting to do but elect the delegates. It would have been useless to have gone through the formality of adopting the National Petition, as that had been for some time in course of receiving signatures. *The People's Charter* was already generally adopted without any question as to its principles or details. Still, it does now seem a little startling to find that the first resolution, instead of embodying a declaration of principles, was a vote of confidence in and thanks to, Feargus O'Connor and Rev. J.R. Stephens. A few words on this resolution, presently. It was moved by Mr. Cock-

burn, remarkable, that, blind from infancy, he was highly intelligent, though that is not very remarkable in the blind, though
he was well versed in the politics of the time, though dependent
for his information on the reading of others, apart from what
he could pick up at lectures and in discussion, for which he had
much relish, being a keen and logical debater. I remember it was a
somewhat painful exhibition to witness his blind eyes instinctively
turned upwards toward the natural light they could not discern.

The resolution was seconded by Mr. Hanson, of Carlisle, who
strongly denounced the Whigs and O'Connell—who from having
been one of the authors of the Charter had now become one of
the fiercest vituperators of the Chartists. The speaker also condemned in the strongest terms, the Birmingham and Edinburgh
critics and censurers of O'Connor and Stephens . Hanson was a
good speaker and (like Marsden in the Convention) a most typical
looking representative of the ill-paid, half-starved weavers. His
gaunt figure and pale face largely excited the sympathy of the
meeting, and added force and fire to his words of wrath—hailed
by the exited assemblage with shouts of applause.

The resolution was carried unanimously, as were all the subsequent motions.

James Ayre moved the second resolution in favour of appointing
Delegates to the 'General Convention of the Industrious Classes'
about to assemble in London. James Ayre, if I remember correctly,
was a stone mason, middle-aged, short, with a careworn countenance, of a most fiery temperament with a speech to match. He
could not see that in another twelve months he would be a fugi-
tive from his native land. After a few years he died, worn down
by the ills of life and disappointment, in the State of New York,
whither he had accompanied Rewcastle and Devyre, and Wilkin-
son of Winlaton. To say that James Ayre's speech was, like himself,
sufficiently fiery, is to say enough.

Edward Charlton, probably under thirty, fresh-looking, but pre-
maturely stout; I think a mason, but subsequently a railway en-
gineer, seconded the resolution, and, in the course of his speech,
significantly observed that *"if the Convention were attacked, the cry
should be 'To your Tents! O Israel!'"*. This Biblical cry was later on

declared to be seditious, and made one of the charges on which some of the Chartist leaders were consigned to prison.

William Parker, whose personal appearance and manner of speech I cannot recall, moved the third resolution, in support of Universal Suffrage. It was seconded by William Thompson, one of the Secretaries of the Northern Political Union. He had gained some local notoriety through having lost his employment, palpably for having taken part in the agitation, though that was denied by the representative of the firm at whose Works he had been employed. He was a somewhat heavy-looking, though still young man. Of what manner his speech was, I have no recollection.

I may say the same for the speech and personality of Thomas Ryan, who proposed Robert Lowery (the name often printed Lowry) as one of the delegates to the General Convention. The motion was seconded by William Cook, of Felling–I think subsequently the portly host of the 'Blue Bell' Gateshead, and who (I think) was Treasurer to a more modern Northern Political Union, well known for many years as a ready speaker at political meetings. Here I must pay a passing tribute to another of the tribe of Boniface, though he was not amongst the speakers on Christmas Day–Mr. Richard Ayre, an admirable man, middle aged, short, square, of very pleasant aspect, warm-hearted, and patriotic–the host of the Charles the Twelfth at Tyne Bridge End.

William Byrne nominated George Julian Harney of London, as one of the Delegates. William Atkinson seconded the motion. I have too imperfect a recollection of the seconded to warrant any attempt at description. The proposer , whose profession, or occupation, I forget, was usually associated with Dr. Hume. There was degree of likeness, though I believe, no relationship. Both were still young, tall of good figure, fair complexion, blue eyed, auburn-haired–both effective speakers. William Byrne was still living a few years ago, the inmate of some institution for 'decayed gentlemen' in the neighbourhood of Newcastle. Dr. Hume, after the collapse, at the end of 1839, engaged as a ship's surgeon, and after several voyages settled in Brooklyn, New York, combining medical practice with pharmacy. In understood he was doing very well when his wife was taken from him by death. That was his ruin. 'We know what we are, but know not what we may be'. In the course of two or three years, or possibly less, he was numbered with the dead.

Ralph Curry, well known to the local Chartists, and whom I must have seen frequently but whom I cannot venture to describe nominated Dr. John Taylor as the third of the three delegates. Thomas Hepburn seconded the motion. 'Tommy Hepburn' as he was familiarly termed, was of middle-age, large, somewhat heavy of look, but an intelligent, energetic leader of the miners. I fancy he occupied a position, though not so well defined, similar to that subsequently held by Martin Jude, and now, and for many years past, by Mr. Thomas Burt—of course I refer to Mr. Burt's position amongst the miners—not to his Parliamentary seat.

The three nominations were unanimously agreed to. Then the delegates addressed the meeting.

Part III

> *The most despised, wrong'd, outraged, helpless wretch*
> *Who begs his bread, if 'tis refused by one,*
> *May win it from another kinder heart;*
> *But he who is denied his right by those*
> *Whose place it is to do no wrong, is poorer*
> *Than the rejected beggar,—life's a slave.*
> *… If we are wrong'd*
> *We ask justice; if it be denied,*
> *We'll take it.*

An apology, not least an explanation due to such of the readers of the *Weekly Chronicle* as may have cared to make acquaintance with these reminiscences. The narrative of the meeting in 'The Forth' at the conclusion of last weeks instalment, looked very like

> *The story of the bear and fiddle,*
> *Which begins, and breaks off in the middle.*

Time may merge into Eternity, and space; and the want of that necessary condition compelled the division of what was intended to be wholly Part II into Parts II and III. The following continues and concludes the narrative.

The Three Delegates

Then the delegates addressed the meeting. They were individually received with enthusiastic cheering. The three spoke in the order of nomination.

ROBERT LOWERY was the first to speak. From the ranks of the working classes (I think he was a tailor) has rarely come a better speaker than **ROBERT LOWERY**. He was at that time a man about thirty, good height, though not tall, well knit, but lame walking with a limp, probably from some malformation at birth. Of rather dark complexion and pleasing appearance. I think his name first appeared in print in connection with South Shields meetings. I understood he was a native of Edinburgh, and had come to Tyneside and was not deficient in its peculiarity of tongue. He was one of the best Chartist speakers generally, without, perhaps the rhetorical power of Vincent, Dr. Taylor, and one of two more. I do not include Stephens, for Stephens was not a Chartist. As the Chartist movement declined, and the 'Complete Suffrage' movement, or attempted movement came to naught, Lowery became more identified with the 'Temperance Movement' as an accredited lecturer. I have understood that in his later years he crossed the Atlantic, and died at the home of a married daughter, in Canada. Though at a subsequent period Robert Lowery became one a more moderate school, he was sufficiently ultra and fiery on Christmas Day, and had made some very 'strong' speeches at preceding meetings. In his speech acknowledging his election he said *"They were to have no sham work; they were to tell the Government and Parliament that if they were to have no part in making the laws. They would not obey the laws. (Cheers)… If after all legal means had been tried and after all their arguments had been used, if they could not get their rights, then they might use their arms"* (Enthusiastic cheering).

The next speaker, the second nominated delegate, was

GEORGE JULIAN HARNEY from London . I must confess, as the writer of these reminiscences, that I have been closely associated for a very considerable period with 'the delegate' just named; in fact if a Family Bible record tell the truth, as may be assumed it does; that connection has so far extended over three score years and ten. Yet I find myself a quite at a loss to describe said 'delegate'. My recollection as far as it may be trusted, through the dim haze of years is of a young man hardly more than a youth, under two and twenty, of medium height, lessened in appearance by a stoop strange in one so young, but accounted for not by any spinal complaint but by former weakness of the eyes which forbade facing the sun or wind. Slender, at once fair and florid, blue eyes, and dark brown hair, sometimes incorrectly described as black. I can say nothing of expression of countenance. Of a fiery temperament, not so much possessing, as possessed by an enthusiasm in more need of experience, discipline and regulation. Not generally a good speaker, not enjoying naturally 'the gift of the gab'–nor that want compensated for by college taught culture. But capable at times of making effective speeches, as at Lancaster in 1843, and at Tiverton in 1847. His speech at the meeting in 'The Forth'–memory serves–by no means one of his best, but received with enthusiasm especially by the Winlatonians, whose abiding friendship said 'delegate' had the happiness to enjoy until the last of the men of 1838-39 had passed away. I speak of the days that are no more. Now the 'delegate' under notice may walk through Winlaton unknown and unmarked save as a 'stranger'. No Winlaton wives would now invite him to rest and partake of their 'singing binnies' as in the days 'When this Old Cap was New'.

I pass to the third of the nominated and elected delegates: a remarkable figure.

DR. JOHN TAYLOR of Ayr, A son, it was understood, of a member of one of the 'best families' in Ayrshire, in the Service of the Government in India, and a lady native of that country. Dr. Taylor showed in his person evidence of his birth–the mingled blood of European and Asiatic, so diverse though both of the Aryan stock. Probably in 1838 rather over than under thirty-five. Tall, at least of good eight, though not of the tallest, well formed, of sallow or dark complexion, of good and striking features, save that his forehead was somewhat low; beautiful dark eyes, a wealth of black curling hair of which he was most vilely and shamefully denuded when arrested and taken to Warwick in July 1839, heavy black whispers, beards were not then in vogue, a winning expression of countenance, and a tongue to match. He carried ladies hearts by storm. His dress was sufficiently outré, or at least uncommon, a bare neck, striped coloured shirt, a collar not so much a la Byron, as like unto that affected by man-o-war's-men when on shore; and here may be added that he walked with a rolling sailor-like gait; a broad–brimmed, low-crowned felt hat, when such hats were unusual. But it is not necessary to make a tailors inventory of the doctors clothes, so I stop here. Byron would have been delighted to have met what he might have deemed an admirable presentment of his Corsaire, or Lara–ready to take the field against any odds. And this reminds me (as Abraham used to say) it was reported, that if not in time to be associated with Byron, the doctor had shared in the Greek struggle for independence. I neither vouch for, nor deny this story. I remember that he was an enthusiastic admirer of the poet, and it would have gone hard with some of our latter day critics–who would deny Byron the title of poet–if they had lived and wrote soon enough to have come under Dr. Taylor's notice. He would have shaken the life out of any such as a mastiff might shake the life out of some yelping cur.

Dr. Taylor was as eloquent as he was a fiery speaker, His voice was melodious, but powerful with a slight tendency to a lisp, which seemed to add to rather than distract from its effectiveness. He did not long survive the collapse of the Welsh insurrection, but retiring with broken health, to (as I have understood) the home of a sister, wife of a minister in the North of Ireland, where he died. A characteristic statue, subscribed for by his Ayrshire admirers, principally working men, stands in the cemetery, Newton, Ayr, where it is lost to view, the cemetery being awkwardly situated, and visited but by few. I suppose snobbishness of the Ayr gentry and authorities would not allow a site where the statue should have stood in Ayr itself.

The character of Dr. Taylor's speech in 'The Forth' will be sufficiently indicated by its peroration:

> *He knew not when the time might come for physical force, but this much he was prepared for, that when the time did come he, for one, would seize the sabre and use it to the very best effect he could. (Loud cheers). That would be no new weapon for him. He had fought with the pen till the apathy of the people had obliged him to lay it down, he had fought on the hustings till his own weakness had forced him to retire; but he would part with the sa-*

bre only with his life, and when all else had forgotten him his own hand would write his epitaph upon a tyrants bow, in characters of blood with a pen of steel. [*Tremendous and long continued cheering*].

Messrs. Lowery and Harney moved a vote of thanks to the chairman–carried by acclamation. In responding, the Chairman made a strong speech, asserting the legal and constitutional right of the people to possess arms, and to use them in self-defence.

And then with bands playing, the assemblage dispersed, and 'The Forth' was left to solitude.

One marked feature of the proceedings had been the consensus of opinion that force would have to be resorted to obtain justice and the acknowledgement of right. This opinion has been placed to the account of certain names, at the head of which stand that of Feargus O'Connor; but I venture to affirm that, if any reader of these remarks has the opportunity to turn to Newcastle papers of the time, he will find in their reports that it was not only Dr. Taylor and others in unison with his views who referred to the probable employment of force, but also those who at least later, acquired a character for moderation, who held the same view and expressed themselves in like terms. The opinion expressed, and the terms of expression may have been unwise; that I am not discussing; but the opinion was general. It was so to speak, 'in the air' The fact is curious and suggestive of reflection.

In the evening there was a 'Tea-party' largely composed of the fair sex, in the New Music Hall. It is said that about 800 persons sat down to tea, and about 200 followed. After tea there was a Public Meeting at which the sentiments given utterance to in 'The Forth' were repeated 'with variations'.

Conclusion

It seems difficult to realise that so much energetic action, confident hope, and burning enthusiasm resulted in failure and disappointment. But, on calm reflection, it is easy now to see there could have been no other issue. The movement for sometime before the meeting of the Convention had been broken into two distinct forces–though of unequal numbers–both at war with the

common enemy, it is true, but fatally at war with each other. As
the reader has seen, the first resolution adopted by the meeting
in 'The Forth' instead of affirming the Charter or setting forth
any other declaration of principle voted confidence in Feargus
O'Connor and the Rev. J.R. Stephens. This was in reply to the
vacillating but significant action of the Council of the Birmingham Political Union, and still more in rejoinder to the Calton Hill
resolutions, so denunciatory of the English agitators, more especially the two above named. To enter upon the consideration of
these matters, to do justice to both parties–nothing extenuating
the course of those with whom I was associated, nor setting down
naught in malice against those to whom I was opposed–would
carry me far beyond the limits of this 'paper', and I must hold my
hand.

> *I have said 'The Forth' was left to its solitude. But:*
> *Where's Troy? And where's the Maypole in the Strand!*

And where is 'The Forth'? It is now more undiscovered than the
Roman Wall. We would have to did up the foundations of the
great Central Railway Station to find its site, or, by the help of
the Antiquarian Society, seek in old plans and views of Newcastle to trace its outlines. Of more human interest to us, at least
to the writer, is the question: Where are the hearts that beat so
warmly on that cold Christmas Day, fifty years ago? Where the
teaming mind and loving sympathy of Thomas Doubleday; the
fierce rhetoric of Dr. Taylor, piercing as Highland swords, burning as the molten lava that runs down the sides of Vesuvius; the
eloquence of Lowery; the bitter outpourings of Hanson's protests
against the cruel lot of his 'order'? Where the thousands of con-
gregated on that day whose aspirations were truly set forth in a
Chartist 'hymn' or 'chant' but of somewhat later production–I
know not who was the author–quite poetical and spirited enough
to have been worthy of the name of the 'Chartist Marsaillaise', as
one stanza will show;

> *By our own our Children's CHARTER,*
> *By the fire within our veins;*
> *By each truth attesting martyr;*
> *By our woes, our tears, our pains!*

By our rights of nature given,
By the voice of liberty
We have sworn before high Heaven–
That we must, we will be free!
That we must, we will be free!
That we must, we will be free!

Where? I need not call upon to Echo to answer! All or nearly gone. Even the very character of the people of that time exists no more! What remains (for the writer)? Only to pray for the preservation of one's country amidst all the coming convulsions, to wish well to mankind through all coming changes, to trim the lamp of life, now fast declining, and wait–wait the inevitable.

Edward Aveling: George Julian Harney– A Straggler of 1848

The Social Democrat No. 1 January 1897.

One of the most effective characters in the repertoire of our great actor, Henry Irving, is that of Corporal Gregory Brewster. Everybody knows it is an extraordinarily finished portrait of a ninety-year-old Guardsman. In 1815, at the Battle of Waterloo, this same Brewster has driven through a narrow lane, the hedges aflame on both aides, a wagon carrying gunpowder for the Guards at Hougoumont. His predecessor in the attempt had been blown to pieces. Brewster wins through somehow, is greatly honored of the regiment, and is here dying of old age and in something perilously near poverty. Among all the wonderful touches in that moat pathetic portrait, there is one that always moves me more than any other–more even than the dying finish, *"The Guards need powder, and by God they shall have it"*. That is where the old man, speaking to the young Colonel of his regiment that was, describes himself with uncertain fingers straying over the table, as *"a straggler"*. I was reminded of the little play, of Irving's beautiful impersonation, when the other day I went down to Richmond to see George Julian Harney. Here is a straggler–a straggler of 1848. Here is a man that carried intellectual gunpowder to the Lifeguards of the Chartist movement. As he sits in his lonely room, crippled by rheumatism, and nearly eighty years of age, it would be difficult to realize that this is the man of whom Ernest Jones said, *"He was the boldest of the champions of the Chartist cause,"* if you did not look at his face.

When you try to get from Harney some reminiscences of that old time, you find the task not too easy. He tells you at the outset *"One may live too long"* and indeed, from the neglect by the English workers of this fighter in the van, he might not unnaturally conclude that he had worn out his welcome amongst them. Harney was born on February 17, 1817, in Kent. That is as near as he will let you get to his birthplace. His schools were the inevitable Dame School of that time, and one or two private schools which be says were of no account. His university, from the age of eleven to fourteen, was the Royal Naval School, Greenwich. After all, his university, like that of the Shakespeare of his adoration, was the big world of thought and action. According to himself, be did not learn much at School, and was very often in poor health. He never had any trade, except that of seafaring, and afterwards drifted generally along into and along with the advanced movement of his time, until he reached the crest of the oncoming wave, and was at once leader and driven. For six months he was at sea going to Lisbon and Brazil. After his return, just as some of us have a great fancy to be a railway guards or circus master, Harney had a great desire to be a printer. But the fates were adverse, although, after all, he was to do more for printing than perhaps any compositor that ever lived.

From than age of sixteen to that of nineteen he was in the thick of the Unstamped Fight. Those were the years of the stamped newspapers. The tax upon knowledge took the official form of a fourpenny stamp upon every newspaper; so the energetic spirits of the time declared roundly for 'unstamped' newspapers. The movement was led by Hetherington, Watson, Collet, Moore, and others, and the fight centered especially around the *Poor Man's Guardian*. Under an Act of Queen Anne, Harney was clapped into prison twice for short terms in London, and then, as there was a vacancy in Derby he went there in place of some unknown fighter, imprisoned. At Derby he sold the unstamped *Political Register*—not on account to be confused with Cobbett's paper of the same name. At Derby he got six months, at the very revolutionary age of nineteen. But his imprisonment was a triumph; for whilst it was still going on, the Government gave way, and the fourpenny newspaper tax was abolished. The victory for education had been won, even if one of the victors was laid by the heels in Derby Gaol. The three prisons that were honored by the temporary residence of Harney were Coldbath Fields, the Borough Compter, and Derby Gaol. They have all gone the way of all bricks and mortar, been transformed or else vanished as completely as the church at Luddington, two miles from Stratford-on-Avon, at which William Shakespeare and Ann Hathaway were married.

The Unstamped men of 1836 became the Chartists of succeeding years. It is an interesting study in evolution—the Unstamped movement, the Chartist movement, the Freethought movement which afforded after the apparent downfall of Chartism the only outlet for the energies of the advanced working men, until the next stage in evolution came, and the socialist movement grew, more or less, directly out of those just named. It is very interesting to see in England how at your socialist meetings, you have especially the old and the young rather than the middle-aged. Some stragglers from the Chartist movement are still with us, and they are the youngest of us all. Their grandchildren, rather than their children form the ever-increasing number of class-conscious workers. On the other hand in many cases, but not in quite all, the children of the Chartists and the fathers of the present race of young workers are, as the inevitable results of their surroundings a few years back, often hide-bound in a hard-and-far Radicalism diluted with Freethought. None of us us will forget, although I have no time to work it out here, the stages of intellectual and political development precedent to the Unstamped movement—the Utopian Socialism of Robert Owen, and from him back through the centuries to the Lilburnes and Kets.

Harney was a delegate to the first National Convention of the Chartists whose full name was the General Convention of the Industrious Classes. In his room there hangs, upon walls full of interesting pictures, a picture of that Convention as it met on Monday, February 4, 1839, at the British Coffee House in Cockspur Street. The British Coffee House has vanished, or undergone such transformation as to have practically vanished. After the second or third day, the Convention removed to the Doctor Johnson Hotel, in Bolt Court, Fleet Street—which is now, says Harney, with a half-cynical humour so characteristic of him, "*a sporting den*".

He was delegate to the Convention from Newcastle, and the Newcastle *Weekly Chronicle*, owned by his faithful friend Joseph Cowen, still retains his services as a writer. Between the Derby prison time and the meeting of the Convention he had been, to use his own language, *"padding the hoof, preaching the gospel of discontent"*. The year 1839 was memorable to him not only for the Convention. At the latter end of July in that year he was arrested again at Bedlington, about eleven miles from Newcastle. It will be observed how faithful he was to Newcastle. This arrest was for a speech made early in the same month at Birmingham. It took place at two o'clock in the morning, and he had to be got across country to Birmingham, handcuffed to a constable of that inspiring town, and hemmed in with Newcastle police. The journey was in a Hackney coach to Newcastle; in a ferry across the Tyne to Gateshead; from Gateshead by rail to Carlisle by stage coach right across Sharp Fell, that highest point among the Westmoreland mountains, up to which the London and North Western engines so slowly climb; finally by rail from Preston, at that time the extreme north of the North Western Railway, to Birmingham. As one heard of the handcuff business, one's eyes involuntary strayed to the poor rheumatic and yet vigorous hands of nearly fifty-seven years after. At Birmingham there was a committal and a letting out on bail. *"I never knew,"* said the veteran, with a laugh, *"how rich I was until then. I was worth one surety of £1,000 and two of £500. The trial did not come off in Warwick in April 1840. The Grand Jury of which for the first time I began to understand the function, and which for the first time I began to have some respect, declined to find a true bill"*:

> *The next taking event was my arrest at Sheffield. I was one of fifty or sixty, all of whom were arrested, in 1842, all over England, for taking part in a Convention at Manchester. The real fact was that this Convention was connected in point of time, but in no other way whatever, with a big trade union strike strike in Lancashire, with which were mixed up plug-drawing and other wicked devices of the workmen. We were to be tried at Liverpool before Lord Abinger, alias James Scarlett. He was Scarlett by name and Scarlett by Nature, and we know that he, like certain judges of today—at least so they tell me—have made up his mind to the verdict before a word of evidence was given. It was necessary to play*

the lawyers with their own cards, and so we traversed, that is we contended for a beautiful legal fiction that as forty days had not elapsed since the time of the arrest, we had not had enough time for the defence. So away to Lancaster—to the Castle, I think—and the Monster Trial at March, 1843. The Judge was Rolfe, and the indictment was riddled through and through by the lawyers on our side. Some of our fellows were represented by Counsel. For those not represented, I 'led'. Fergus O'Connor brought up the rear of the self defenders, and everybody knows that the big actor always likes to have the stage at the end of the play.

The chief Counsel for the prosecution was the Attorney General, Sir Frederick Pollock, of whom Harney speaks with the greatest respect. "*He was a prosecutor, not a persecutor*". Ultimately Harney and O'Connor were found guilty on one of the innumerable counts and the others upon two. Goodness only knows now, and nobody whatever cares, what the counts were, as there was an arrest of judgment—which was turning the tables by the arrested with a vengeance—and a quashing of the whole business in the Court of Queen's Bench, as far as Harney and the rest were concerned, on the ground that the indictment was bad.

'Tom' Cooper, as Harney calls him, was not so lucky. I have a dim memory of Cooper, when I was very small youth, lecturing to me and a lot of other people, and more or less converting us from the error of our orthodox ways. Cooper had two years in Stafford Gaol, and took them out of humanity in general by writing *The Purgatory of Suicides*. He became converted in his later days to Christianity and general respectability. In the summer of 1841 Harney went in for his first political contest against Lord Morpeth, and the arena was the West Riding of Yorkshire. To get rid of the political contests once for all there was another opened on July 30, 1847, against that arch-friend of Russia, Lord Palmerston. The Palmerston constituency was Tiverton, and Harney swears that for his fame (Harney's not Palmerston's), "*he should have after*". When he went out to America later, even such a man Horace Greeley knew him chiefly on the ground that he opposed Palmerston. Of course these more or less abortive runnings of candidates were chiefly with the intention of making propaganda by speech. For example, the opposition to Morpeth gave Harney the opportunity of speaking at such towns as Huddersfield, Bradford, Dewsbury, Wakefield. There was never any serious intention of going to the poll.

The rest of this life of struggle and event is chiefly journalistic. Thus in 1843, he joined the *Northern Star* at Leeds, and was first sub-editor and afterwords editor. This connection was ended by disagreement with Fergus O'Connor. The grounds of the disagreement were, according to Harney, that he made too much of the foreign refugees, whilst O'Connor made too much of the old political ideas, and was too much of a King, Lords and Commons man. One epigrammatic summary of O'Connor by Harney is worth preserving. *"He was like William Cobbett, without his particular form of genius"*. The *Democratic Review*, 1849, the *Red Republican* and the *Friend of the People* (June 1850 to July 1851) were his next journalistic and pugilistic ventures. From 1855 to July 1862 he was in Jersey, looking after the *Jersey Independent*. He seems to have been attracted to the Channel Islands chiefly because Victor Hugo (whom he knew and loved well afterwards) had been expelled from Jersey to Guernsey. *"The first week I was in Jersey,"* says Harney. *"I heard the Bailiff reading the Proclamation of Peace with Russia"*. Since the Jersey time, there have been the little interludes in such a life as this of journey to and a sojourn to America, and return to this country. I do not think I can give any better idea of the intellectual, moral, and political characteristics of Harney than by telling telling the reader of the portraits and the like that crowd his walls. I take them just as I saw them, working round his room. Fergus O'Connor; Frost; Joseph Cowen; Oastler, the Factory King; 'Knife and Fork' Stephens, the physical force man, who spent eighteen months in Chester Castle; W.J. Linton, engraver and Chartist; Harney himself (he is even now a delightful bit of a beau in his way, as scrupulously dressed and groomed as ever), as a Yankee with a moustache, only, instead of the present venerable beard; Lovett, who drew up the *People's Charter*; Frederick Engels and Karl Marx, very fitly by the fireside (Harney had the high honour of their friendship); 'Ironsides' Adams of the Newcastle *Weekly Chronicle*.

All these are on the walls by his bed and the fireplace that runs to the window, looking south. Over the mantlepiece is a group

that reminds some of us younger workers in the workers movement that perhaps we hardly pay much attention to pure litera-
ture as our political forefathers did–Byron, Scott, Burns, Shelley,
Moore, Pope, Dryden, the grave of Fielding, and, high over all,
Shakespeare. Between the windows looking south are Miss Elea-
nor Cobbett, now ninety-one years of age, a letter from Cobbett
himself, and the *People's Charter*, between the windows and the
door, Magna Carta, Darwin, Ruskin, Sidney, Chaucer, Raleigh, De
Stael, Mary Wollstonecraft, together with a bust of Shakespeare
again. And, by the door, there is a picture of Uncle Toby and the
Widow Wadman.

The words of Harney about Engels and Marx (I put them in the
order in which he began to know them) will be of interest:

> *I knew Engels, he was my friend, and occasional correspond-
> ent over half a century. It was in 1843 that he came over from
> Bradford to Leeds and enquired for me at the* Northern Star
> *office. A taIl. handsome young man, with a countenance of al-
> most boyish youthfulness, whose English, in spite of his German
> birth and education, was even then remarkable for its accuracy.
> He told me he was constant reader of the* Northern Star *and
> took a keen interest in the Chartist movement. Thus began our
> friendship over fifty years ago. In later years he was the Nestor
> of International Socialism. Not more natural was it for Titus to
> succeed Vespasian than for than for Frederick Engels to take the
> place of his revered friend when Karl Marx had passed away.
> He was the trusted counsellor whose advice none dared to gain-
> say. Probably the private history of German Socialism could tell
> how much the party is indebted to his wise counsels in smooth-
> ing acerbities, preventing friction, mildly chastening ill-regulated
> ambition, and promoting the union of all for each and each for
> all. The author of* Das Capital *was supremely fortunate in hav-
> ing so devoted a friend. The friendship of Marx and Engels was
> something far from the common. If not positively unique we must
> go back to ancient legends to find a parallel. Either would have
> emulated Pythias offered sacrifice for Damon. In their public
> work as champions of their ideas they were like the 'Great Twin
> Brethren who fought so well for Rome'. Engels, like I believe, most
> short-sighted people, wrote a very small hand; but his calligraphy*

was very neat and clear. His letters were marvels and he wrote an immense number in spite of his longs hours of original composition or translation. He attended Demonstrations in Hyde Park [all, except that of 1895, the year of his death, and was always on the International platform, of which I had the great honour to be chairman; E.A.]– but I doubt if sixteen hours covered his average days work when he was at his best. With all his knowledge and all his influence, there was nothing of the 'stuck up' or 'stand–offishness' about him. He was just as modest and ready for self-effacement at the age of seventy-two as at the age of twenty-two when he called at the Northern Star office. Not only his intimate friends, but all loved him. Although Karl Marx was his great friend his heart was large enough for other friendships and his kindness was unfailing. He was largely given to hospitality, but the principal charm was his own 'table talk', the 'good Rhine wine', of his felicitous conversation and genial wit. He was himself laughter loving and his laughter was contagious. A joy-inspirer, he made all around him share his happy mood of mind

A letter from Harney to Marx just found by us among the papers of the latter is of great historical interest (look at the dates and names), and is here published for the first time.

Dear Marx, I have been and am very unwell, so can only say that the propositions for holding a Democratic Congress in Brussels in September next have been unanimously adopted by the Fraternal Democrats, the German Workingmen's Association and the Metropolitan Chartist Committee, and the Chartist Executive. I will write again in the course of the first week of 1848. London Dec.18.1847. G.J.H"

Turning back from this beautiful retrospect upon one of his own kin by Harney, calling to mind many happy days when I met him at Engel's house, I am conscious that the two men, Engels and Harney were cast in the same mould, soldiers in the same regiment. As I look in this darkening room at Richmond at this old warrior with his carefully brushed hair and beard, his strongly marked face, his clear eyes—as I listen to the clear voice that expresses his clear thought—my mind goes back to years before he was born, and forward to years after both he and I will be dead, and I see in this old man an unbreakable link between the years and the years. I know that long after the rest us us are forgotten the name of George Julian Harney will be remembered with thankfulness and with tears. A Straggler of 1848. But a straggler who cried then, and who will cry with his latest breath that which shall be the motto helping us to remember him, *"The people want powder, and by God they shall have it"*.

Index

Lightning Source UK Ltd.
Milton Keynes UK
UKOW050349220512

192993UK00001B/3/P